The Reparative Effects of Human Rights Trials

Justice in domestic courts is one of the most prominent aims of victims seeking to obtain accountability for human rights violations. It is, however, also one of the most difficult to achieve. In many Latin American countries, as well as elsewhere, activists have put human rights prosecutions forward as a fundamental means to end impunity, build democracy, strengthen the rule of law and address victims' rights. But there is still little knowledge about what actually happens when these judicial mechanisms are effectively put to work. Can prosecutions of mass human rights violations contribute to overcome the effects of state violence and impunity? Can trials enable meaningful reparative changes for victims in their local contexts? Analysing the human rights trials in Argentina established to prosecute those responsible for human rights violations during the military dictatorship, this book addresses how and why domestic prosecutions can operate as a means for reparation and contribute to dealing with the damage caused by crimes against humanity. Based on a series of interviews conducted with victims participating in these prosecutions, as well as with lawyers, prosecutors, judges and other relevant actors in five provinces of Argentina, this book will be of considerable interest to those studying and working in the interdisciplinary field of transitional justice and human rights. The PhD thesis on which this book was based was awarded with the 2016 Doctoral Studies Award of the Philipps University of Marburg in Germany.

Rosario Figari Layús is based at the Philipps University of Marburg in Germany from where she holds a PhD in Political Science. Her areas of work and research are transitional justice, human rights and political violence.

Transitional Justice

Series Editor: Kieran McEvoy
Queen's University Belfast

For a full list of titles in this series, please visit www.routledge.com

The study of justice in transition has emerged as one of the most diverse and intellectually exciting developments in the social sciences. From its origins in human rights activism and comparative political science, the field is increasingly characterised by its geographic and disciplinary breadth. This series aims to publish the most innovative scholarship from a range of disciplines working on transitional justice related topics, including law, sociology, criminology, psychology, anthropology, political science, development studies and international relations.

Titles in this series:

Transitional Justice in Latin America
The Uneven Road from Impunity towards Accountability
Elin Skaar, Jemima Garcia-Godos and Cath Collins (2016)

Violence, Law and the Impossibility of Transitional Justice
Catherine Turner (2017)

Resistance and Transitional Justice
Edited by Briony Jones and Julie Bernath (2017)

Amnesties, Pardons and Transitional Justice
Spain's Pact of Forgetting
Roldán Jimeno (2017)

Transitional Justice and the Politics of Inscription
Memory, Space and Narrative in Northern Ireland
Joseph Robinson (2018)

The Reparative Effects of Human Rights Trials
Lessons from Argentina
Rosario Figari Layús (2018)

The Reparative Effects of Human Rights Trials

Lessons from Argentina

Rosario Figari Layús

Routledge
Taylor & Francis Group
LONDON AND NEW YORK

First published 2018 by Routledge

2 Park Square, Milton Park, Abingdon, Oxfordshire OX14 4RN
52 Vanderbilt Avenue, New York, NY 10017

Routledge is an imprint of the Taylor & Francis Group, an informa business

First issued in paperback 2018

a GlassHouse book

British Library Cataloguing-in-Publication Data
A catalogue record for this book is available from the British Library

Library of Congress Cataloging-in-Publication Data
Names: Layús, Rosario Figari, author.
Title: The reparative effects of human rights trials : lessons from Argentina / Rosario Figari Layús.
Description: New York, NY : Routledge, 2017. | Series: Transitional justice series | Includes bibliographical references and index.
Identifiers: LCCN 2017014356 | ISBN 9781138079045 (hbk)
Subjects: LCSH: Prosecution—Argentina. | Transitional justice—Argentina. | Trials (Crimes against humanity)—Argentina. | Human rights—Argentina. | Trials (Political crimes and offenses)—Argentina. | Trials—Argentina—History. | Reparations for historical injustices—Argentina.
Classification: LCC KHA5836 .L39 2017 | DDC 345.82/02322—dc23
LC record available at https://lccn.loc.gov/2017014356

ISBN: 978-1-138-07904-5 (hbk)
ISBN: 978-0-367-19183-2 (pbk)

Typeset in Galliard
by Apex CoVantage, LLC

To my wonderful grandmother Anita Ventina Dora

Contents

Illustrations

Figures

Tables

Acknowledgments

This book is the product of my PhD dissertation which would not have been possible without the support and collaboration of many people and institutions. First and foremost, I wish to thank to Professor Kirsten Mahlke, director of the European Research Council-funded research project "Narratives of Terror and Disappearance" at the University of Konstanz (Germany), in which I had the opportunity to develop my thesis. Thank you for your generosity and intellectual support, which made this research possible. I would also like to express my immense gratitude to my PhD supervisor, Susanne Buckley-Zistel, Professor at the Centre for Conflict Studies at the Philipps University of Marburg, for your support, advice and motivation throughout the difficult process of writing a dissertation in the political sciences. I was so fortunate to have you as my PhD supervisor. The continued encouragement and guidance from you both were very important to the completion of my thesis and this book. I wish to express my gratitude to the European Research Council [European Union's Seventh Framework Programme (FP/2007–2013)/ERC Grant Agreement n° 240984], that supported my PhD research with three years of funding.

Many people have collaborated in different ways to make this book possible. I appreciate the knowledge, ideas, interest, patience and encouragement of the many people who have helped me in my research. First, my deepest thanks to all interviewees and contributors in Argentina, specifically Buenos Aires, La Plata, Rosario, Córdoba, Tucumán and Santiago del Estero, who generously trusted me with their life stories that often included difficult and painful experiences. My research would not be possible without them sharing their insights and knowledge with me. As is shown throughout this book, human rights trials are the result of years of struggle and persistence of survivors, relatives of disappeared and human rights organisations in Argentina. They all have my greatest respect and deepest admiration.

I also want to thank the team who participated in the research project "Narratives of Terror and Disappearance" at the University of Konstanz who accompanied the writing process: Estela Schindel, Silvana Mandolessi, Mariana Perez and Liliana Feierstein. Thank you for your constant advice, your essential support and encouragement during all the stages of this thesis. I learned so much from each of you, not only on a professional level but also on a personal one. In the course of this project I gained theoretical and methodological knowledge but also, and most importantly, a group of friends that I hope will last forever. Thank you for your friendship and especially for the many hours of discussions that we shared in all means of transport – trains, cars and airplanes – throughout these years. I really miss those trips with all of you. Especially, I want to thank Estela Schindel for great support in the different stages of the research, for your thorough reviews of the most difficult chapters, as well as your enlightening suggestions, which highly enriched this work.

A very special thank you for Alejandra Carreras, who took the excellent photograph that appears on the cover of this book. The picture shows four former political militants after hearing the judgment of the first human rights trial in the province of Santiago del Estero in 2010, in which three former policemen were convicted of the torture and murder of the student and political militant Cecilio Kamenetzky in 1976. The four *compañeros* in the picture are: Pedro Ramírez, Oscar Bader, Mario Habra and Lucas Néstor Alejandro Zerdán. Thank you to all of you for sharing this unforgettable moment.

I also want to thank some important persons, who are irreplaceable referents for me, for their support, advice and unfailing inspiration across all these years in Argentina and Germany: Horacio Ravenna, Wilhelm Heitmeyer, Daniel Feierstein, Ruth Stanley. All your wisdom and teachings on human rights and social sciences during different times of my life helped me to write this study. Along with them I wish to thank the Permanent Assembly for Human Rights (APDH), an organisation that was crucial in helping get in contact with several interviewees and experts. My special thanks to Veronica Jeria, Estela Assaf, Ines Izaguirre, Antenor Ferreyra, Gabriela Águila, Ana Longoni, Rubún Kotler and Norma Rios, who were an invaluable support during the field work in the cities of Tucumán, Rosario, Santiago del Estero and Buenos Aires. Thank you for sharing your time and perspectives, which gave me great insight into the complexities of the human rights trials in different regions of the country. Very special gratitude goes out to the friends and colleagues who have contributed their reflections, comments and relevant information to the research. Among them, I want to thank Johanna Treblin, Julieta Lampasona, Marc Pradel Miquel, Florencia Diaz, Sebastian Huhn, Cath Collins, Friederike Mieth and Pilar Calveiro for your careful, intelligent and critical reading of the chapters of this book, as well as for their insightful comments that helped deepen, concretise and order key aspects of this work.

Further, a special thank you to my colleague and friend Ulrike Capdepon for all your support and outstanding comments on chapters of this book. It was a pleasure to work with you on the organisation of different panels and discussions on the topic of human rights trials. Many thanks also to all my colleagues who very generously shared their ideas and gave me constructive feedback on my work during different workshops and presentations. Specifically, I would like to thank Narda Henriquez, Sonja Perkič, Wolfgang Kaleck, Jo-Marie Burt, Nina Schneider, Marcia Esparza, Gabriel Pereira, Francesca Lessa, Alke Jens, Par

Engstrom, Camila De Gamboa and Stephanie Golob. Your expertise, enthusiasm and engagement with this difficult topic were a great inspiration for my research.

It is often said that doctoral research is a lonely endeavour. Luckily, during that time I have been fortunate to work in different fantastic academic institutions, where I counted on the great inspiration and support. Specifically, I would like to thank Prof. Anika Oettler and Bettina Wallon at the Philipps University of Marburg, Prof. Peter Imbusch at the Bergische University of Wuppertal and my former colleagues Boris Wilke, Ciaran Wron-Passmann and Sabine Passon at the Bielefeld University.

Thanks to Prof. Elazar Barkan for giving me the chance to be a visiting fellow at the Institute for the Studies of Human Rights at the Columbia University in 2012 in New York. Thanks to him, I had the chance to exchange and share my ideas with other colleagues and benefit from the wonderful resources found at their university library.

Crucial for this book were also the contributions of Rosana Kordylas, whose extraordinary support and engagement in the translations of many of the interview quotations as well as for her great copy editing of chapters of this book. Many thanks also go to Dr Philip Derbyshire and Charlton Payne, who very patiently edited the previous drafts of the chapters presented here. Their detailed corrections and precise suggestions greatly improved this text, making it much more legible, clear and rich.

These acknowledgments would be incomplete without me expressing my deeply felt gratitude to my friends and family. While I cannot mention everyone, I want to thank Sophia Lenhardt, Carolina Ghio, Andrea Faganello, Corina Anisko, Gunda Meyer, Mina Baghai, Ana and Gero Lenhardt, Alicia Gershanik and Hugo Mercer, Mariana and Jakob Greichen, Sigrid Akkerman, Christiane Schwarz, Alexandra Huck, Eugenia Jeria, Olatz Ispizua, Lena Davila, Patricia Dorado; Alejandra Villaseñor and Elina Aguiar for your friendship, encouragement and advice. Thank you for listening and for your unfailing support in all these years.

I also wish to express my sincere gratitude to the Routledge team, who assisted and advised me at various stages of the publication process, particularly to Collin Perrin, Hannah Lovelock, Marie Louise Roberts and Kieran Mc Evoy. Thank you for this opportunity. It was a pleasure to work with you.

Most of all I want to thank my parents. My father, Guillermo Figari, thank you for your unwavering belief in me, your wisdom and teachings, lifelong support and love at long and short distances. To my mother, Stella Maris Layús, your warm-heartedness, wisdom and patience always remind me that tenderness and empathy are amongst the highest values in life; and my sister Maria Eugenia Figari Layús, the person who makes me laugh more than anyone in the world. You always inspire me. Finally, I want to thank my dear uncle, Carlos Layús, who was always there for me when I needed him, even when I had the crazy idea of coming to Germany for the first time ten years ago. Thank you is not enough. This book is dedicated to you all.

Abbreviations

A: It refers to the answers of the interviewees in a quotation of an interview
ANDHES: Abogados y Abogadas del Noroeste Argentino en Derechos Humanos y Estudios Sociales (Human Rights Attorneys of Northern Argentina)
APDH: Asamblea Permanente por los Derechos Humanos (Permanent Assembly for Human Rights)
CELS: Centro de Estudios Legales y Sociales (The Centre for Legal and Social Studies)
CDCs: Clandestine Detention Centres
CONADEP: Comisión Nacional sobre la Desaparición de Personas (National Commission on the Disappearance of Persons)
EATIP: Equipo Argentino de Trabajo e Investigación Psicosocial (Argentine Work Group for Psychosocial Research)
ERP: Ejército Revolucionario del Pueblo (People's Revolutionary Army)
ESMA: Escuela de Mecánica de la Armada (Navy Mechanics School). ESMA operated as a clandestine centre of detention and Extermination in Buenos Aires throughout the entire military dictatorship.
HIJOS: Hijos por la Identidad y la Justicia, contra el Olvido y el Silencio (Children for Identity and Justice, against Oblivion and Silence)
Int (s): Interview (s)
ICC: International Criminal Court
ICTR: International Criminal Tribunal for Rwanda
ICTY: International Criminal Tribunal for the former Yugoslavia
Q: It refers to my questions in the quotation of an interview
UP1: Unidad Penitenciaria Número 1 (Prison Unit Number 1)

Introduction

"Small victories"

Justice in domestic courts is one of the most prominent mechanisms that victims strive for in order to obtain accountability for human rights violations. However, it is also one of the most difficult to achieve. In many regions of the world, human rights activists have put prosecutions forward as a means to end impunity, build democracy, strengthen the rule of law and address victims' rights. Yet, there is little knowledge about what happens when these judicial mechanisms are put to work effectively. Can prosecutions of mass human rights violations make a difference and help victims? If so, in which ways? This book looks to contribute to this question by analysing how domestic prosecutions can help to repair the damage caused to victims of systematic state crimes in Argentina, where trials to prosecute those responsible for human rights violations during the military dictatorship (1976–1983) began in 2006 and are still ongoing.

After many years of impunity, the introduction of these trials nationwide against those responsible for human rights violations in the 1970s and 1980s marked a very significant change in state policy regarding the crimes of the past, their perpetrators and victims. The government of Néstor Kirchner (2003–2007) re-oriented the state's attitude towards victims and the consequences of systematic state violence committed between the late 1970s and the early 1980s. From then on, a gradual change of direction by state institutions and actors led to the effective dismantling of previous official barriers to prosecution. The amnesty provisions of 1986 and 1987 were declared unconstitutional by the Congress in 2003, annulled by the Supreme Court in 2005, and in 2010 the Congress unanimously declared the human rights criminal trials to be a "state policy." The justice breakthrough was, however, not only the result of government initiatives but also the work of a civil society, which considers these trials to be the result of years of struggle. Hence the title of this introduction: "Small victories." This is the way a human rights activist and survivor of a former clandestine torture and detention centre in Buenos Aires (whose partner was made to disappear) explained her feelings about the trials: "One feels that our struggle (. . .), that despite the pain, the losses, the sorrow, the defeat, we are having our small victories. The trials are small victories."

The analysis of the impact of accountability at local level has social and political relevance since dealing with a legacy of gross human rights violations after a transition from authoritarianism to democracy or from war to peace presents not only challenges but also opportunities to enhance human rights and the rule of law in society and its various state institutions. The harm caused by systematic human rights violations does not disappear with the end of an authoritarian regime. The role of the following governments and society is crucial in either reinforcing the consequences or dismantling them. This book shows how prosecuting crimes against humanity can play a key role in redressing victims and attempting to overcome – at least partially – the damage caused by state violence.

The study of criminal trials as a mechanism for reparation considers their legal and social impact, since changes in society are echoed in victims' feelings and everyday lives. The Argentine case provides an extraordinary opportunity to explore these phenomena since it is the only country in Latin America where there have been regular, oral and public criminal trials of human rights violations on such a scale.[1] The testimonies compiled in this book show why and how domestic human rights trials can become a centrepiece of social and personal reparation. Without ignoring historical and cultural differences, the trials in Argentina have become a reference for other societies where accountability for systematic human rights violations is pursued.

The Argentine case: state repression and the path to human rights trials

On 24 March 1976 a military Junta seized rule of the country by a military coup, the so-called *Proceso de Reorganización Nacional* (National Reorganisation Process). The coup d'état institutionalised a system of repression that the military justified as a "struggle against subversion." Though assassinations and even disappearances had already taken place in 1974–1975, after 1976, the repression acquired a systematic and widespread character. This state repression was based on an apparatus of covert torture centres in which military and police forces kidnapped and mostly murdered those regarded as opponents. Members of armed groups, their families, as well as representatives of student groups, labour unionists and all of those who expressed criticism towards the political and economic policies of the government were abducted, tortured and ultimately made to disappear. According to human rights groups, 30,000 people were forcibly disappeared by the regime.

When Argentina returned to civilian rule in 1983, survivors, relatives of the disappeared and human rights organisations demanded investigations into the crimes and prosecution of those responsible. During 1984 and 1985, the government of elected president Raúl Alfonsín took some initiatives to address the demands for justice and truth. It created *Comisión Nacional sobre la Desaparición de Personas* (National Commission on the Disappearance of Persons, hereafter CONADEP) tasked with investigating the whereabouts of the disappeared and the human rights violations committed during the military dictatorship. Furthermore, the commanders-in-chief of the first three Argentine Juntas of 1976–1983 were put on trial and some of them were sentenced to life imprisonment (1984–1985). However, hopes of justice were dashed by the adoption of amnesty laws that foreclosed any successful prosecution of ex-military leaders for human rights crimes. The *Ley de Punto Final* (Full Stop Law) and the *Ley de Obediencia Debida* (Due Obedience Law) were passed in 1986 and 1987, respectively, and pardons were granted by former president Carlos Menem in 1989 and 1990. Even though prosecutions were now impossible, human rights groups continued to gather evidence on the disappeared with the goal of demanding justice. During the twenty years of impunity, the disappeared and survivors were stigmatised and even blamed for the crimes they endured, because of their previous political militancy and activism. Some sectors of the population did not see them as victims but rather as "subversives" or "terrorists" who had done something to deserve the crimes they suffered. In 2003, the Argentine Congress finally revoked the amnesty laws (a decision confirmed by the Supreme Court in 2005), giving rise to a new period of trials for human rights violations, which are currently taking place across the country. Along with the work of human rights organisations, the government of former president Néstor Kirchner (2003–2007) and Cristina Fernández de Kirchner (2007–2011, 2011–2015) initiated a new policy focusing on the criminal prosecution of human rights violations before and during the military dictatorship. These legal procedures are a unique example of retributive justice efforts. Between 2006 and 2016, 174 decisions were issued by different federal courts in almost every province. During this period, 813 former members of the security forces (military and police) and some civilians were convicted and eighty-seven were acquitted (Procuraduría de Crímenes contra la Humanidad 2016). After many years of impunity, the systematic conducting of human rights trials marked a significant change in state policy regarding the crimes of the past, the perpetrators and the victims.

Reparative justice

In this book, I engage with the relation between domestic prosecutions and a new conceptualisation of reparation: reparation as change. The changes brought about by the trials can acquire different meanings depending on personal experiences and perceptions and the local history and context in which victims are immersed. However, in spite of these variations, some common references to meaningful positive changes can be found in the interviewees' statements presented here. When I asked the interviewees how they would define the reparation they experienced during and after the trials in which they participated, many of them said that it was a positive feeling but difficult to describe. Others link the feeling of reparation to different emotions such as feeling better, healthier, glad, stronger, empowered and also feeling listened to, respected, acknowledged, accompanied, encouraged, supported, relieved and satisfied. As is explained in this book, the events leading to such emotions have a significant impact on the dignity, rights and quality of life of the survivors, political prisoners and relatives of disappeared people in different regions of the country.

In order to be reparative, that change should modify those legal, political and social conditions that either generated the original violence or perpetuated their victimisation. By a reparative–restorative effect I understand a process of change that contributes to the empowerment of victims, providing them with new possibilities of action and enabling them to have the same guaranteed rights to justice as other citizens. Reparative changes can take place at different levels in victims' lives. I will focus on three kinds of reparations or changes that human rights trials may provide when they are properly held: civic–legal, personal and social redress. Overall, the research is structured around the following questions: can prosecutions go beyond their traditional narrow retributive role and enable meaningful reparative changes for victims of human rights violations? If yes, why and in what way?

Civic–legal reparation refers here to the enforcement and guarantee of previously denied human and citizen rights to victims, such as the right to justice and truth. I also analyse whether trials can generate personal reparation for victims by empowering them and foster the restoration of their social ties. In the specific context of Argentina, this implies analysing if and how trials are a means to overcoming fear, breaking silence, strengthening social ties and changing social attitudes towards victims in their communities.

A main assumption underlies these questions. The first of them is that when dealing with mass human rights violations, law in its different forms (amnesties or trials) can influence social perceptions and relations by creating specific frameworks of interaction and meaning in which victims are immersed. The law, as an expression of the position of the state, can contribute to the reproduction and reinforcement of some of the effects of systematic authoritarian state violence even under subsequent democratic governments or can alternatively contribute to (partial) reparation for those injuries. The different kinds of laws or justice policies implemented to deal with state crimes tend to foster – or undermine – certain kinds of social understanding of and attitudes towards victims. The law operates as an instrument of communication that influences the ways in which society deals with human rights violations and their victims. The law may, for example, promote indifference or respect and solidarity; it may stigmatise or recognise, blame or support victims, all of which has great importance for the question of how victims deal with the damage they have endured. In this framework, an understanding of the power and social function of law is essential to explaining how justice policies dealing with human rights violations reflect different power relations and varying ways of addressing state crimes. In the following chapters I show how, in contrast to impunity laws, trials can produce positive changes in victims' lives inside and outside the courtroom. By "inside" the courtroom I refer to all the possibilities that judicial processes enable for the victims regarding access to truth, giving testimony and official acknowledgement of state responsibility for the past violations. By "outside" the courtroom I refer to the impact trials have in other sectors of society, on social perceptions and attitudes, which in turn affect the victims' lives. In giving an account of the reparative processes undergone by the victims within the framework of domestic prosecutions, I also consider their limitations. However, it is important to note that despite the difficulties that criminal prosecutions present, none of the victims would prefer these trials not to take place. All victims interviewed expressed their support for the trials, whatever their degree of engagement and participation.

The best way to access knowledge about these judicial processes is to listen to the experience of those directly involved (as plaintiffs and witnesses). Therefore, the main source of original data I draw on in order to answer the research questions is a data bank of seventy-five unique, semi-structured interviews conducted between 2011 and 2012 with victims participating in these processes in the recent period (in practice, between 2006 and 2012) as well as of other key informants such as lawyers, prosecutors, judges and other relevant actors in six different cities across Argentina. By means of the victims' perceptions, I could also glimpse some of the changes in other portions of society, since at least some of the changes in victims' lives have been driven by a shift in the attitudes or perceptions of people around them such as neighbours, local political authorities and the media in their communities.

Considering the importance of the reparative potential of domestic prosecutions is not the same as treating it as a universal experience. To what extent retributive justice can acquire reparative dimensions will depend on several factors and the social contexts in which trials are conducted. A trial does not necessarily lead to reparation. The way and modality in which it is conducted, the treatment of plaintiffs and witnesses, the flexibility of the judicial personnel as well as their relevance for each social situation can vary according to specific contexts. As a matter of fact, prosecutions in other regions such as Rwanda or the former Yugoslavia do not seem to have these kinds of effects on victims (Corey and Joireman 2004, Staggs Kelsall and Stepakoff 2007; Campbell 2007). In this vein, criminal trials are not the only possible form of justice to deal with mass violence or reparation for victims. The importance or need for them is closely linked to the political, cultural and historical meaning that each society ascribes to the legal system in general and the criminal justice in particular as an instrument of power and conflict resolution. In other contexts, such as Asia or Africa, the use of criminal law as a state instrument of conflict resolution may not necessarily have the same relevance as, in fact, it has in the Argentine society.

Similar considerations arise regarding the meaning ascribed to reparation. The notion of reparation is defined by international legislation but to be effective it needs to address its local meaning and needs. It is important to consider what damage reparation is aimed at in every specific case. For this reason, in Chapters 2, 3 and 4, I analyse Argentina's local context including an assessment of the extent of damage caused by state terror and impunity in order to determine what can be considered reparative in this case. In Chapters 5, 6, 7 and 8, I specifically address the human rights trials and their reparative dimensions.

The vast empirical analysis of human rights trials and their reparative effects on victims in Argentina can inform lawyers, participants, justice system actors and policymakers about key problematic aspects of current trials practice. It can thereby contribute to the formulation of changes that may better protect victims' rights and physical and psychological integrity through the trials process, via consideration of what victims describe and experience as "effective," reparative or unhelpful in regard to the pursuit of justice.

Victimhood and justice

Victims and victimhood have been the subject of significant policy attention in recent years (e.g. United Nations 1985; Van Boven 2005; Bonacker and Safferling 2013). Many scholars observe a notable global shift in regard to the relevance and participation of victims in judicial processes since the mid-1980s and, especially, over the last fifteen years (Bonacker, Oettler and Safferling 2013). Much social research on victims has focused on topics such as their classification (as individual or collective actors, and direct or indirect victims), perspectives, agency and/or instrumentalisation in post-conflict scenarios and transitional justice initiatives (Redress 2001; Huyse 2005; Picker 2005; Madlingozi 2010; Bonacker 2012; McEvoy and McConnachie 2012; McEvoy and McConnachie 2013).

As for the status of victims in judicial processes, there has been a gradual displacement of the focus from the perpetrators to a victims-centred perspective. Whereas in the Nuremberg and Tokyo Tribunals the main goal was to assign individual responsibility for international crimes by identifying perpetrators (Ainley 2008), over the next decades the focus changed and gave more space for the participation of the victims and their narratives (Teitel 2003; Bonacker 2012; Bonacker, Oettler and Safferling 2013). The so-called rise of the victims refers to the increasing valorisation of victims as well as their growing institutionalisation and integration into instances of justice, to the development of international norms and to the transnationalisation of human rights movements (2013, 282–283). In fact, there is an ever-growing literature on victim-related issues, such as the modalities of inclusion and the risks and limitations for the participation of victims, at the level of international and hybrid tribunals (Findlay 2009; McGonigle Leyh 2011; Doak 2011) such as the International Criminal Court (ICC) (Findlay and Henman 2012; McCarthy 2012; Kelly 2013; Eckelmans 2013; Garbett 2013), the International Criminal Tribunal for Rwanda (ICTR) (Koomen 2013), the International Criminal Tribunal for the former Yugoslavia (ICTY) (Fletcher and Weinstein 2002; Mannergren Selimovic 2010), and the courts in Cambodia (Pham, Stover and Vinck 2009; Bonacker, Form and Pfeiffer 2011). However, the literature on victims' perspectives on national human rights trials is still very scarce. Against this background, and since the victims' perceptions are one of the main aspects considered in this research, it is necessary to draw some attention to the question: What does it mean to be a victim of human rights violations?

The notion of "victim" can have multiple meanings depending on the theoretical framework or discipline from which it is addressed. International human rights legislation offers some approaches which also show important differences. On the one hand, one of the narrowest international definitions of "victim" is provided by the ICC. In the Rules of Procedure and Evidence (RPE) of the Rome Statute of the ICC "victims" are defined as "natural persons who have suffered harm as a result of the commission of any crime within the jurisdiction of the Court" (International Criminal Court 2002, Rule 85). As several scholars note critically, the Rome Statute follows a narrow definition of victim, since family members are not included. Furthermore, the interpretation of "harm" is very vague, so that it remains questionable whether psychological effects and the emotional suffering of a person are sufficient to qualify him or her as a victim before the ICC (Kelly 2013; Bonacker, Oettler and Safferling 2013). In this definition, there is no reference to the perpetrators since under the ICC not only state but also private actors are considered as such. A more wide-ranging definition of "victims" is given by the UN General Assembly resolution 60/147 of 16 December 2005 on the "Basic Principles and Guidelines on the Right to a Remedy and Reparation for Victims of Gross Violations of International Human Rights Law and Serious Violations of International Humanitarian Law," according to which "victims" are all those

> persons who individually or collectively suffered harm, including physical or mental injury, emotional suffering, economic loss or substantial impairment of their fundamental rights, through acts or omissions that constitute gross violations of international and national human rights law (. . .). The term "victim" also includes the immediate family or dependents of the direct victim, and persons who have suffered harm in intervening to assist victims in distress or to prevent victimisation.
>
> (Van Boven 2005, Art. 8)

Similarly, the International Convention for the Protection of All Persons from Enforced Disappearance, introduced in December 2006 and with special relevance in Argentina, states in Article 24 that "victim" means "the disappeared person and any individual who has suffered harm as the direct result of an enforced disappearance" (United Nations 2006, Art. 24.1). This includes not only all those persons who were and are still disappeared, but as in the case of Argentina, also survivors – persons who were disappeared for a certain period of time – as well as the relatives of both of these categories.

These definitions rely on a broad concept of victim, which extends beyond the individual who suffered the direct physical and mental harm to a larger universe of people that includes family members. In this regard, Huyse makes the distinction between direct and indirect victims: whereas the first are those who have suffered the direct effects of physical and psychological violence, the latter are those who are linked to direct victims in such a way that they too suffer because of that link (Huyse 2005, 54). Considering that enforced disappearance was the main means of repression used in Argentina, which affected not only the direct disappeared persons but also other related sectors of society, I adopt a broad definition of victim. I consider as such not only those who directly disappeared but also their relatives, the survivors, who were disappeared for a certain period of time, as well as the former political prisoners who were illegally detained during the period under study.

Debates on the social and political construction of victims

Victimhood is socially and legally constructed, within social and political contexts that simultaneously frame and influence that definition. In many cases the definition of victimhood also implies the construction of an ideal type of victim, which ascribes to it certain characteristics that often do not correspond to the reality of violence. This ideal type usually constructs the victim as a passive, vulnerable subject in need of protection (Bouris 2007). These assumptions deny their agency and simultaneously may present severe consequences for all those who do not fit into the category of passive victims of state violence. This can lead to the stigmatisation of politicised victims and also to the denial of the victims' status and hence reparation.[2] Thus, the construction of victimhood is often embedded in the debate about "guilt" or "innocence." This can be disturbing in cases of political violence in which several actors are involved. Victims are primarily associated with those who are "innocently" caught in the crossfire of warring groups (in Latin America: guerrilla versus state security forces). In many cases this kind of conceptualisation results in a hierarchy of victims, where those who consider themselves, or are considered by others, to be "innocent" victims dispute whether other "bad" or "impure" victims can be recognised as deserving the same status (McEvoy and McConnachie 2012; Madlingozi 2007; Meyers 2011). The political and discursive construction of a dichotomy of "innocent" versus "guilty" victims (the latter being politically engaged) is very common in post-conflict countries. As McEvoy and McConnachie (2012, 532) explain, there is a view according to which *only* those designated as "completely innocent" can be considered to be victims at all. Of course, in societies in which political conflicts prevail, not every victim will fit neatly into such separate boxes and individuals may move between these categories. Thus, a hierarchy of victimhood, predicated on distinctions between what Madlingozi (2007) has termed "good" and "bad" victims, often maps onto both subjective views on the 'justifiability' of the suffering that was visited upon such victims and the strategies and tactics deployed by them in the transition and their attitudes towards dealing with the past. International human rights law appears to find it difficult to contend with victims who are not in fact entirely "blameless" (Bouris 2007). The concept of "innocent" victims relates to apolitical people, who did not actively challenge the prevailing power relations. However, it is curious that the fact that someone has resorted to violence or was engaged in oppositional activity seems to take away the status of victim. It raises the following questions: Why are the specific conditions under which the person was victimised not considered in the definition instead of their personal and political characteristics? What is the difference between a person who was member of a guerrilla group and another who was not, if both were killed in a situation where they were utterly helpless, such as in a clandestine detention centre (CDC) or concentration camp? Why does their political character make some of them "less" victims than others? This kind of construction of victimhood tends to displace the responsibility of the crime from the perpetrator to the victim: who was *really* the victim? What did he or she do to be victimised? Such constructions and hierarchies of victims often map closely onto the national political sphere. There are often close relationships between political constituencies and victims' groups, which may in turn be linked to disputed interpretations of the violence of the past and its justifiability (McEvoy and McConnachie 2012). As will be discussed in this work, the dichotomy between "innocent" and "guilty" victims plays an important role in the political and social attitudes towards victims of state violence in Argentina. During the impunity years, the disappeared and survivors were stigmatised and even blamed for the crimes they endured, because of their previous political militancy and activism, whereas current human rights trials have questioned the ideal type of victim construction officially acknowledging that victimisation refers to the acts carried out by the perpetrator rather than to those of the victim.

The relevance of the victims' perspective in Argentina

The participation of victims in the Argentine human rights trials is one of the main features of these processes. Victims know the field of trials very well. Thus, the one-dimensional legal taxonomies mentioned above cannot capture the complexity and diversity of the victimised subject in other dimensions of his or her life. People victimised through state violence are not just victims or merely recipients of public policy but also powerful agents of change. In Argentina, the fight against impunity first and the human rights activism around trials now show that victims are not necessarily passive. As a matter of fact, many victims belong to what Cath Collins calls "accountability actors" (2010), that is to say, all individuals, entities or groups, domestic, external or international, who promote judicial accountability measures in either (criminal or civil) form. Almost all Argentine human rights organisations dealing with the trials have victims among their members. The activism and work of human rights organisations, such as HIJOS (Children for Identity and Justice, against Oblivion and Silence), *Justicia Ya!* (Justice Now!), *Abuelas de Plaza de Mayo* (Grandmothers of Plaza de Mayo), *Centro de Estudios Legales y Sociales* (Centre for Legal and Social Studies, hereafter CELS), and *Asamblea Permanente por los Derechos Humanos* (Permanent Assembly for

Human Rights, hereafter APDH) have been and continue to be essential for the implementation of the trials. In this context, as I explain in detail in Chapter 5, it is possible to distinguish different types of civil engagement and participation, which range from acting as a plaintiff, providing professional support, giving testimony, accompanying and supporting other witnesses during hearings, to investigating and providing evidence, publicising the trials, their content and outcomes (such as the courts' decisions) in public places and institutions such as schools.

Fieldwork and data collection

The best way to access knowledge about the impact of these judicial processes is to listen to the experience of those directly involved. Thus, a total of 75 interviews with different actors participating in the trials were conducted – with victims and key informants as well as lawyers, academics, judges and prosecutors. Primary data was generated using qualitative methods, semi-structured interviews, observations at trials, informal discussions and the analysis of NGO reports, journalistic material and legal documents.

For the in-depth interviews, I prepared an interview guide with the main topics and foci of my research. Interviews with survivors and relatives of disappeared people were specifically structured into three sections. The first part of the interview contained questions regarding their experience of violence and victimisation, which addresses the reasons why they decided to participate in the trials. Interviewees narrated their personal history and how they had been victimised by state violence. In cases of survivors, they described their activities prior to being illegally detained (most of them were social activists or affiliated with a political party, a trade union, or a student organisation). Then they went on to speak about their experience of captivity, the time in which they were detained – disappeared – and how they experienced their liberation from the detention centres. In the case of relatives of the disappeared such as mothers, partners, siblings and children, they also narrated how their family members were kidnapped and disappeared. In many cases they were not present at that moment, so they explained what had been told to them by others. They also recounted about their desperate search and unsuccessful demands for information on the whereabouts of the disappeared. In the second section, the questions referred to their experience during the decades of the 1980s and 1990s in which successively the CONADEP was established, the Juntas Trial took place and then amnesty laws and presidential pardons were promulgated. The third section of the interview focused on the interviewees' evaluation of their personal experience in the trials, how they felt during and after, and whether they fulfilled their expectations and if not, the reasons why. In this instance they were asked about their own case(s) but also about other cases and the trial universe more generally. The questions also sought to discover how they got involved in the trials, and in what role (plaintiff, witness, lawyer, supporter), what critical and reparative aspects they identified in the implementation of trials, and what changes they perceived not only in their private environment but also in the public sphere of the areas where they live. All the sections included questions regarding their relations to state institutions, their community and neighbourhood as well as to their families before, during and after their participation in the trials. Here it was important to find out if they identified any changes in their lives after the trial and where the response was affirmative, what kind of change it was. Information provided by research participants has been treated very carefully, maintaining confidentiality. Data was stored safely and not used for other goals aside from scholarly dissemination and discussion. In this regard, names, occupation and other sensitive information of the interviewees have been anonymised.

The fieldwork also had a multi-regional perspective, since interviews took place in six cities: Buenos Aires, La Plata, Rosario, Córdoba, Tucumán and Santiago del Estero. These cities are located in five different provinces of Argentina.[3] They also combine capital and urban perspectives (Buenos Aires, La Plata, Rosario and Córdoba) with those of the countryside and small towns (Tucumán and Santiago del Estero). The motivation for conducting interviews in different regions of the country was to see whether interviewees' views on trials were broadly similar or whether it is possible to identify nuances in the way the trials are being perceived in the different regions. The technique of regional sampling sought to avoid a capital-centric approach.

The six locations chosen correspond to places where at least one trial has been conducted and finished at the time of the interviews (2011–2012). Ten interviews were conducted in each of these cities with victims, lawyers and officers of the judiciary. All of them are urban centres and, except for the city of Rosario, they are all provincial capitals. However, the degree of urbanisation of cities such as Buenos Aires, Rosario and Córdoba is much higher in terms of population, services and infrastructure such as transport, media, etc. than other urban centres such as the city of Tucumán and Santiago del Estero, which combine urban and rural characteristics.[4]

Structure of the book

This book is structured into three parts. The first part outlines the different main strands of research into scholarship dealing with human rights prosecutions. In doing so, in Chapter 1 I look at the main works on international and national human rights tribunals and their positive and critical views on their impact. I also draw on theoretical and legal approaches regarding the meaning of reparation as well as the role of law as an instrument of power and communication which has the potential of reconfiguring social relationships.

The second part of this research, consisting of Chapters 2, 3 and 4, provides a historical and empirical analysis of state violence and the justice policies (Juntas trials and amnesty laws) implemented in Argentina once the dictatorship ended as well as their different consequences for victims. Since the meaning of reparation is a context-linked phenomenon, the reparative impact of domestic trials can only be understood by situating these effects in a certain political and historical context

(Palmer 2012, 157). In other words, to understand what reparative changes trials can produce on victims' lives, it is first necessary to identify the damage caused to them both by the military repression and by impunity. Therefore, in Chapter 2, I provide an analysis of the characteristics of the state terror and its impact on victims and on other sectors of society in Argentina between the late 1970s and the early 1980s. In Chapter 3, I analyse the well-known "*Juicio a las Juntas*" (the Trial of the Juntas or, hereafter, the Juntas Trial between 1984–1985), when an investigatory legal process was set in motion under the first constitutional administration after the military dictatorship – the government of Raúl Alfonsín (1983–1989) – in an attempt to come to terms with the crimes of disappearances. The trial brought to court the nine Junta leaders deemed responsible for planning and ordering systematic violations of human rights, and had an important role in symbolically marking the transition to democracy. Focusing on that trial, I consider its social impact and its meaning for the victims. In doing so, I analyse some of the important contributions of this trial but also its limitations. In Chapter 4 I address the implications that impunity, in the form of amnesty laws and pardons, had on the victims and other segments of society. I show how the formulation and implementation of amnesty laws contributed to the reproduction of social perceptions and attitudes that were detrimental to the victims and highly beneficial to perpetrators, many of whom were still powerful in the 1990s in Argentina. The analysis of the serious implications of impunity for victims is crucial to understanding why trials are so important for them today and how they can develop a reparative potential.

In the third part of this book – Chapters 5, 6, 7 and 8 – I focus on the analysis of trials for crimes against humanity in Argentina and their concrete reparative changes on victims' lives. Through these chapters, I show how trials have the potential to transform, at least partially, the legal, social and institutional context in which the victims are immersed. The public and official establishment of limits and responsibilities sends an important message not only to the victims but also to society as a whole. In Chapter 5 I provide an introduction to the specificities of human rights trials in Argentina and I look at the political and legal conjuncture in which these trials first started. In addition, I provide a general overview of the main actors and I discuss the advances and difficulties surrounding the trials in the past ten years. In Chapter 6, I focus on the more formal type of reparation that the trials provide for the victims: civic and legal redress, which refers to the restitution of the rights of which victims were deprived before. I also give an account of how the enjoyment of these rights, such as the right to justice, also echoes in the victims' feelings of inclusion in the state as full citizens. In Chapter 7, I examine how human rights trials, when conducted with a victim-centred approach, pave the way for new attitudes and practices that were unattainable for the victims before and that are now experienced as a process of empowerment. When in Chapter 7 I refer to personal reparation, I do not mean an isolated or merely individual process of reparation, but rather a process through which a person, as a result of changes in his/her social and institutional context, is able to undertake and confront situations which were not possible for him/her before.

In Chapter 8 I engage with the specific changes in local community attitudes towards the victims, both during and after the trials held in their cities. I examine the social and institutional impact of the trials on the victims' lives, as they encounter new attitudes of respect, openness and inclusion. Additionally, in accounting for the reparative processes that the trials are generating, I consider the difficulties and limitations that they involve. Finally, by underscoring the reparative role of domestic prosecutions, I make some concluding reflections presenting the similarities and differences between ordinary criminal trials and what this work considers to be a specific category of prosecutions: human rights trials.

Notes

1 In Chile there have also been prosecutions to deal with the crimes committed during the Pinochet dictatorship, but these trials are not oral and public but written. This modality has undermined their social impact (Collins 2010). Trials have also been held in Peru and Guatemala, but they are much fewer in number in comparison with Argentina (Collins, Balardini and Burt 2012; Blake 2014).

2 While the labelling of "victim" may provide a person who experienced violence in times of repression access to reparations, both material and symbolic (Buckley-Zistel 2013, 96), denying him or her this status can hinder that right. However, this is not a clear-cut issue. Throughout South America, reparation programmes for victims of human rights violations have adopted different approaches, depending on each context. In Argentina, reparations were granted to victims of state violence whether or not they had belonged to opposition political armed organisations. In Perú, while victims of violations by state actors or illegal armed groups are entitled to reparations, members of illegal opposition organisations are excluded. The Peruvian Commission of Truth and Reconciliation (CTR), established that those who "belonged at that time to a subversive and terrorist organisation cannot be considered victims" (Comisión de la Verdad y Reconciliación 2003, 1503). Individuals belonging to armed groups, who were injured, even if not in the frame of armed confrontations, are not considered victims. Similarly, the families of victims belonging to illegal organisations, who were killed or disappeared, are not entitled to any reparation programme.

3 The provinces of Buenos Aires, Santa Fe, Córdoba, Tucumán and Santiago del Estero.

4 Rural locations were excluded from the sample since the federal courts where the trials are being conducted are only located in urban centres. However, some of the interviewees who participated in the trials did live in rural areas, especially in the cases of Tucumán and Santiago del Estero.

Part I

Theoretical approaches to reparative criminal justice

Chapter 1

Justice and reparation of human rights violations

This chapter proposes some theoretical framings in order to understand why trials can work as a reparation mechanism. A cursory glance at the literature on human rights prosecutions reveals three features. First, studies on the effects of human rights trials in domestic courts are very scarce. Most focus on international or hybrid tribunals, their dynamics, the advances they have achieved in terms of international law, and their incorporation of international law into domestic norms; the impact and effects of such trials remain under-researched. Second, the few examples of such scholarship on the scope and effects of human rights trials focus mainly on their impact on legal norms and institutions, usually from a quantitative perspective (see e.g. Olsen, Payne and Reiter 2010; Sikkink 2011; Collins, Balardini and Burt 2012), but not sufficiently on their reparative function. In turn, those studies that understand domestic trials as an appropriate state-sponsored instrument to redress victims provide a well-intentioned approach but without enough empirically based results to support their conclusions. Third, among those authors concerned with the implications of transitional justice initiatives – not only trials – there is a very narrow view of the effects of criminal prosecutions on the victims of mass human rights violations. Indeed, many scholars have excluded tribunals as an appropriate mechanism for granting reparation to victims, arguing that criminal justice focuses on punishing perpetrators (Zehr 1990; Walgrave 2003). Advocates of restorative justice initiatives (e.g. truth and inquiry commissions) question the reparative function of criminal trials by claiming that there are greater benefits in other alternatives, where punishment of perpetrators is excluded (McElrea 2013; Mallinder 2013).

This chapter addresses these research gaps and provides alternative theoretical approaches in order to understand how and why human rights trials can enable a process of reparation for victims. In Section 1, I outline the contributions and limitations of the existing literature on the impact of human rights trials as well as the arguments for and against retributive justice. In Section 2, I analyse the concept of reparation (which is used in international legislation but also discussed by several scholars specialised in the field), and the three different types of reparation provided by human rights trials: civic, personal and social. Finally, in Section 3,

I address different theoretical approaches to the power of law and why it has the potential for reparative effects on the victims of mass atrocities. An understanding of the functioning of the law in society is fundamental to seeing why trials can work as an effective instrument for the redress of victims' harm and rights.

1.1 Research on human rights prosecutions

An overview of the existing scholarship on criminal trials dealing with human rights violations at international and domestic levels and a discussion of its contributions and gaps reveal how little has been written about the reparative effects of domestic human rights trials. This can be due to the fact that it is indeed a relatively new field. Since the deployment on a large scale of domestic justice for past human rights violations is itself a recent phenomenon with most of the cases – though not only – concentrated in Latin American countries (e.g.: Chile, Argentina, Perú, Colombia and Guatemala), empirical evidence has to date been scarce.

1.1.1 The post Second World War trials

From a historical perspective, much focus has been placed on the scope of trials: What, for instance, are trials supposed to achieve and what are they not? These debates go back to the immediate period after the Second World War in Europe. It was not until then that war criminals were held accountable for their crimes. The Nuremberg trials (1945–1946) tried 22 leading Nazi officials, acquitting three of them. Twelve of the defendants received the death sentence. In Tokyo, Japanese war criminals were prosecuted in a similar manner. The legacy of Nuremberg was very important for further judicial developments since it was the first serious attempt to punish individuals for such crimes. In fact, the Nuremberg trials are generally seen as the starting point of a worldwide human rights movement. They inspired such justice endeavours as the Eichmann trial in Jerusalem in 1961 and the Holocaust trials in France in the 1980s.

However, in none of these cases were trials seen as an instrument to redress victims. Their scope has been reduced to the allocation of individual responsibility of perpetrators. One of the most influential scholars advocating for the limited role of prosecutions was Hannah Arendt. In *Eichmann in Jerusalem: A Report on the Banality of Evil*, Arendt insists that the purpose of trials is to render justice and nothing else. According to her, the main function of trials is to administer justice, understood as determining the guilt or innocence of an individual, and to punish the guilty (1964). Also Tzvetan Todorov (1996), when referring to the successive trials of Paul Touvier in France in the 1980s and 1990s, stresses that prosecutions should only focus on the trials of the accused. According to these scholars, the law should not attempt to have other functions than prosecution. Other potentialities of trials, such as restorative outcomes or the reconstruction of history, would not apply to the judicial processes. These debates did not consider justice as a form of reparation for victims.

1.1.2 The transitional justice approach

From another perspective, one of the main approaches to human rights trials is that of transitional justice (hereafter TJ). This perspective analyses the relationship between political changes or transitions and judicial initiatives, that is to say, how the nature of a political transition can influence the modality of the trials to be implemented (e.g. O'Donnell and Schmitter 1995; Huyse 1995; Teitel 2000; Hayner 2002; Arthur 2009; Olsen, Payne and Reiter 2010). The TJ approach often considers the introduction of "special" justice measures in the period immediately after a change of regime. In their focus on the immediate transitional period, scholars have tried to identify what factors may activate, promote and/or hinder the early adoption of domestic criminal trials for human rights violations committed by previous regimes. Political science approaches have tended to emphasise factors of path dependency and political agency such as how the previous regime ended, the balance of power at the time of transition (Binningsbø, Elster and Gates 2005; Lie, Binningsbø and Gates 2007), the role played by elites, (Huntington 1991; O'Donnell and Schmitter 1995; Posner and Vermeule 2003), the duration of the period of illegal repression (Huyse 1995), the level of popular support for the new regime (Gloppen 2005), the nature of the ideological preferences of the political elite, the political commitments of the new regime (Barahoma de Brito, Gonzalez-Enriquez and Aguilar 2001), the increasing involvement of domestic non-governmental organisations (Collins 2006), the influence of transnational actors, international courts and networks (Risse 1995; Sikkink 1993; Sikink 1998; Finnemore and Sikkink 1998; Keck and Sikkink 1998; Risse and Sikkink 1999; Call 2004; Collins 2006; Hafner-Burton, Tsutsui and Meyer 2008; Burt 2009), and bilateral and multilateral foreign policy sanctions (Lutz and Sikkink 2000). Given their date of production, the early examples of this literature were primarily focused on decisions made about trials (or other mechanisms such as truth commissions) right after a political transition had occurred (O'Donnell and Schmitter 1995; Huntington 1991; Huyse 1995; Zalaquett 1995). These approaches left largely unexplored questions about the likely future evolution and effects of judicial policies and practices in what some would describe as "post transitional contexts" (Collins 2010), or at least, contexts where formal regime change or cessation of open hostilities took place decades ago. Such is the case in present-day Argentina, where formal political transition took place in 1983, as in much of the rest of the Southern Cone of Latin America, which also emerged from periods of military dictatorship through the course of the 1980s (or in the case of Chile, in the 1990s). In this sense, the recent trials for crimes committed by the military in Argentina offer a useful opportunity to observe the effects at a significant distance in time after the change from a dictatorial to a constitutional regime, in the context of continuous reworking and renegotiation of initial transitional settlements. In the case of Argentina, it should be noted that the current prosecutions are not considered by their main actors – witnesses, plaintiffs, attorneys, prosecutors, judges, etc. – as an instance of TJ. Even though many scholars have tried to classify the ongoing human rights trials as such, this labelling is a critical point. While mechanisms of TJ are regarded as special, temporary and extraordinary, and trials are seen as just one option among others, the Argentine trials are being conducted in regular and domestic institutions of the local criminal justice system. As a matter of fact, most of my interviewees, with the exception of some judges and lawyers, did not even know what the concept of transitional justice means (Figari Layús 2015).

1.1.3 The debate for and against prosecutions

The analysis of the reparative repercussion of prosecutions is highly relevant since scholarship on this field is scarce. In order to gain a better understanding of the advances but also the gaps in research on the impact of these trials, I will briefly summarise the most relevant works produced so far on the effects of prosecutions at international and domestic levels.

In the first place, one should note that there are important debates among those scholars who argue in favour of the positive impact of trials, in both international tribunals and domestic courts, and those who oppose them and question their scope and effects. Authors stress, on the one hand, that trials are not as effective as other justice mechanisms due to their limited scope on individual perpetrators and responsibility. The focus of trials on individual criminals responsible for ordering or carrying out acts of mass violence would not address all the responsibilities involved: particularly, perhaps, the systematic quality of those violations and/or state instigation or complicity (Arendt 1964; Malamud-Goti 1996; Hayner 2002; Drumbl 2005). On the other hand, scholars such as Forsberg assert that "there is little evidence that prosecutions and forgiveness perform any better than forgetting" (2003, 68). By trying to challenge these critical perspectives on the scope and efficiency of trials, Katryn Sikkink identifies in the literature four repeated assumptions in terms of their possible negative impact: 1) trials would destabilise democracy and lead to new military coups, 2) prosecutions would increase human rights violations, 3) trials would prolong violence or conflict, 4) prosecutions would impede the consolidation of the rule of law (Sikkink 2011, 142). Similarly, Samuel Huntington argues "[D]o not prosecute, do not punish, do not forgive, and above all, do not forget" (Huntington 1991, 231). Underlying this statement is the concern that efforts to prosecute the military in the midst or right after a negotiated transition to democracy might result in the military re-entering politics. Taking power again in the face of prosecution, military leaders would then be even more reluctant to return power to a civilian administration and might react violently in an effort to avoid being brought to court (Roehrig 2009, 723). Rather than risk any of these problems, others argue that civilian governments should choose to avoid prosecutions (Neier 1990). Leslie Vinjamuti and Jack Synder identify this stance as the "pragmatist approach," noting that "the consequences of trials for the consolidation of peace and democracy trump the goal of justice *per se*, since the future prospects for justice depend on the establishment of social peace and unshakeable democratic institutions" (2004, 353). Other scholars argue that justice has to be sacrificed in order to establish the truth about the past (Hayner 2002; McElrea 2013; Mallinder 2013). The "justice versus truth" model corresponds to the politics implemented in South Africa and Colombia, where in exchange for full confessions, perpetrators received reduced or lower sentences or no punishment at all (Laplante and Theidon 2007; Figari Layús 2010). As I show in the next chapters, in Argentina, as well as in several other cases such as Colombia, reduced sentences or the total absence of punishment have not guaranteed that perpetrators would tell the whole truth about their crimes. Finally, those who oppose prosecution usually maintain that a successful transition to democracy requires a society to move on from a horrible past and seek reconciliation between victims and perpetrators (Ibid., 724). According to these authors, prosecutions open old wounds and increase the desire for retribution, both of which make it more difficult to create consensus and a functioning democracy (Huyse 1995, 63).

On the other hand, those who are in favour of prosecutions and the so-called legal paradigm consider the use of law as the most appropriate tool to provide reparation for the victims. Many scholars and activists conceive trials and the right to justice as the centrepiece of social reparation in response to victims' rights and needs (Beristain 2009, 33; Edelman 2010, 107; Lagos 2010, 116; Bekerman 2010, 131), in an effort to promote the rule of law after mass atrocity (Roht-Arriaza 1990; Orentlicher 1991; Sikkink 2011). According to them, trials may contribute to rebuilding communities after mass atrocities by attempting to: 1) discover and publicise the truth of past atrocities; 2) punish perpetrators, thereby producing a deterrent effect, preventing future human rights abuses; 3) respond to victims' needs or wishes; 4) promote the rule of law in emerging democracies; and 5) promote reconciliation (see De Greiff 2008; Sikkink and Booth Walling 2007; Van Boven 2005; Orentlicher 1991 and Roht-Arriaza 1990 for a representative sample of these views).[1] Moreover, according to Juan Méndez, allowing military leaders to escape justice fosters an impunity that "will only encourage new abuses in the near or distant future" (Mendez 1997, 3–4). In recent years, especially in Latin America, there has been a greater consensus on the positive effects of properly conducted human rights trials (Kordon et al. 2010; Sikkink 2011; Collins, Balardini and Burt 2012). In this respect, Diana Orentlicher suggests that when trials are initiated by domestic regimes instead of international courts, the government's willingness to hold wrongdoers accountable signals to citizens that the country is entering a period of reform (1991).

One of the main contributions about the institutional consequences of domestic trials, from a quantitative perspective, is the series of studies by Kathryn Sikkink and other scholars on what they call a "justice cascade," meaning the increase of criminal accountability for human rights violations worldwide (Lutz and Sikkink 2000; Sriram 2005; Sikkink and Booth Walling 2007). Sikkink and others such as Chandra Lekha Sriram have acknowledged and documented the growing deployment of trials for mass atrocities in diverse countries. This increase in prosecutions was even described by Sriram as a "revolution in accountability" (Sriram 2005). As for the concrete effects of prosecutions, Sikkink has analysed the impact of domestic trials in different countries and evaluated whether the growing number of trials is actually associated with positive developments in democracy and indices of human rights (Sikkink 2011). Using a quantitative approach, they demonstrate that prosecutions can indeed have positive effects on human rights practices and in promoting democracy. These scholars perceive a growing normative consensus away from blanket amnesty or impunity and towards the inclusion of some dimensions of judicialisation. This shift would be mainly attributed to the national adoption of international norms in favour of prosecutions and human rights norms. However, this "internationalist perspective" underestimates local or national factors such as power configurations and the fight of the local human rights movement and victims, as well as other efforts by civil society to promote memory and justice. From a different perspective and focusing on Chile, Cath Collins (2013) shows that domestic trials have, at least partially, "educated" judicial personnel and contributed to the incorporation of international human rights standards into Chilean judicial practice and the legal framework to deal with mass atrocities (2013, 77–80).

All these works provide a strong motivation for the analysis of trials. However, most of them do not analyse the reparative function of prosecutions on victims in national settings. In order to analyse why and how judicial accountability dealing with mass human rights violations can be reparative, it is necessary to explain what the concept of reparation means in general and in particular in relation to human rights trials.

1.2 What does reparation mean?

Traditionally, reparations consist of administrative or judicial proceedings providing monetary compensation to redress harm resulting from an unlawful act that violates the rights of a person (García-Godos 2008; Laplante 2014). However, the meaning of reparation has expanded in the last decade. Recent international legislation and academic scholarship define "reparation" as a set of material and symbolic modalities of redress for victims of human rights violations (Shelton 1999, 2006; Van Boven 2005; De Greiff 2008; Beristain 2009). International law has established an obligation on the state to provide redress to victims of human rights abuses. One of the best known and most comprehensive documents is Theo van Boven's UN Basic Principles and Guidelines (2005). The Basic Principles provide a framework predicated on a growing body of jurisprudence concerning the right to reparations.

Van Boven's guidelines outline four forms of reparation: 1) restitution, 2) compensation, 3) rehabilitation and 4) satisfaction and guarantees of non-repetition. Van Boven clearly understands the notion of reparation in a wider sense than the mere pecuniary one. According to the Basic Principles, the victim's right encompasses among other things (a) access to justice (Section VIII) and (b) access to factual information concerning the violations (Section X). The right to justice is also recognised as an important form of symbolic reparation. The modalities of reparation can have multiple meanings according to the consequences of state violence in a particular context. For that reason, it is essential to undertake an analysis of the local scenario in order to know what might be considered as a reparative outcome in that case.

From the experience of Argentina, it is possible to see a more expansive vision of what prosecutions can achieve in terms of reparation in terms of reparation, going beyond the traditional narrow concepts of retributive justice or monetary compensation. Trials contribute to a new concept of reparation: reparation as change. This concept implies a change in victims' lives which is perceived by them as positive. In order to be reparative, that change should modify those legal, political and social conditions that either generated the original violence or perpetuated victimisation over time. Impunity was one of the main conditions preventing such change in Argentina. This change also depends on the perceptions and social reality of those affected. Human rights trials have the potential to work for change if they are conducted with a victim-centred approach. In analysing domestic prosecutions as a means for reparation, I will focus on three types: civic, personal and social–restorative redress. While these changes will be thoroughly explained in the next chapters, in what follows I will briefly outline their main features.

1.2.1 Civic and legal reparation

The notion of civic reparation refers to the formal restitution of rights to victims, re-establishing their status as citizens. Basic civil rights are typically violated under authoritarian regimes. Citizenship invokes the relationship of an individual to the state and involves access to rights. To belong to a political and legal system within the modern state means access to equal rights for all its members (De Greiff 2008, 460). As shown in Chapter 2, the experience of the dictatorship in Argentina involved a highly restrictive form of citizenship for the whole society, but for the direct victims it involved its total erasure. Arbitrary and illegal arrests, torture and the enforced disappearance of people became widespread. Later, impunity prevailed and survivors and relatives of the disappeared became second-class citizens, or what Guillermo O'Donnell defines for Latin America as "low intensity citizens," (O'Donnell 1993, 5). Victims became a marginalised group of citizens legally deprived of rights enjoyed by others in society.

As I discuss in Chapter 4, the impunity of perpetrators automatically converts their victims into a different kind of citizen. They are legally deprived of access to justice, of having judicial investigations and of knowing the truth about what happened to their loved ones. By contrast, human rights trials operate in the opposite way, recognising these individuals as citizens. Thus, the formulation and application of laws to deal with human rights violations, in the form of amnesties or trials, express an official state position towards victims: either of denial and exclusion or recognition and inclusion. This official position in each different political conjuncture has concrete consequences for the victims, their perceptions, and their interaction with the state. Impunity is the greatest expression of inequality of citizens before the law; human rights trials entitle victims to rights they were previously denied. Restoring citizens' rights enforces the principle that all have the right to equal treatment by the courts, a crucial condition in post-dictatorial contexts. On the other hand, state policies that inhibit the prosecution of human rights perpetrators question whether citizenship belongs to those who endured state crimes. In this way, trials, through the restitution of citizens' rights, constitute a fundamental reparative element in terms of the inclusion of victims in institutional, legal and political spaces of a regime that claims to be democratic.

The right to know the truth is an integral part of the right to justice. Knowing what happened is also considered to be a fundamental human right, especially in cases of enforced disappearance, as established by the UN Convention establishes (United Nations 2006, art 32).

The right to know the truth is an emerging principle contained in several legal documents. International law entitles the families of disappeared persons to know the totality of circumstances surrounding the fate of their relatives and imposes an obligation of investigation on states.[2] Along with the restitution of rights, trials provide an opportunity for the victims to access new information. Beyond their retributive character, trials can operate as truth-seeking mechanisms since they allow victims to make accusations and thus enable investigations of human rights violations. Judicial investigations contribute to reconstructing the past, which, as revealed in the Argentine case, has a reparative effect. The importance of knowing the truth about what happened is based upon the fact that the ongoing suffering of survivors and families of disappeared people is caused to a certain extent by not knowing what happened to them (Parlevliet 1998; Robben 2007).

In the literature dealing with past violations, truth is generally understood to entail not only *knowledge*, but also *acknowledgement*: the determination of facts about the past, and a full, public and official acknowledgement thereof (Weschler 1990; Parlevliet 1998). Acknowledgement entails an official recognition of what happened. This acknowledgment is attained by prosecutions through their investigations and rulings that give account of the seriousness of state violence. Advocates of criminal trials assert that retributive justice provides a means through which victims are recognised and receive redress (Roht-Arriaza 1990; Orentlicher 1991). Bonacker, Oettler and Safferling point out that one of the main reasons why survivors participate in criminal proceedings is in order to be recognised as victims (2013, 286). By prosecuting those responsible for human rights violations, the trials express a clear rejection of the context of repression. The state officially supports the rights of the victims. As Parlevliet (1998, 3) outlines, the strength of acknowledgement seems to have an impact on several levels: on a psychological level, since "it means an affirmation that one's pain is real and worthy of attention." On a social level, it can put an end to the isolation and fear that accompany survivors of gross human rights violations. On a political level, it symbolises that the state takes responsibility for what happened in the past. In this way, and as will be shown in the following chapters, the significance of truth as a means of reparation in relation to human rights violations goes beyond sheer factual knowledge. Truth, understood as knowledge and acknowledgement, may have a strong moral, political and social impact. Attitudes towards victims can be influenced by official acknowledgement which confirms what victims were affirming for years. Truth does not only point out who or what was wrong in the past, but also how people should relate to one another. As Parlevliet (1998, 4) explains: "it provides, as it were, a sort of normative blueprint for the organization of society and the state in the future." This may bring about a different way of interaction between those who were directly affected by violence and other people in their social context.

1.2.2 Personal reparation

By the term "personal reparation," I refer to a process of empowerment of those who were victimised by violence. The whole judicial process, from the investigations and public hearings to the verdict, can produce reparative effects by facilitating a process of recovery of their rights and dignity. One of the key aspects of human rights trials is their retributive function (i.e. they hold perpetrators accountable for their acts). By prosecuting those responsible, trials empower victims and contribute to diminishing the fear many of them still feel. While the literature on the topic is scarce, many factors indicate that, by prosecuting those responsible for state violence, human rights trials challenge fear and thus help to empower victims. As Chapter 7 shows, one factor that led to a decrease in fear is the conviction of perpetrators who while being at liberty – even after the end of the authoritarian regime – continued to threaten and intimidate the victims. Incarcerating the perpetrators involves also removing them not only from the social sphere of the victims, but also from their continued positions in public institutions such as the security forces. As I show in Chapter 7, with the perpetrators in prison, victims gain new freedoms. The risk victims felt before decreases, empowering them and giving them wider scope for action and speech not only in the courts but also in public places. In the course of the trials, survivors and relatives of those who disappeared in Argentina began to tell their stories, assigning names to previously unmentionable events and people (most of them perpetrators).

Trials also provide an opportunity for the victims to speak in public about their experiences, and thus take on an active involvement in the judicial process. The reparative power of truth-telling has been stressed by various scholars (Goldstone

1996; Hayner 2002, Lawry-white 2015). According to Payam Akhavan, a former prosecutor at the ICTY, "truth telling will also enable victims to hear and see their stories told – either their own personal stories or stories like theirs – in an officially sanctioned forum" (1998, 766). The public and official exposure of the truth is itself a form of reparation.

1.2.3 Social reparation

Domestic human rights trials can expand the traditional notion of retributive justice, normally associated with ordinary criminal prosecutions, and have crucial restorative effects. Restorative justice is defined by its advocates as a strategy of justice aimed at redressing the harm done not only to the victims but also to communities. Restorative justice is usually characterised as "relational" since it aims to address and restore the harm that violence caused to social relationships (Zehr 1990; Walgrave 2003; McCold, Llewellyn and Van Ness 2007; Mallinder 2013; Laplante 2014). Thus, the notion of restorative justice refers on the one hand to specific methods or initiatives – which are not retributive – implemented to deal with past atrocities and, on the other hand, it describes the narrow social healing scope of individual prosecutions. As shown in this book, I argue that criminal trials, when properly conducted with a victim-centred approach, can also produce some of the goals adjudicated to other TJ strategies. When violence is intense and systematic, with impunity prevailing for many years, social bonds, trust, systems of norms, social and family solidarity and political participation are severely affected (Lechner 1992; Salimovich, Lira and Weinstein 1992; Feierstein 2006). After the dictatorship and through the impunity period in Argentina, survivors and relatives of the disappeared saw many of their relationships with others in their communities and even within their own families broken. Here, the social scope of trials plays an important role since it not only has an impact on the victims but also on other parts of society and can resonate in the everyday lives of all those who are affected. As stated in Chapter 8, human rights trials have the potential to transform, at least partially, the social and institutional context of the victims. Argentina's trials have an important impact on the social perceptions and ties in which the victims are embedded, particularly because of the way in which they are carried out, in oral and public hearings, with space for storytelling, and with the presence of the public and media.

However, much literature on restorative and retributive justice ignores these kinds of experiences. As a matter of fact, the "restorative versus retributive justice debate," which is addressed in detail in Chapter 8, calls into question that criminal justice can have a reparative potential for victims at all. The reparative function of criminal trials is questioned by claiming that there are greater benefits in other justice alternatives in which punishment of perpetrators is excluded, such as truth and inquiry commissions. Retributive justice instead is seen as a mere confrontation between victims and perpetrators (Sherman and Strang 2007; Parent 2010). Although these arguments might be adequate when applied to the regular criminal system for minor offences, they do not seem appropriate when dealing with systematic human rights violations.

Advocates of the restorative justice approach continually compare the advantages of initiatives such as truth commissions with public hearings or local traditional practices or rituals which are more common in African countries with the fruits of ordinary criminal justice and consider the former as the best option to repair the damage caused to victims. Supporters of this position criticise what they call "the punishment-centred perspective" of trials, arguing that sanctions are not the only means to resolve conflict in society: in their view restorative justice is a more adequate way to repair the personal and social damage caused by violence (Zehr 1990; Clamp 2014) and deter future crimes (Sherman and Strang 2007, 21). It is sometimes argued that mechanisms such as inquiry and reconciliation commissions or public apologies deliver a differently textured accountability by moving beyond overly proceduralised forms of adversarial justice as adjudications of individual guilt toward a more complex account of individual, communal and institutional accountability (Bell and O'Rourke 2007, 40). According to this perspective, justice should not be understood only as punitive but should aim instead at restoring victims' and communities' social ties (Mallinder 2013, 145). However, my study shows that this reflects a very restricted and unnuanced view of criminal justice, especially when applied to mass human rights violations, since it fails to acknowledge the full extent to which retributive justice can contribute to offering redress to victims. This study does not deny the limitations of the trials or the reparative aspects of restorative justice initiatives. Nevertheless, some literature on restorative justice – though not all of it – tends to present an idealised picture of the scope of restorative justice in only stressing the failings of trials. As Bell and O'Rourke stress in their critique to this notion of restorative justice:

> what appear to be compromises with liberalism's rule of law requirements, such as "truth for amnesty," are hereby reconceptualised, away from a notion of a problematic "justice gap" and towards a notion of an innovative "bottom up" mechanism capable of squaring the circle between strict punishment and total amnesty.
>
> (2007, 40)

Of course, retributive justice presents also important limitations and per se is not sufficient for a holistic reparation of victims. It has, however, many potentialities for reparation and it can vary greatly according to the ways in which it is implemented in every specific context. To consider the importance of the reparative function of trials in Argentina is not tantamount to making it a universalising experience. There is no need to deny or minimise the potential benefits of retributive justice in order to highlight the positive elements of restorative justice, especially when dealing with human rights violations. In fact, both can be implemented in a complementary manner where the victims and the community agree to do so.

Yet, when asserting that trials can have reparative and restorative effects on victims' lives, it is important to make clear what I mean by restorative in the Argentine case and what not. First, it should be noted that by "restorative" I do not mean a restoration of the *status quo ante* or the situation prior to the violence, since that is impossible. Second, much of the literature equates restorative justice with the complex concept of reconciliation. However, this is a vague term which is used in extremely different ways by many scholars and practitioners and can widely express divergent things.[3] While there is critical literature on the idea of reconciliation (Humphrey 2000; Schaap 2005; Little 2012), attempts to define reconciliation and highlight its normative benefits abound in the scholarship. There is also a tendency in academic research to think of reconciliation as a positive process towards the accommodation of political difference in divided societies (Little 2012). The question then arises as to who is supposed to reconcile with whom and on which bases? As I show in the following chapters, survivors and relatives of the disappeared in Argentina have no intention to have any link with former perpetrators who, as a matter of fact, after 30 years, are still convinced that the crimes they committed were justified. None of them have regretted their acts, apologised or provided important information on the disappeared that could bring relief to their families. In this scenario, the only relationships to be restored at least at a basic level are the ones of victims, as members of the community, with other members of their social environment, but not with perpetrators.

Thus, reconciliation is a multi-faceted concept which may acquire different meanings and political implications in different contexts (Hermann 2004). As Adrian Little asserts, a key issue at stake when using the concept of reconciliation is the need for a specific and deeply contextual understanding of the meaning of reconciliation to unpack the ideological, political and legal consequences that reconciliation may invoke within a specific context (2012, 83).While in countries such as South Africa or Rwanda reconciliation may have been linked with projects of nation-building, non-violent cohabitation of victims and perpetrators within communities, as an instrumentalistic or pragmatic way of living together, including what Susanne Buckley-Zistel describes as a "chosen amnesia" (2006), or even with development and poverty reduction (Zorbas 2004), in the Latin American context in general and in the Argentine one specifically, this notion has been used as synonym for impunity and was primarily used to justify a public stance of "forgive and forget" towards past crimes (Roht-Arriaza 2004; Figari Layús 2015). Indeed, in Argentina, "reconciliation" has often been invoked as both the objective of and justification for enacting amnesty laws and pardons (Druliolle 2013, 260).[4] This explains the deeply contested nature of the concept there. The notion of reconciliation is certainly not universally beneficial and can be harmful where the implications of its application is detrimental to victims, as is the case in Argentina.

For all these reasons, when I describe the restorative effects of trials, I am not referring to the concept of reconciliation that could even be adequate to describe other case studies. Reconciliation is not an appropriate term for understanding the social scope of trials in the Argentine case. Rather, by restorative effects I refer to the emergence of new attitudes of respect, inclusion and solidarity between victims and other members of their communities which give victims the possibility of new practices and integration into social and institutional settings from which they had been excluded for years.

Therefore, human rights prosecutions should not be viewed in opposition to restorative justice. Instead, when properly implemented, retributive justice can borrow and blend elements from it. As the next chapters show, the boundaries between both approaches are blurred in practice when the concrete social and restorative effects of domestic human rights trials are analysed. In this way, the case of Argentina demonstrates the important reparative potential of prosecutions and provides meaningful insights for other societies where mass atrocities took place.

Finally, before engaging with the questions of why human rights trials can have reparative–restorative effects on victim' lives, it is important to stress that reparation is in itself an incomplete process. The immeasurable harm caused by torture, sexual violence, extrajudicial killings and enforced disappearance is irreparable and irreversible. The facts resulting from the traumatic experience of captivity in a torture and detention centre cannot be changed. It is impossible to make people reappear or to erase the pain of their loss. Thus, it is important to note that although trials can contribute to reparation for victims in different aspects of their lives, the consequences of violence do not vanish.

1.3 Why do human rights trials provide reparation?

The question now is why human rights trials have a reparative potential for victims. Much of the literature on prosecutions offers vague explanations of the underlying mechanisms that enable retributive justice to produce reparative effects. In the case of the restitution of rights (to justice and truth for instance) it is clear why trials can redress victims. In other cases, especially when it comes to the restorative potential of trials in the recognition of the suffering, the diminution of fear, and the change of social attitudes and perceptions towards the victims, the mechanism is not so clear. In order to address this point, it is necessary to pay attention to two fundamental functions of law: its influence on social behaviour and potential as a mechanism of acknowledgement, briefly mentioned above.

1.3.1 Communicating and shaping social behaviour

As an expression of the authority of the state, the law has the power to influence attitudes and perceptions regulating different aspects of social and political life, including norms and values. As Tyler asserts, "the purpose of creating law and empowering legal authorities is to establish and maintain social order by regulating public behaviour" (Tyler 2006, 269). To be authoritative, legal rules must affect the actions of those towards whom they are directed. Through the formulation of laws, the authorities have the power to shape public behaviour and aim to do so. Laws are the product of historical, social and political processes and represent a system of rules and mandates, enforced through social institutions, to govern behaviour (Tyler 2006, 16–19; De Gregorio 2007, 172–173; Crawford and Hucklesby 2013, 1–2). From a sociological perspective, Pierre Bourdieu affirms that the law operates as a powerful discourse that is coupled with physical means (punishment)to impose compliance on others, which might be understood as an instrument to normalise social behaviour (1987, 848). According to Bourdieu, the law aims at towards exceptions and vagueness by imposing clear and strict borders in society. Juridical formalisation would thus introduce clarity and predictability into social relations and interaction (Bourdieu 1987, 849). Similarly, according to political scientist Guillermo O'Donnell, the legal system is a constitutive part of the state that "penetrates and textures society, furnishing a basic element of predictability and stability to social relations" (O'Donnell 1998, 15).

Now, if the formulation and application of the law convey a mandate to be obeyed, it becomes clear that the law is, in the words of Antony Duff in his famous book *Punishment, Communication and Community*, an instrument of communication (2001). According to Duff, communication involves a reciprocal and rational engagement: it requires someone with whom we try to communicate. It aims to engage that person as an active participant in the process, one who will receive and respond to the communication, and it appeals to the other's reason and understanding – the response it seeks is mediated by the other's rational grasp of its contents (Duff 2001, 80–81). As Duff asserts, criminal law seeks not just the obedience of the population to its demands, but its understanding and acceptance of what is required of them as citizens.

The signal that the message(s) conveyed by the law was/were *received* by society is translated into social attitudes. The most explicit of these attitudes is compliance with the explicit text of the law, such as "Do not kill." However, the law may communicate more than one explicit message, or convey implicit messages which produce multiple forms of conduct that go beyond the explicit compliance with the command "Do not kill." The law not only communicates explicitly that a certain act-crime is permitted or prohibited, but also conveys underlying implicit messages. When it comes to mass human rights violations, the enforcement of laws, whether for impunity or for trials, involves concrete consequences and – explicit and implicit – messages which influence social attitudes towards victims. As I show in the next chapters, the amnesty laws and their consequences (such as the fact that perpetrators remained at liberty) in the 1980s and 1990s in Argentina sent a strong message to society that endorsed "forgetting, forgiving and reconciliating." By legally excusing perpetrators, these laws helped legitimise the repressors' actions and allowed them to justify their crimes while reinforcing the trend of blaming the victims. This had serious repercussions on victims' lives and their relation to some sectors of society as the effects of state terror were reproduced over time, engendering fear, social silence and stigmatisation.

By contrast, human rights trials, by expressing official disapproval of the crimes and acknowledging the damage and the victims' status, tend to foster different social attitudes such as a higher sensitivity, solidarity and interest for the suffering of others. The law can influence the way a society deals with human rights violations, their perpetrators and their victims.

1.3.2 Symbolic effectiveness: legitimacy, acknowledgment and its social implications

The social legitimacy of the law seems to be the "magical" element of its impact and effectiveness in society. The reasons underlying the legitimacy of the law as the expression of the authority of the state, which enables it to shape social attitudes and obtain compliance, are still hotly debated by contemporary social scientists (see for instance Tyler 2006, Crawford and Hucklesby 2013). According to them, legitimacy in the eyes of the public is a key precondition for the effectiveness of power. Changes in legitimacy would affect the degree to which people comply with laws in their everyday lives. But what makes the law authoritative and provides it with legitimacy to influence social perceptions?

According to Antony Duff, the relevance and authoritative element of the message inscribed in the law's command is given by the sanction or punishment that non-compliance with the law would entail. For this author, punishment, as one of the central aspects of criminal law, serves an expressive and communicative purpose (Duff 2001). Similarly, for Feinberg punishment "is a conventional device for the expression of attitudes of resentment and indignation, and of judgments of disapproval and reprobation, on the part either of the punishing authority itself or of those 'in whose name' the punishment is inflicted" (Feinsberg 1970). Without denying the relevance of punishment, Pierre Bourdieu (1987, 849) argues that the legitimacy of the law but also of what he calls the "juridical field" comes from the growing internal rationality, professionalisation and rhetoric of impersonality and neutrality which comes to characterise the judicial language and produces two major effects: *neutralisation* and *universalisation*. These are designed to mark the impersonality of normative utterances and to establish the speaker as a universal subject, at once impartial and objective (Ibid., 820). For instance, he argues, the use of indefinites and of the eternal present expresses a generality or omni temporality of the rule of law, the existence of an ethical consensus is presupposed, and there is a recourse to fixed formulas and locutions, which give little room for individual variations. Neutrality and universality would be the expressions of the work of rationalisation to which the system of juridical norms is continually subordinated (Ibid.). The development of a body of rules and procedures with a claim to universality and neutrality, a product of a rationalisation process in the juridical field, provides the law and its judgments with *symbolic effectiveness and legitimacy* in society. This legitimacy ignores or hides the political arbitrariness of the law. For Bourdieu, this rationalisation process increased the separation between legal judgments based upon the law and others belonging to other institutions or common sense of justice. The result of this is that the legal system and its laws appear both to those who impose them and to those upon whom they are imposed, as totally independent of the power relations which such a system sustains and legitimises. This apparently bias-free logic and rhetoric of rationalisation is what provides the law with the authority and legitimacy and, in Bourdieu's words, the "quasi-magical power" (Ibid., 839) to effectively communicate specific explicit and implicit messages to the population whose behaviour it aims to influence.

Michel Foucault also gives an account of how legal discourse becomes a powerful producer of legitimate knowledge and truth (2007). Foucault analyses the link between systems of power, systems of knowledge and juridical discourse as a productive system of a truth that plays a legitimising role in a society's narratives. The way in which legal processes reconstruct and represent a past of systematic human rights violations perpetrated by agents of the state can have important symbolic and performative effects on victims and society, and on the construction of collective memory. Indeed, some scholars present the legitimacy of judicial narrative in producing historical truth as unquestionable: "the most authoritative rendering of the truth is possible only as a result of judicial inquiry, and major prosecutions can generate a comprehensive record of past violations" (Orentlicher 1991, 32).

1.3.3 The power of the law

The concealment of the political nature of the law is fundamental to guaranteeing its legitimacy, compliance and thus effectiveness in society. Although the state aims through the law to provide the image of representing the common, general interest, it actually provides the authorities behind it with the power to regulate and influence social behaviour in favour of a certain social order according to the prevailing power relations in each historical context. Therefore, the messages and social attitudes that the law seeks to communicate and foster are not neutral, as the groups behind it often claim. Following Bourdieu, the law has the symbolic power to name and to create the things it names: "The law creates the social world, but only if we remember that it is this world which first creates the law" (Bourdieu 1987, 839). Thus, authorities in different historical contexts have looked for various legitimising explanations in order to justify their authority and power over a certain population and to obtain compliance by promoting social behaviour which was functional and beneficial to their interests.

The formulation and application of criminal justice reflects the results of political struggles between different political and social interests in society. Those who prevail in these struggles are the ones who for the most part impose the law: law and judicial procedures thus operate as an instrument of power or, according to Foucault (2004), as one instrument among the multiple forms of domination. The law encompasses a set of practices, discourses and institutions, which, on the one hand, are the reflection of the relations of power existing in the social body and, on the other, disseminate and reproduce these relations of power and domination. As Foucault states, the law is a product of wars and social struggles:

> War obviously presided over the birth of state: right, peace, laws were born in the blood and mud of battles. (. . .) The law is born of real battles, victories, massacre, and conquests.
>
> (Foucault 2004, 50)

The state is constituted by social and power relations, and depending on the kind of legal system and policies, it promotes and establishes a certain legal order which can never be neutral. In a similar vein, political scientist Guillermo O'Donnell stresses the political bias of the legal system as one of its main features:

> The legal system is a constitutive dimension of the state and of the order that it establishes and guarantees over the given territory. That order is not an equal, socially impartial order; (. . .) it backs, and helps to reproduce, systematically asymmetric power relationships.
>
> (O'Donnell 1993, 3)

O'Donnell has further analysed how in Latin America the law is characterised by its discretionary, and often exactingly severe, application upon marginalised sectors of the population as an efficient means of oppression (O'Donnell 1998). The flip side of this is the ways in which the privileged sectors, whether directly or by means of appropriate personal connections, exempt themselves from abiding by the law. In Latin America, there is a long tradition of ignoring the law or, when acknowledging it, twisting it in favour of the elites, and for repressing or containing marginalised groups, usually considered as "dangerous." In O'Donnell's words: "to be powerful is to have impunity" (O'Donnell 1998, 13). In this context, the violence of the state, economic elites or powerful private actors such as business companies is not usually submitted to regular administrative procedures and gains criminal impunity.

However, power and legal structures can always be challenged. The law is not the fruit of a consensus that puts an end to all conflicts but the product of multiple and complex social relations of power which can change over time. Thus, the state and the justice system become a space of political and social dispute for conflicting groups' interests and values, with strong symbolic and material consequences for society.

A trial represents a paradigmatic staging of the symbolic struggle inherent in the social world: a struggle in which antagonistic world-views confront each other (Bourdieu 1987, 837). Thus, prosecutions in human rights cases do not only rely upon the presentation of facts and witnesses but also express an interpretation of those facts, creating either a new narrative of the past or reproducing an old one. Judges, who are not neutral but influenced by the social and political context in which they are immersed, evaluate all the evidence and make a selection between competing historical explanations of the past (Wilson 2005, 918). A legal judgment brings to an end, or at least limits, (however provisionally) the struggle over the disputed view of that past and its main actors. It allocates clear responsibilities and thus defines aspects of that violent past, producing, for instance, a clear division between victims and perpetrators, and setting out the causes of violence and its effects on the victims and society. Thus, legal narratives of the past contribute to the production of a conclusive past: they are also an active force that determines relationships between different actors and power relationships in the present. In this sense, the battle for a certain interpretation of the past is also a battle over the legitimacy of the power relations of the present. In Argentina, the judicial field has become one of the most important institutional frames in which the battle for the control of a legitimate representation of the state repression of the 1970s takes place.

Amnesties and trials concerning human rights violations express opposed official state interpretations and positions, not only towards the crimes in question but also towards the victims and the perpetrators. While amnesties deny recognition to victims and their rights, trials grant it. In both cases, this implies an official position with concrete consequences for the victims and the way how they are perceived and treated by other sectors of society. Pablo de Greiff asserts that recognition is both a condition and a consequence of justice (2008, 461). If recognition through the trials is so important, it is precisely because they clearly and publicly define who are the perpetrators and who the victims, and the latter regain their rights as citizens. This recognition of individuals as victims has a significant and restorative meaning for them, especially in contexts, such as Argentina, where some sectors of the population did not see them as victims but rather as "subversives" or "terrorists" and often stigmatised them or made them invisible during periods of impunity. The symbolic effectiveness of the law as an instrument of communication as well as a punitive mechanism can contribute to understanding why in contexts such as the Argentinean one the recognition provided by the law is so crucial. The law has the legitimacy and force to shape social attitudes and perceptions in society in general and also specifically when dealing with human rights violations.

Therefore, many actors throughout history have fought to have an influence on the formulation and application of the law, since the law allows changes in the social order in which they are immersed. Indeed, as this research demonstrates, a legal system which enables criminal trials to prosecute agents of the state responsible for human rights violations promotes a very different social order from one which prohibits those kinds of procedures and provides amnesty for perpetrators. While laws that create impunity tend to promote a social order that favours perpetrators and stigmatises victims, human rights trials foster the emergence of what here is considered a framework for reparation and the recognition of victims, with the latter being respected and included. As will be shown in the next chapters, the struggle of victims and human rights organisations in Argentina also entails a struggle to change the law and fulfil victims' rights, and therefore to change, in a positive and inclusive way, the social context. Now, to understand the meaning of reparation provided by human rights trials, it is first important to consider what damage is to be repaired in each specific case. Thus, in what follows I provide an analysis of the damage caused to victims first by state terror (Chapter 2) and later by impunity in Argentina (Chapter 4).

Notes

1 Some of these goals can also be found in the preamble of the Rome Statute of the ICC, which links prosecution of grave crimes with the goals of "peace, security and well, being of the world," and "ending impunity contributing thus to prevention of such crimes." (United Nations General Assembly 1998).

2 See Art. 24, 2 of the International Convention for the Protection of All Persons from Enforced Disappearance (United Nations 2006).

3 For instance, Hamber and Van der Merwe (1998) describe how in the South African case in the 1990s reconciliation was equated with a number of diverse goals such as non-racial ideologies, an agenda of inter-communal understanding and a form of community building among others. Depending on which of these approaches was paramount, very different meanings of reconciliation emerged with varying knock-on effects for policy and practice (Litle 2012). What is more, Hamber and Van der Merwe state that at different times the Truth and Reconciliation Commission (TRC) articulated different understandings of reconciliation to meet their objectives (see also Doxtader 2001; Hayner 2002; Litle 2012)

4 As discussed in Chapter 4, in Argentina former president Carlos Menem justified the approval of pardons of military perpetrators in 1989 and 1991 in the name of "national reconciliation."

Part II

Implications of state terror, limited justice and impunity for victims of human rights violations

Chapter 2

The hallmarks of state terror on victims and the wider Argentine society

The reparative impact of domestic trials on victims' lives can be constructively examined by situating it within a particular political and historical context (Palmer 2012, 157). Therefore, this chapter provides an analysis of the damage caused by the military government on victims and other sectors of society. The dissemination of terror was one of the most important political strategies used by Latin American dictatorships in the social disciplining and control of the population (Corradi, Fagen and Garretonet 1992, 89; Malamud-Goti 1996, 111–120). The dictatorship in Argentina made use of psychosocial repressive methods to spread terror in order to produce lasting structural changes, deactivate revolutionary political forces and destroy collective identities, relationships based on solidarity and practices of resistance (Lechner 1992; Duhalde 1999; Feierstein 2006; Izaguirre 2009; Bayer et al. 2010). Though in different ways and degrees, protracted repression caused fear and anguish not only among the relatives of the people who were killed and disappeared but also reached other segments of the population. Therefore, to limit the damage of state terror only to the category of victims (disappeared, survivors, political prisoners) is to fail to apprehend its social repercussions. State terror, while deployed against individuals, is also directed at the larger social body (Suarez-Orozco 1992). Used as a tool of political domination, terror was instilled and multiplied by those holding power, through extreme violence, stigmatising discourses (the political construction of a dangerous "other"), the control of the media and changes in school curricula. Dominant narratives were intended to silence the voices of the victims, and to manipulate public opinion with the aim to legitimate state-sponsored violence. In Argentina the spread of terror by the systematic torture and enforced disappearance of people was a crucial mechanism in the control of society, the disarticulation of social links and the elimination of opposition.

In order to give a clear and detailed understanding of the impact of state terror on victims and society, I will present my analysis in five sections. The first provides a description of the Argentine political context of the 1970s that gave rise to the military dictatorship as well as its *modus operandi*. The second section deepens the analysis by describing the specific characteristics of the enforced disappearance of people in Argentina. In the third section I address, on the one hand, some of the legal political implications of state terror which derived from the absolute deprivation of rights. On the other hand, I provide an overview of the crucial collaboration of the judiciary with the military regime as well as the resistance practices mounted by relatives, victims and human rights organisations. In the fourth and fifth sections I give an account of how terror affected the connections of victims to society by breaking social bonds and practices of solidarity, while it created an image of victims that contributed to their stigmatisation and a displacement of responsibility. The analysis of the impact of terror on society helps to explain why the terror that prevailed during the dictatorship continued in the form of fear years after the military regime came to an end and why trials can contribute to redress these phenomena.

2.1 State organised violence in Argentina

The military regime which began in Argentina in 1976 is not an isolated experience, but the most extreme expression of a series of military interventions (1930–1932, 1943–1946, 1955–1958, 1962–1963, and 1966–1973) not only in the country but also in the continent. Indeed, the history of military dictatorships in Argentina should be understood within a larger socio-political context, as the regimes were part of a conflict on regional scales (Zarankin and Salerno 2008). Since the victory of the independence movements, Latin America swayed between democratic and authoritarian governments (Meyer and Mena 1989). During the 1960s and 1970s, several countries in Central and South America came under rule of dictatorships.[1] These used repressive forces to combat and eliminate all forms of political opposition. In turn, the use of state repression did not always take place under dictatorial regimes but also under constitutional ones.

In the specific case of Argentina, from 1930 onwards, the armed forces regularly intervened in politics with military coups, often in alliance with the landowning and urban elites. This tendency was reinforced by the ten years of the first Peronist governments (1945–1955). While President Juan Domingo Perón gained the support of the working class, he also met with the opposition of conservative sectors within the armed forces, as well as of important sectors of civil society. In 1955 Perón was overthrown by a military coup backed by the Catholic Church hierarchy, all the non-Peronist parties, and important sectors of the middle classes and of the rural and urban economic elites (Cavarozzi 1997, 19). Another military coup took place in 1966. The goal of the military was to impose a political and social "order" and stabilise the economy, a policy involving the reduction of the role of the state that had become central under the Peronist governments (Tedesco 1999, 9, 17). During this dictatorship, known as the *Revolución Libertadora* (Liberating Revolution) and which lasted until 1973, political polarisation deepened. The suppression of civil and political rights, in combination with the international context of the Cold War, sparked resistance movements among workers, students and the lower ranks of the Catholic Church, motivated by ideas of social justice and revolution (Van Drunen 2010). Sources of inspiration were as diverse as the Cuban Revolution, the experience of May 1968 in France and the liberation struggles in the colonised world. There was a process of political radicalisation among these sectors in Latin America, in which the armed struggle was increasingly seen as a means of achieving social change. The United States saw the growth of left-wing movements in Latin America as a threat to their national interests and thus supported the aspirations of military elites in the region (Lernoux 1980).[2]

At the beginning of the 1970s in Argentina, political-military (or guerrilla) organisations emerged, the Marxist-Leninist *Ejército Revolucionario del Pueblo* (People's Revolutionary Army, hereafter ERP), and the Peronist *Montoneros* being the two most important ones. The *Montoneros* received the support of Perón, who had become the central figure of the opposition during his exile in Madrid (Gillespie 1982, 40). The organisation experienced an exponential growth following its strategic alliance with the *Juventud Peronista* (Peronist Youth, JP). This alliance provided the organisation with a mass movement, which came to be identified as the *Tendencia Revolucionaria* (Revolutionary Tendency) within the Peronist movement (Van Drunen 2010). These political-military organisations, as well as other forms of protest such as mass strikes, riots, and demonstrations, put the military regime under extreme pressure (Gillespie 1982, 113). As social protests increased, the regime felt obliged to clear the way for elections. Frenetic political activity characterised the period of the electoral campaign, which lasted until March 1973. The Peronist *Tendencia Revolucionaria* played a key role in the campaign, mobilising impressive numbers of people on the streets, and at demonstrations and rallies in favour of Héctor Cámpora, the Peronist candidate running for president as Perón had been proscribed (Gillespie 1982; Marchak 1999). Cámpora won the elections and was inaugurated as President of Argentina on 25 May 1973. During his short presidency, the *Tendencia Revolucionaria* acquired a number of important political positions within the government, the National Congress, provincial governments, local legislatures and in higher education (Gillespie 1982). But tensions also grew with the right wing of the Peronist movement, represented by the trade unions. After Perón took over presidency in September 1973, these unions became increasingly dominant within the government, gradually displacing the representatives of the left (Gillespie 1982; Verbitsky 1985).

The death of President Perón in July 1974 heralded a great escalation in violence. His wife, Isabel Perón, who was his vice president, assumed the presidency. From then, attacks on the left became more violent and were directed at targets far beyond the guerrilla forces. The activities of para-police groups such as the *Alianza Anticomunista Argentina* (Argentine Anti-Communist Alliance, Triple A[3]), which had started in 1973, intensified and reached their peak in 1974 and 1975 (Van Drunen 2010, 17). These death squads, which included members of the security forces, abducted, tortured and killed more than 1,000 activists and left their bodies on the roads to instil terror in society. Numerous opponents went into exile after seeing their names on the death lists of the Triple A (Van Drunen 2010, 17; Robben 2007, 136–138).

The political situation worsened when in January 1975 the involvement of the army in matters of internal security was extended in the operation against the rural guerrilla forces of the ERP in the northern province of Tucumán which the military designated as "Operation Independence."[4] Many of the repressive practices that would be carried out during the military dictatorship of 1976–1983 were applied for the first time in Tucumán (Izaguirre 2004; Feierstein 2006). At that time, newspapers reported daily on acts of political violence, real and alleged armed confrontations between guerrillas and security forces, political assassinations and bombings (Novaro and Palermo 2003, 80). Social protests, especially from the workers' movement, also marked the period (Gillespie 1982, 203–204). In this context of economic crisis, social protest and political repression, an alliance began to emerge between powerful economic groups and the armed forces with the purpose of reorganising the country to further their economic and political interests. The operations to suppress social demands and mobilisation which preceded the 1976 coup produced 15 per cent of those killed, disappeared and victimised during the repression of the period (Izaguirre 2004, 8).

2.1.1 The military dictatorship

On 24 March 1976, a military coup overthrew the government of president Isabel Martínez de Perón. A Junta consisting of Lieutenant-General Jorge Rafael Videla, Admiral Emilio Massera and Brigadier-General Orlando Agosti took power. The *Proceso de Reorganización Nacional* (National Reorganisation Process) as the military called the dictatorship, institutionalised a system of repression justified by an alleged "struggle against subversion." The military government stressed that Argentina was increasingly dominated by "terrorism, violence, and chaos" (Junta Militar 1980, 11). This discourse aimed at justifying the dismantling of popular resistance through the physical annihilation of all those considered enemies.

Within this dictatorial framework, the state combined a façade of legality with the clandestine or para-legal activities of special "task forces." There was a co-existence of two simultaneous but opposite faces of the state, one legal and the other clandestine (Duhalde 1999). Abductions, tortures, assassinations and even disappearances had already taken place in 1974–1975, but after 1976, the repressive practices acquired a systematic and widespread character. The armed forces took over command and responsibility for carrying out repressive and coordinated actions at the national level.[5] They drew inspiration from the Doctrine of National Security, the experience of the French military in Algeria and from the training sessions in counterinsurgency warfare that they had received in the School of the Americas in Panama (Armony 1997; Novaro and Palermo 2003; Robin 2004). More than 450 CDCs for the secret detention of prisoners were scattered throughout the entire country. *Grupos de tareas* (task groups) were responsible for the repression within and outside the CDCs. These operations groups comprised young officers, policemen and civilians. Both the task groups and the clandestine detention facilities were dedicated to the tracking, detention, torture and jailing or execution of alleged "enemies." In general, each task group was assigned to a specific geographical area and CDC as basis of operations (Armony 1997). As will be shown in the following chapters, many survivors and relatives of the disappeared refer to the CDCs as "concentrations camps" since the captivity conditions were very similar to those of the concentrations camps during the Holocaust.[6]

The definition of potential enemies was so broad that it could encompass many different groups: militants of the most diverse social and political organisations, including labour union representatives, shop stewards on factory committees, members of student centres, welfare kitchens, neighbourhood centres, politicians, priests, nuns, professionals, intellectuals, journalists, relatives or friends of the victims. Those targeted ranged from Peronist groupings to the entire gamut of the left, and even several independent movements without any clear partisan affiliation (Feierstein 2006, 150; Van Drunen 2010, 15). The dictatorship sought to neutralise all opposition to the government's economic and political project (Servetto 2004, 1–2).

The objective of the so-called *Proceso de Reorganización Nacional* was the liberalisation of the economy, a goal that underlay the wave of repressive military regimes experienced across the region at the time (Pucciarelli 2004). The coups in Argentina, Chile, Uruguay and Brazil were in part a response to the rise of left-wing politics (whether armed or not) throughout the 1960s. These military governments defended existing elite privileges but also aimed, in many cases, to establish new, free-market economic models which would benefit a new elite and/or the international financial sector to the detriment of domestic industries. The new regimes represented a return to a free and open market, a mercantilist developmental logic after the autarchic import-substitution industrialisation (ISI) emphasis of the 1960s (Canelo 2004; Pucciarelli 2004). For this project to work, it was necessary to terminate the earlier interventionist state model that had accompanied ISI with its particular logic of modernisation. It was also considered necessary, therefore, to contain social and political costs by disempowering or deactivating strong unions and other types of social and political organisations that had grown under the state-centric model. A fuller discussion of the political economy of the Argentine dictatorship and its regional counterparts lies beyond the scope of this work, but it is important to note that Argentina at this time had strongly corporatist political traditions and high levels of urban working-class political and union organisation. Although the regime was accordingly less willing or able than others to impose a fully neoliberal, open-market model – the neoliberalisation of the Argentine economy having been, if anything, completed and deepened under the post-dictatorship government of Carlos Menem (1989–1999) – state terror was both used and widely perceived as a repressive political tool designed in part to carry out a process of deindustrialisation that intended not only to benefit the financial sector of the economy, but also, in conjunction with the repressive actions, to dismantle and eliminate the social and workers' movements that lay behind the high levels of social conflict (Canelo 2004,

Pucciarelli 2004). Thus, many interviewees, including victims and non-victims, remarked on the strong links between the practices of terror and repression meant to transform the country's economic policies and its beneficiaries. The conceptualisation of human rights violations as instrumental in obtaining further goals makes it possible to understand the reasons underlying repression. The link between specific economic goals and human rights violations is emerging during current human rights trials that have gradually begun to prosecute those civilians and entrepreneurs who, to further their economic interests, actively supported state violence by financing illegal activities, for example, or by handing over trade unionists to the security forces. One well-known case involved complaints against the German motor company Mercedes Benz (Weber 1999). By 1980, the guerrilla groups were wiped out, as were a variety of political parties, trade unions and social movements.

2.1.2 Reconstructing the meaning of state violence

The repression and enforced disappearance of those considered as opposition was the result of a state policy of violence in Argentina, which was planned and systematically executed. The way this state violence is labelled, defined and interpreted is the object of discussions in many social and political realms, and also reflected in the current human rights trials and their judgments. This reconstruction and classification of the past can vary according to the actors, ideologies and interests. Narratives of the past construct reality not only in the form of memory, but also as an active force that establishes relationships between different actors in the present. Different scholarly terminology has been used during the last decades to explain the illegal repression of the 1970s and 1980s in Argentina, such as "dirty war," "irregular warfare," "antisubversive war," "dictatorship," "state terror," "state terrorism," "terrorist state" (Duhalde 1999), "crimes against humanity" and "genocide" (Feierstein 2006, 2011).[7] The terms referring to the state violence as a "dirty," "counterrevolutionary," "antisubversive" or "irregular" war have been historically raised by the military to justify illegal detentions, tortures, murders and disappearances Indeed, this argument of "irregular warfare" has been held by the military and those who supported them up to the present, even in the current trials as part of their defence strategy. At this point, however, it is already out of discussion and even proven and supported by many judicial decisions[8] that what happened in Argentina was not a war of any kind, but a systematic plan of extermination against all those considered as opposition.

The other nominations which make clear that military repression was a vertical, top-to-bottom kind of violence – such as state terrorism, crimes against humanity and genocide are part of a fervid debate among survivors, relatives of disappeared persons, human rights organisations, lawyers and academics in Argentina. Therefore, as will be seen in the interviews throughout this work, these different interpretations – excluding of course the one of a "war" – are reflected in the way in which the interviewees refer to that period. While some of them describe the military repression as genocide, others refer to it as state terrorism or simply as dictatorship.

2.2 Forced disappearance in Argentina

The forced disappearance of persons was the dominant instrument of terrorisation used by the military. According to the legal definition of the UN International Convention for the Protection of All Persons from Enforced Disappearance:

> Enforced disappearance is considered to be the arrest, detention, abduction or any other form of deprivation of liberty by agents of the state or by persons or groups of persons acting with the authorisation, support or acquiescence of the state, followed by a refusal to acknowledge the deprivation of liberty or by concealment of the fate or whereabouts of the disappeared person, which place such a person outside the protection of the law.
>
> (United Nations 2006, Article 2)

This general definition acquires specific features in different social and political contexts. The specificities of enforced disappearance in Argentina involved a series of interconnected acts (illegal detention, official denial of that detention, torture, and concealment of the person or the body in case of murder). While some of these acts were visible to society – this is the case of military and police raids in the streets, the abduction of persons in public places in broad daylight and the screams of detainees being tortured in CDCs located in the middle of the city – others were kept in the shadows, such as the murder of persons and the concealment of their bodies. This logic of showing and concealing as a basis of terror is very well explained by Pilar Calveiro: a part of what is otherwise concealed is shown in order to disseminate terror, with the immediate effect being silence and immobility (Calveiro 1998, 26). The imposition of terror through the double facet of showing and concealing has been commented upon by several interviewees from different provinces. For instance, a plaintiff from Rosario, whose first husband was disappeared, recalled the social climate in her city at the time:

> No sooner had the coup occurred than they [the military] were already in the streets seeking us out, trying to abduct us. Then they operated in full view of everyone, they killed people in the street in broad daylight. They banned the assembly of three [or more] people in the street, people were even afraid when they waited for the bus. The tanks were in the streets and the neighbourhoods were taken over, you went shopping for groceries five or six blocks away from home and when you returned, you could not go in, and there was no knowing what you could find at home because they [the military] did as they liked and they broke into and looted houses, whether or not they found the people they were looking for (. . .). They instilled an

> immense terror in the population. At that time they began to take people away and, in general, when they abducted someone, as no answers were given, the first thing one thought, rather naively at the time, was that he or she was being held *incommunicado*.
>
> (Int. 27, March 2011, Rosario)

This was a commonplace scenario in many provinces. Police and military raids in the streets operated as another means to display terror and the risk of arbitrary arrest on suspicion of being a potential "subversive." As stated by an activist from the province of Tucumán:

> There was terror in the streets, they [the military] would stop people on buses, trains, undergrounds, they would close [bus and train] stations, stop trains and everyone [had to get] off, they would ask for IDs and take away people just because they had the "wrong face," or looked "suspicious." Things were getting more and more difficult.
>
> (Int. 70, October 2012, Tucumán)

State-sponsored violence was too obvious for people not to know about it. The army frequently set up road blocks and few people felt beyond suspicion when all the occupants of a car were ordered to get out, menaced by carbines, in order for an officer to quiz the travellers (Malamud-Goti 1996, 103). Especially in semi-rural areas of the country such as the province of Tucumán, the government made no secret of its violent actions: it wanted to terrorise the rural population, which it viewed as "subversive" and potential enemies. A common example is the dumping of mutilated bodies in public spaces following the abductions and unwitnessed secret murders of the disappeared, thus generating terror in the local population. Corpses were also found in deep gullies, rivers or clandestine graves. Certain liminal places, such as crossroads and river banks, became regular dumping grounds.

In the harshest period of the military dictatorship, from 1976 until 1979, disappearances occurred on a daily basis. The CONADEP has documented 8,960 cases of disappearance but the numbers are believed to be much higher (2013, 297). Human rights organisations have put forward a number of 30,000 disappeared, estimating that for each known disappearance, two had not been made public (Filc 1997, 37). Other estimates vary between 12,000 and 20,000 persons (Calveiro 1998, 29).[9] A number of disappeared died from torture inside the CDCs. However, most of them were killed outside the CDCs. They were either shot at close range or dumped at sea while sedated but still alive. The throwing of captives from planes over the sea was one way to make bodies disappear. In provinces far away from sea, as in the north of Argentina, many prisoners were executed and their corpses were burnt or buried as unidentified persons – *Nomen Nescio* (name unknown, NN) – in different cemeteries. Many bodies were also abandoned along country roads. Most often, they were cremated or interred in cemeteries.

It is important to stress that enforced disappearances in Argentina did not always imply the murder of the disappeared person. Many people, today survivors, were also "disappeared" into CDCs for a certain period of time and then obtained their liberty in different ways. Some escaped. Others were released but under *libertad vigilada* (controlled liberty), meaning that they had to report their actions and they were not allowed to leave the country. Others were given the opportunity to leave the country but were not allowed to come back. They joined the huge group of exiles who had already fled to Europe, the United States and other Latin American countries (Van Drunen 2010, 18). A final group had their confinement made legal and became political prisoners at the disposal of the *Poder Ejecutivo Nacional* (National Executive Authority, hereafter PEN), becoming part of the already large group of political prisoners, many of whom had been imprisoned in the years preceding the military coup. Even though legal confinement, release or escape meant "re-appearance," for the time they were kidnapped and held, these people were effectively disappeared. Nobody knew where they were. Even though the large majority of people who were kidnapped remain "disappeared," that is, are still "disappeared" today, one should keep in mind that the survivors, who, as I will show in the following chapters, have a crucial role to play in the current trials, were also disappeared for a certain period of time.

Enforced disappearance is a crime of interconnected acts and phases. The CDCs were a central component. There were more than 450 CDCs distributed around the country. The specific procedure of kidnapping and captivity in these CDCs usually had the following pattern. Targeted persons were brutally abducted from their houses or in the street by a group of heavily armed military and policemen wearing civilian clothes and driving cars without licence plates, the so-called *patotas* or task groups. In most cases, the victim's house was ransacked. Numerous persons witnessed kidnappings in the streets or abductions from houses. The blatant and violent ways in which these were carried out ensured that they did not go unnoticed by the public. Often houses were plundered during or after the operation, with trucks taking away the furniture, in full view of the whole neighbourhood (CONADEP 2013, 20–24, 284–295). Once abducted, the victims were taken to the CDCs, where they were kept in subhuman conditions and subjected to all types of torture and humiliations. According to the testimonies of survivors, during the systematic torture sessions, sexual abuse against detainees, particularly women, were systematically practiced in all CDCs (Balardini, Oberlin and Sobredo 2011, 119). The use of this kind of violence always has a political function. With the pioneering study by Susan Brownmiller "Against our will. Men, women, and rape" (1975), it became clear that rape operates as a means of social control over women, and therefore as a form of violence that goes far beyond an individual act. It aims at exercising power over another. The role of sexual violence as an instrument of subjection that involves the constant sexualisation of domination relations is reflected in the concept of "sexualised violence." This acquired different modalities in Argentina. In addition to constant rapes, women who were abducted while still pregnant were kept alive in extremely harsh conditions until they had given birth. Immediately afterwards, most of them were killed and their babies were given to families connected with the military or police to be re-educated according to “true” Argentine values. Approximately three hundred of these cases have been officially reported, but other estimates run to five hundred (Ginzberg 2002).

In the CDCs torture was used as a political tool to have an impact on the individual as well as the broader society. According to Salimovich, Lira and Weinstein, torture is applied to selected individuals identified as representatives of specific social groups such as political parties, organisations and unions, or those who sympathise or collaborate with such groups (1992, 78). The individual physical and psychological harm to the victim acts as a psychological mechanism of control over their social group and organisation, and over society as a whole. Similarly, Sveaas and Lavik (2000) contend that the destructive psychological effects of violations such as torture also function at a large-scale socio-political level. Trust, predictability, a sense of control, belief systems and norms, they argue, are severely affected or destroyed in societies where such violations occur.

The aim of enforced disappearance was basically to cause terror and to prevent people from acting and becoming involved in social and political activities. Social bonds are thus broken and collective identities lose their structure. Social participation is discouraged. Phrases such as “If I get involved in politics, I’ll get killed” or “S/He must have done something” when someone was disappeared fostered feelings of mistrust, while reinforcing and legitimising the dissolution of social bonds, as will be discussed below. Therefore, the dissemination of terror and the disappearance of those considered by the military to be dysfunctional are, as pointed out by Calveiro, efficient instruments for social discipline and the production of submissive subjects and societies (Calveiro 1998, 70). Thus, the enforced disappearance contributed to: 1) erase evidence of criminality, 2) create uncertainty and false hopes among those searching for their relatives, 3) stall investigations into the whereabouts of the disappeared, 4) paralyse public protest, and 5) prevent feelings of solidarity between society and those searching for their relatives (Robben 2007, 278). Enforced disappearance also turned the relatives of the disappeared into victims. Families were extremely affected by factors such as the illegal arrest of the victim (generally carried out in the presence of the family or people related to them); the anxious search for news in public offices, courts, police stations and military garrisons; the hope that some information would arrive; and the fantasy of a bereavement that is never confirmed: “Behind each disappearance, there is often a family that is destroyed or dismembered” (CONADEP 2013, 335).

2.2.1 Repression and denial

As the UN definition of enforced disappearance stresses, one of its main characteristics is the refusal of the state to acknowledge the deprivation of liberty (United Nations 2006, Article 2). The military government and its institutions refused to give any information about the disappeared or take responsibility for them. While national and international human rights organisations such as Amnesty International claimed that political prisoners were being secretly held in clandestine prisons, the government denied the allegations saying that they were biased and based on rumours. Indeed, as the CONADEP report years later showed, while the judiciary rejected writs for *habeas corpus* pursued by the families of the victims and insisted that they knew nothing of the whereabouts of the disappeared, the corpses were to be found in the judicial morgue with the full knowledge of the Appeals Chamber (CONADEP 2013, 401).

The calculated unleashing of terror also produced denial in the population. As some scholars assert: "knowing what not to know is a major response in coping with terror" (Zur 1994, 15; Suarez-Orozco 1992, 219). The secrecy and ambiguity of the repression made it possible for many people to deny what was going on (Novaro and Palermo 2003, 135). Thus, running parallel to the regime's position of denying involvement in brutal violence, there was also a strategy used by citizens to avoid confronting what they knew, or at least, suspected. Many people simply decided to ignore what was happening and to look the other way, as if pretending that nothing was going on would erase the violence. The military's propaganda to make guerrilla groups responsible for crimes committed by the state was in common use. The same holds true for the staging of combat between the military and illegal groups in which the dead bodies of persons who had been disappeared were skilfully arranged so as to give the impression that they had died in combat. While this type of practice intensified the population's fear of the guerrilla groups, it covered up the state's repressive actions. Likewise, many of the mass media, supportive of the dictatorship, cooperated in this denial by publishing fake articles or by giving publicity to phoney operations. Thus, the regime denied the existence of disappearances, simultaneously demonised the victims and claimed the repression was justified.

2.2.2 Psychosocial consequences

The state's denial of any information on the whereabouts of disappeared people is a key element of forced disappearance, which led their families to a desperate search, as was expressed by several of those interviewed. The wife of a militant disappeared from Rosario explained to me:

> It was hard (. . .) we saw that nobody showed up anywhere, they were not in prison. (. . .) It was frustrating because people don't disappear, you can't get it into your head that you're talking to someone today and the day after you never see him again in your life. It is not a natural or logical thing.
>
> (Int. 27, March 2011, Rosario)

Not to know what happened to the disappeared has been a form of continual torture for their relatives. Even though the families of the disappeared are certain that their relatives have died, for many their torment has not diminished since their relatives first disappeared. The desire to know every detail, the uncertainty of what happened to their relatives and the awareness of its incomprehensibility became a continuing psychological torture suffered by most surviving relatives. From a psychological perspective, the absence of the body and the impossibility of carrying out the funeral rituals make the process of mourning difficult and increases the psychological trauma that relatives might suffer as a result of the disappearance of their loved ones (Abudara et al. 1986; Kordon and Edelmann 1988; Sieder 1995). Death in the abstract can never be as convincing as the body of the dead person. This state was called by psychologists Stewart and Hodgkinson the "questioning syndrome" (1988). They claim that

> in the total absence of the body, there exists for the bereaved a terrible struggle between the need for certainty, to allow an ending, and inevitable "irrational hope." Without seeing the body, the death cannot be accepted as final, doubt exists.
>
> (Stewart and Hodgkinson 1988, 11–14)

This non-acceptance of the death and an irrational waiting for the disappeared, even in the knowledge that the person would not return, persisted for several years after the dictatorship. A survivor whose partner is still disappeared narrated:

> My only goal was to wait for him, I kept waiting for many years, even though I had a [new] partner, I still thought he could come back (. . .) I kept waiting for him to come back, but very deep inside I knew that no, he wouldn't come back, but I still had hope. (. . .) His mother kept celebrating his birthday every year, she bought him gifts, she had a closet full of gifts for him.
>
> (Int. 63, September 2012, Buenos Aires)

Uncertainty persists through time, from the initial moment of disappearance onwards. Several scholars also claim that disappearance eliminates speech and bars any dissenting narrative, silencing people (Kordon and Edelman 1986). Terror affects the perceptions of events; it fragments the vision of social reality, thus breaking down social communication (Malamud-Goti 1996, 119.120). A common refrain at the time of the dictatorship was "*el silencio es salud*" (Silence is health) which reflected what was required from society (Feitlowitz 1998, 34; Cohen 2001, 155). The silencing of speech was an order from the dictatorship whose effects continued for several years, especially in some regions of Argentina, as shown in the next chapters. This social silence led to the rupture of social and interpersonal relationships (Kordon and Edelman 1986). This generated what different authors call a "culture of terror," based on silence, in which those who have seen or heard something do not react or avoid speaking about it, terrified of suffering the same fate (Corradi 1987). As Zur explains (1994, 16), these effects have repercussions for years because the silence is internalised; emotions are suppressed and repressed, partly as a result of state oppression. People take a distance from the victims and their relatives and, as explained below, many prefer to believe the idea disseminated by the Army that the victims themselves, and not their perpetrators, were responsible.

In what follows I will examine the effects of these strategies of state repression on the victims and society in two main dimensions. The first refers to the legal and political sphere which entails an analysis of how repression impacted on the victims' relations to the state. The second, the social field, refers to the consequences of state terror on the social sphere of. I will look at how repression contributed, on the one hand, to the destruction of social relationships and, on the other hand, to the generation of attitudes of silence and stigmatisation towards the victims.

2.3 The erasure of rights and the attempts at resistance

The restriction of citizens' rights was, at the same time, a clear condition and consequence of the dictatorship. Civil and political rights were curtailed and participation was seen as undesirable. These restrictions, typical of a state of siege and a military government, affected the whole Argentine population, albeit in different ways and to different degrees. While it involved a highly restrictive citizenship for the whole society, for the direct victims it involved a total erasure of it. As soon as the military took power, the most basic civil and political rights were suppressed: strikes, collective bargaining and students' organisations were forbidden, unions came under government control, censorship was imposed on the media and political parties were suspended (Águila 2006). Arbitrary and illegal arrests, torture and the forced disappearance of people became a widespread practice.

The families of the disappeared exhausted nearly all the available legal procedures to search for their relatives. In a majority of cases, they repeatedly filed complaints and raised writs of *habeas corpus* before national authorities and courts, to establish where their relatives had been taken and who was detaining them.[10] These were systematically rejected and no investigations were conducted. The judiciary was largely silent, ignoring pleas for *habeas corpus* and justifying the suspension of civil liberties (Roht-Arriaza 2004, 97).[11] With few exceptions, the judiciary endorsed the discretionary application of powers of arrest under the state of siege and accepted the validity of secret reports from the security services as a justification for the detention of citizens for an indefinite period. At the same time, it turned the writ of *habeas corpus* into a mere formality, rendering it useless as a means of combating the policy of arbitrary and illegal detentions (CONADEP 2013, 296). The judiciary became a sham legal structure and almost inoperative as a means of appeal. Many judges who could have limited the abuses of arbitrary detention instead displayed a complicity with the abductions and disappearances by their indifference or even support of the regime.

Thus, the performance of the judiciary was reduced to indifference and ineffectiveness or active support for the military regime. This situation led many families of the disappeared to an overwhelming feeling of impotence. On top of their fear, pain and grief, they had to endure the frustration of having no adequate legal channel to protect their rights (CONADEP 2013, 405). Therefore, due to the systematic rejection of their judicial appeals by the courts, relatives of the disappeared resorted to all kinds of unofficial or extra-official procedures to discover the whereabouts of their loved ones. They appealed to the country's rulers and the most influential people in society; they went through all the administrative channels, they even asked the various churches to intervene (Lernoux 1980). However, only on very few occasions did these measures bring any positive result. Thus, these claims soon spread to local and international human rights organisations such as the Organisation of American States (OAS) or the United Nations (Crenzel 2008, 36).

State repression could not stop all attempts at resistance by civil society. It was during the dictatorship that some of the most important human rights organisations emerged which, despite comprising small groups of people, have had a fundamental role in reporting and condemning these crimes. They became the most important actors agitating for justice and truth during and after the dictatorship. These organisations were often, but not solely, made up of relatives of the disappeared. Indeed, when referring to human rights organisations in Argentina, some scholars make the distinction between victims and non-victims organisations, with the latter sometimes also called advocacy organisations (Jelin 1995; Humphrey and Valverde 2007). Victims organisations refer to those organisations formed in direct response to the loss of family members by the dictatorship's policy of enforced disappearance. Their demand in the first years was to "Bring the disappeared back, alive!" (Bosco 2004, 390). These associations became one of the public faces of human rights opposition to the regime, alongside the non-victim or advocacy human rights organisations, and documented individual cases to bring them before the courts and publicise and condemn the crimes committed in Argentina at a national and international level.

The following are some of the so-called victims organisations that emerged during and after the dictatorship *Madres de Plaza de Mayo* (Mothers of Plaza de Mayo, founded in 1977), *Abuelas de Plaza de Mayo* (founded in 1977), *Familiares de Desaparecidos y Detenidos por Razones Políticas* (Families of the Disappeared and Detained, founded in 1976), HIJOS (founded in 1995) and *Ex-Detenidos Desaparecidos* (Ex-Detained Disappeared, founded in 1984). The main advocacy organisations active during the dictatorship included: SERPAJ (Service for Peace and Justice, founded in 1974), CELS (founded in 1979), APDH (founded in 1975), and *La Liga Argentina por los Derechos del Hombre* (Argentine League for the Rights of Man, founded in 1937). Many of these advocacy organisations had been established before the dictatorship.

2.4 Terror and the rupture of social bonds

Despite the struggle of the human rights organisations, repression continued to undermine citizen rights and seriously affect the interaction between groups and individuals in society. Terror can be extremely isolating. Social fragmentation is one of the consequences of what Malamud-Goti calls a "disarticulating power," typical of state terror, which aims at preventing coordinated opposition (1996, 125–126). Norbert Lechner describes the instrumentalisation of terror as one of the principal mechanisms of social discipline, a strategy of depoliticisation and social normalisation of those labelled as critical or dangerous to the regime (Lechner 1992, 27, 31). Solidarity and trust are thus effectively destroyed, and collective identities and social mobilisation undermined. In Argentina, groups such as trade unions, students' organisations, community soup kitchens and political associations were regarded by the state with suspicion. The main goal of repressive policies and terror thus becomes the destruction and atomisation of the individual as an active political being, severing links with family and other social and political groups (Salimovich, Lira and Weinstein 1992, 74). Terror sought to intimidate a wider target population beyond the immediate victims. As many scholars assert, the purpose of state terror was in great part to discourage people from any form of political activity, cowing them into political submission (Corradi, Fagen and Garreton 1992; Calveiro 1998; Schindel 2012). Isolation is one of the conditions necessary to exercise control over human beings as political beings and it also constitutes one of the main tools that allows the dismantling of practices of confrontation-resistance. This relationship between terror, isolation and power was explained by Hannah Arendt (1985), who states that terror can rule absolutely only over those who are isolated. The hallmark of isolation "is impotence insofar as power always comes from men acting together (. . .) isolated men are powerless by definition" (Arendt 1985, 172).

The political construction of an "other," by the military, that is, a potential and invisible enemy who could strike anytime and anywhere, was functional to the weakening of social bonds in Argentina. The vague concept of the "internal enemy" used by repressive forces in Argentina promoted the image of a "defenceless society" which was endangered by the activities of "subversion" or "terrorism" (Águila 2006, 175). The category of "terrorist" was as broad in scope as it was blurred, and was made to include both the militants of guerrilla organisations and the members of other social and political movements, generally of a left-wing nature. The definition of "terrorist" was articulated by Junta president Videla in a press conference in 1978: "A terrorist is not just someone with a gun or a bomb, but also someone who spreads ideas that are contrary to western civilisation" (quoted in Duhalde 1999, 67). Anyone could be considered a terrorist if they did not fit with the military's concept of "Western civilisation." Thus, a person was a "subversive criminal" because he or she was "active" in student centres, in neighbourhoods or in the internal committees of trade unions, or because he or she was found to participate in what the intelligence services called "insurgent activities," political acts such as painting slogans on walls, throwing leaflets on the street or simply possessing or reading a publication of those organisations (Águila 2006, 172). Within this framework, the military dictatorship depicted public life as dangerous because of the presence of the invisible enemy. The enemy could be one's neighbour, a school teacher or a priest. All members of society were potential "subversives."

Thus, terror provoked specific and diverse social behaviours that some scholars have described as "adaptative responses" (Salimovich, Lira and Weinstein 1992, 74). Public spaces were emptied of collective action and offered no room for popular demonstrations (Schindel 2012, 5). The dissemination of terror and mistrust gnawed at society as people became afraid to talk to neighbours, make new friends and socialise with colleagues, let alone engage in collective political action. Many people were even reluctant to join social or leisure activities such as a theatre or study groups and threw away possibly "incriminating evidence," such as books. A significant portion of the population abandoned public space to seek shelter and support in the private realm. Social networks became impoverished and many people were thrown back upon a diminishing circle of trusted relatives and long-time friends (Águila 2006).

This social isolation was intensified by the official prohibition of informal social gatherings and political associations. The public sphere shrank and the private sphere was under strain (Robben 2007, 275). Repression reduces the public space, which is an essential condition for democratic political action, and thus contributes to the demobilisation of sectors of civil society. In this connection, state terror in Argentina laid the groundwork for the construction of a new political subject – obedient and passive. With the closure of the spaces where individuals could identify with broader collectives (political parties and political activities were banned, and so were trade unions and trade union activities), individuals became isolated and defenceless: the culture of terror was thus imposed on an immobilised society (Servetto 2004, 2). In this way, depoliticisation, where no one is committed to anything or anybody, leads people to feel socially uprooted. Rootlessness is manifested in the mistrust and indifference that gradually pervade social relations generating a privatisation of social life that drastically restricts the field of common actions. The resulting atomisation and isolation of individuals leads to what Lechner described as the "erosion of collective identities": a distance between the interests and values of the individual and the common values and interests of society (Lechner 1992, 29–30). The "climate of terror" also plunged the survivors and the relatives of the disappeared into a kind of social isolation, in many cases even involving indifference or rejection by their own families. As stated by a relative of disappeared persons:

> After my son and his wife disappeared, I never heard again from any of my seven sisters or my brother. They all avoided us. It has been seventeen years since I last saw them. They were terrified that the same thing would happen to them.
>
> (quoted in Robben 2007, 275)

Other relatives of disappeared persons in different provinces across the country have provided similar accounts. The whole family (parents and siblings) of one of my interviewees disappeared in Tucumán in 1977. For this reason, she and her husband were forced to flee to Buenos Aires:

> I was in Buenos Aires throughout 1977. There was not much I could do, I phoned my family here [in Tucumán] and no one answered, quite simply, there was no answer. They were scared to death, such was the effect of terror. They [the military] had had no qualms about taking away all the family.
>
> (Int. 70, October 2012, Tucumán)

This isolation, which began during the dictatorship, continued to be reproduced for several years in different sectors of society after the military regime ended. The dissemination of a stereotype of "subversive" criminals as well as the continuous propaganda urging citizens to "report extremist elements" encouraged the prejudices of the community and had the open objective of enjoining society to participate in its repressive activities. Thus, the dictatorship established an oppressive atmosphere in which denunciation and suspicion became widespread, while a largely silent and/or indifferent society acted as if nothing was happening.

2.5 Victims under suspicion: displacement of responsibility

Terror was not the only reason for the isolation of victims. Under the dictatorship and even many years later, victims were often held responsible for the violence they endured. Illegal repression is usually accompanied by the construction of narratives that are intended to deny and/or justify the perpetrators' actions. Such social representations may have a strong impact on other social sectors that may adopt and reproduce them. Indeed, in Argentina large sections of society looked on victims of repression as the object of blame. People shifted the focus of their anguish and fear from the perpetrators to the victims (Malamud-Goti 1996, 141). Before and after the dictatorship in Argentina, different explanations and campaigns of defamation were developed to justify the repression and actions deployed against the victims. As discussed above, one of these justifying discourses was the view that in Argentina there was a "war against subversion" or an "irregular warfare," concepts that served to justify the use of "irregular war strategies" such as forced disappearance. Another discursive strategy of justification consisted in labelling repression as a legitimate proceeding even if "mistakes and excesses" were committed in the task of "saving the homeland" from impending subversion. This idea of "mistakes and excesses" denies the state's responsibility and the fact that the human rights violations were planned and organised (Feierstein 2006).

In this context, the military, supported by many politicians and sectors of the media, developed extensive propaganda campaigns that tried to present social and political activists as "demons" who aimed to destroy the social order, meaning

Western and Christian values. Thus, victims were made responsible for the violence they and their relatives suffered under the so-called "theory of the two demons," which equates the repression of the armed forces with the violence carried out by the opposing armed political groups. Under this theory, there were two "bands" that confronted each other while society remained uninvolved. Such a discourse seeks to equate the victims with the perpetrators by giving a "symmetrical treatment" to state repression and guerrilla actions, as if alleging that there is a conflict of symmetrical forces – which, in any event, was not the case – could justify state repression (Feierstein 2011). This theory constructed an image of the disappeared as terrorists, demonising them as "subversives" who "had surely done something." That "something" referred to what was considered as suspicious behaviour such as the involvement in political activities opposed to the regime that justified people being abducted, tortured and finally made to disappear. This image enhanced the idea that the victims, and not their perpetrators, were responsible.

Consequently, people were afraid to get close to those who had been touched by a disappearance. However, the reasons for taking distance from such victims as relatives of the disappeared were not only the fear of being made to disappear but also the stigmatisation of the victims due to their political activism. An interviewee from Rosario, whose husband was member of a guerrilla organisation and disappeared in 1976, recalled her difficult position with two little children when her husband disappeared:

> And after my son was born (. . .) I took a job as a live-in maid. [My daughter] had to live with her grandparents, my husband's parents, because my mother was dead, and so was my father. [The rest of] my family did not readily accept the wife of someone who was a member of the guerrilla organisations and they closed many doors on me, as happened to everyone else. (. . .) many people acted out of fear or because they did not agree with our ideas, they thought we had got into this, and that we were responsible for what was happening.
>
> (Int. 27, March 2011, Rosario)

Similarly, another interviewee, whose parents and brothers were disappeared, and was also persecuted during the dictatorship, explained how the family on her father's side broke all contact with her, a breach lasting until now, due to her political activism:

> Even to this day I have lost all ties with my father's family (. . .) They completely ignore me because they claim that I'm responsible for that [the disappearance of her father] due to my militancy.
>
> (Int. 70, October 2012, Tucumán)

2.5.1 The stigma of surviving

While the relatives of disappeared persons with a history of political militancy were isolated – even by their own families as recounted by the interviewee above – the situation of stigmatisation of and distrust towards the survivors was – and in many cases still is – much more extreme. The survivors had been abducted and disappeared and later released from the CDCs, and thus survived. Already during the dictatorship, the survivors began to give testimony to different human rights organisations of their experiences in the CDCs and the conditions prevalent in them. However, the first testimonies were not well received (Calveiro 1998). One of the reasons for such rejection was that many relatives and even human rights organisations accused the survivors of collaborating with the military (Crenzel 2008, 43). Questions were raised as to why they had survived while the disappeared had not. This aroused suspicion over their conduct in clandestine centres, and led to the suggestion that the survivors might have collaborated with the military and betrayed and informed on other detainees in order to be released. Those who survived are suspects in the eyes of society. Their resistance and their practices of solidarity with the other detainees, do not matter. As Calveiro asserts, society wants to understand why survivors are alive and is unable to explain it. Thus, survivors are automatically condemned to exclusion and the very fact that they are alive is the evidence of their alleged guilt. As explained by a survivor:

> Once my ex-mother in law asked me, "why are you alive and my son isn't?" "I don't have an answer," I said, "the answer should be given by the repressors;[12] I don't know why I'm alive. I would have wanted to be here with your son, but he isn't, I don't know why." You could hear it in the demonstrations, we've heard Hebe de Bonafini[13] many times, she always said her children were heroes because they were gone (. . .), and those of us who returned were all collaborators. She has said it many times.
>
> (Int. 63, September 2012, Buenos Aires)

Survivors do not know for certain why they survived, and much as they may torment themselves trying to find an explanation, they will never know for sure. It was their captors who made the decision. However, many in society saw survival as proof of treason, of having provided information that led to other people being captured (Longoni 2007). Yet, the decision to release or murder the detainees cannot be explained by reference to the victim's conduct. Reporting on others did not result in release. As noted by Calveiro, many collaborators died and there were survivors whose resistance was tenacious and relentless (1998, 160). In the same vein, survival did not depend on the degree of involvement in guerrilla organisations. Again, as Calveiro explains, individuals unrelated to guerrilla organisations survived, as did others that had a close relationship with such organisations and high-ranking leaders. On the other hand, others in the same position were murdered. There were no methods of selection, as processes were conducted at random (Calveiro 1998,160). However, feelings of guilt are commonly found among survivors:

> I'm free, they [the disappeared] are not and for me it was very hard to accept that I was not responsible for being alive. The decision was theirs [the oppresors'], they were the ones who decided "You live, and you die."
>
> (Int. 63, September 2012, Buenos Aires)

As explained by the survivor – and asserted by many scholars – the CDCs and the reasons for entering or leaving them belong to the logic of the perpetrators (Calveiro 1998, 160). Survivors have no say in that decision. Yet another reason for rejecting the survivors had to do with the content of their testimonies. Survivors said things that others, especially the relatives, were reluctant to hear. At a time when the human rights movements and the relatives fought for "the disappeared to reappear alive," the survivors did not speak about disappeared but dead people; they described the living conditions in the concentration camps and stated that there was no perverse concealment of the prisoners but they had simply been eliminated without trace (Calveiro 1998, 161). While the truth in this case was cruel and disturbing, it gave knowledge of what had happened. Thus, the survivors, who were released by their own captors, had to endure not only their own feelings of guilt for having survived and the traces of torture on their bodies and minds, but also the stigmatisation by a society that was unable or unwilling to listen to them (Crenzel 2008). They were demonised for their political militancy, suspicions were cast over their release and their testimonies were rejected by those who refused to accept that their relatives had been murdered. Both the experience of previous political activism and surviving state terror have in many cases resulted in distrust, stigmatisation and isolation of the survivors (Longoni 2007; Lampasona 2012).

Displacing responsibility from the perpetrator to the victims and then blaming them can have a psychological and self-protective or defensive function for society. As Malamud-Goti asserts, blame constitutes a way of distancing ourselves from those who suffer (1996, 142–144). By claiming that the victim "did something" that we did not, we attempt to diminish the fear that we will be the next to be victimised. The underlying message is "We are not like them." The victims belong in this way to a social and political category that is different from our own (Ibid, 142). In attaching blame to those who have undergone torture and have been disappeared, society tries to deny its own responsibility for what happened to them. However, the attempt to differentiate themselves from the victims by blaming them also makes evident that those sectors of society did not oppose the actions of the dictatorship.

Notes

1 For instance, Bolivia (1964–1982), Brazil (1964–1985), Chile (1973–1990), Ecuador (1963–1966), Honduras (1963–1971, 1972–1982), Panama (1968–1989), Perú (1968–1980) and Uruguay (1973–1985).

2 Dictatorships were expected to control any dissidence. The United States often provided political, economic and military support to these regimes, including intelligence services and military instruction, such as at the well-known School of the Americas (Gill 2004). In fact, many similarities exist in the repressive methods employed by Latin American dictatorships between the 1960s and the 1980s. Some of these patterns account for the existence of a coordinated strategy among several countries of the region. It is well established that South American

governments elaborated a joint plan of political repression in 1975. *Plan Cóndor* (Operation Condor) was a military program developed in the Southern Cone. It included Argentina, Brazil, Chile, Bolivia, Uruguay, Paraguay and, peripherally, Perú and Ecuador. *Plan Cóndor* was designed to conduct intelligence activities and to persecute and exterminate political opposition (Nilson 1998).

3 Triple A was a death squad, many of whose members, though not all of them, were police officers.

4 In February 1975, the government of Isabel Perón gave its official approval to army involvement, as key members of her government signed Decree Law No. 261, which authorised the armed forces to "annihilate" the rural guerrilla insurgency in the northwest province of Tucumán.

5 The armed forces also integrated these national operations with international ones since they collaborated with other military regimes in the repression of their citizens through "Operation Condor," a collaboration between the intelligence services of Chile, Argentina, Paraguay, Bolivia, Uruguay and Brazil, which also received assistance from the CIA and other state security agencies (Armony 1997).

6 For more on this comparison, see Feierstein 2006.

7 For a detailed analysis on the social and political implications of using each of these different ways of understanding the military repression in Argentina, see Feierstein (2006, 2011).

8 See for example Judgment Julian Simon 2006, 16–38, Judgment massacre of Fatima 2008, 45–65, Judgment Mansion Sere 2008, 198–215, Judgment Vargas Aignasse 2008, 77–84.

9 Even today, it is still impossible to know the exact number of disappeared persons in Argentina. In addition, Schindel asserts that even the democratic government does not have this information because to this day former military officers have refused to provide any information (Schindel 2002, 114).

10 In Argentina, *habeas corpus* is one of the main guarantees in the constitution. It is the basic right to ask a judge to order, through an expedited summary proceeding, the cessation of any action by an official which restricts the right of personal freedom. The judge must receive all the information regarding the state of the beneficiary of *habeas corpus* (i.e. if he is detained, where; which officials are holding him; the legitimacy of the detention; and also whether there is reasonable cause for arrest, even when ordered by the National Executive under a state of siege (CONADEP 2013, 405).

11 The number of habeas corpus actions filed in the period 1976–1979 in Buenos Aires alone reached 5,487 against 1,089 for the period 1973–1755 and 2,848 for the period 1980–1983 (CONADEP 2013, 405). The same proportions, but with lower absolute figures, apply in the main provincial cities.

12 That is the usual term to refer to military perpetrators in Argentina.

13 Hebe de Bonafini is one of the founders of the organisation Mothers of Plaza de Mayo.

Chapter 3

Darkness and light of the military Juntas trial

This chapter analyses the well-known "*Juicio a las Juntas*" (the Trial of the Juntas or, hereafter, the Juntas Trial) (1984–1985), when an investigatory legal process was set in motion in the first constitutional administration after the military dictatorship in an attempt to come to terms with the recent past. The trial brought to court the nine Junta leaders deemed responsible for planning and ordering systematic violations of human rights, and had a meaningful role in symbolically marking the transition to democracy. Focusing on that trial, I consider its social impact and its meaning for the victims. The discussion of the contributions and limitations of the Juntas Trial is crucial to my subsequent analysis of the reparative potential of the new criminal proceedings for the victims, many of whom are constantly aware of the difference between the two models of justice.

The chapter is divided into three sections. First, I provide an account of the transition from dictatorship as well as the attempts by the military to obstruct accountability and the shift of the Juntas Trial from the military to the civil courts. Second, I reflect on the social and political relevance of the Juntas Trial in terms of acknowledging the systematic state violence. Finally, I focus extensively on the legal, political and social conditions that limited the scope and reparative potential of the Trial. As shown below, in that period the judiciary was also a reflection of the social and political context which was still very adverse for survivors and the relatives of the disappeared.

3.1 The transition and the military obstacles to accountability

The collapse of the military regime started in 1982 with disagreements within the armed services over the financial crisis, rising external debt and a crumbling economy. All of which, combined with the unpopularity of the military after the defeat in the Malvinas/Falklands conflict, hastened the transition to democracy (Novaro and Palermo 2003, 462–468). Before that, however, the military government took several legal steps to prevent future prosecutions of their crimes. One such step was the formulation of the "Final document of the military Junta on the war against subversion and terrorism" of 23 April 1983. In this document, the armed forces established their position on human rights violations, and justified any potential "mistakes" or "excesses" that might have been committed in the context of the "war against subversion." The same day the military issued an "Institutional Law" in which they stated that all repressive acts committed by the armed forces against "terrorism" should be considered legitimate acts of military service and, therefore, not punishable (Nino 2006, 113–114). Finally, on 23 September of the same year, the *de facto* president Gen. Reynaldo Bignone signed law No. 22924, known as *Ley de Autoamnistía* (Self-Amnesty Law) or *Ley de Pacificación Nacional* (Law of National Pacification). In the first article of this law, the military sought to grant the security forces full amnesty for all crimes committed between May 1973 – this date giving evidence that repressive actions had begun before the 1976 military coup – and June 1982 (Zalaquett 1995, 18–20).

The return to democracy in late 1983 brought the restoration of constitutional legality. Legitimacy, however, was a different question and, in any case, something to be built by the new government. This uphill task required the adoption of a critical vision of the military – and civilian – authoritarian past, and the restoration of the rule of law (Floria and Garcia Belsunce 2005, 267). Raúl Alfonsín, leader of the *Unión Cívica Radical* party, was the first democratically elected president after the end of the military rule. Largely running on a campaign that promised to address past violations, Alfonsín proclaimed that the Junta "will not only have to be judged by history, but also tried by regular civilian courts" (McSherry 1997, 110 quoting the Buenos Aires Herald, 3 May 1983). Fifty-two per cent of the electorate handed Alfonsín a decisive victory on 30 October 1983 (Di Paolantonio 2004, 353–354). Alfonsín took office with a debilitated democratic infrastructure and a strong military party that actively resisted accounting for its past actions. The promise to seek legal accountability was, however, a more vexing issue that eventually positioned Alfonsín in opposition to the demands of most human rights groups.

Once in office, Raúl Alfonsín's administration brought in a series of measures that re-opened the question of responsibility for the crimes committed by the military. First and foremost, on 22 December 1983, Alfonsín sent a bill to Congress calling for the nullification of the de facto "Law of National Pacification" and the abrogation of the Self-Amnesty Law sanctioned by the military government just before it left power. The Congress approved the measure unanimously, setting an important precedent for similar laws in the future. At the same time, decrees No. 157 and No. 158 were issued. Decree No. 157 ordered the prosecution of the leaders of guerrilla organisations, thus reinforcing what in the previous chapter has been described as the "theory of the two demons," which equates the criminal actions of the guerrilla forces to the military's repressive actions.[1] In December 1983, Decree No. 158 ordered the prosecution of the nine members of the three military Juntas from the period 1973–1983 (Nino 2006, 124).[2] Alfonsín's plan for prosecution attempted to steer a middle ground between carrying out extensive prosecutions throughout the ranks and allowing the amnesty of the military to stand. Thus, the initial idea voiced within Alfonsín's circle was to bring to trial only a handful of high-ranking officers who had ordered the criminal acts (Osiel 1986, 154). Exempt from prosecution were low-ranking soldiers and police who claimed to have been following orders. Alfonsín hoped that by limiting the scale of prosecutions, he would ensure the transition to democracy while avoiding a military backlash (Roehrig 2009).

Finally, with decree No. 187, the executive created the National Commission on the Disappearance of Persons (CONADEP), tasked with investigating the whereabouts of the disappeared and the human rights violations committed during the military dictatorship. Reporting to the executive, CONADEP comprised 13 members and five secretaries, including legislators, public figures and members of human rights organisations. CONADEP analysed thousands of cases, including testimonies from family members and survivors who had been released from detention centres. The official report *Nunca Más* (Never Again), released in Spanish in 1984, became a best seller (Crenzel 2008). Amid thousands of testimonies of heinous crimes, the commission made a series of recommendations for initiating legal actions against those responsible, while it presented evidence before the courts and offered a partial list of the names of disappeared persons as well as members of the Armed and Police Forces mentioned by the victims. To date, those files continue to represent a key piece in ongoing prosecutions (Filippini 2010). According to sociologist Emilio Crenzel, CONADEP aimed to function as an intermediary between the Argentine state and civil society (2008, 60). However, many members of the human rights movement, such as Mothers of Plaza de Mayo, were initially reluctant to accept CONADEP, which was a commission constituted by notable individuals. Instead, they argued for a legislative commission because they considered that it would be more legitimate and representative if the corresponding investigations were conducted by the state. This led to the creation of some provincial parliamentary commissions, as with the case of the *Comisión Bicameral Investigadora de las Violaciones de los Derechos Humanos* (Bicameral Commission of Inquiry into Violations of Human Rights, or hereafter Bicameral Commission) in the province of Tucumán, a similar legislative investigative commission in Santiago del Estero and another one formed by deputies in the province of Chaco. They were receiving complaints at the same time as CONADEP was (Kotler 2007).

As for the prosecutions, Alfonsín and his advisers drafted Law 23.049, which formally established that jurisdiction for the trials belonged to the highest military court. Under this law, the supreme council of the armed forces – a military court composed of retired officers – was vested with original jurisdiction to prosecute the military personnel (McSherry 1997, 120). However, after months of stalling, the council sided with the perpetrators and returned not-guilty verdicts based on what it claimed was insufficient evidence (Pion-Berlin 1997, 82). In addition, the military court was very hostile to the victims, who felt threatened and mistreated, undermining in this way their testimony. As stated by a prosecutor in the current trials:

> With the return to democracy, the military courts were given jurisdiction to prosecute the crimes. [When] witnesses were called to testify; guns were cocked in front of them, and so on. The military courts did terrible things following this logic.
>
> (Int. 50, April 2011, Tucumán)

The intimidating character of these courts inhibited testimony: how can someone testify in front of those who could have been perpetrators or at least their accomplices? The complicity of the supreme council of the armed forces with those they were supposed to prosecute became evident when in September 1984 this military court declared in an official document that the orders issued by the military leadership for repression were "unquestionably legitimate," thus releasing the ex-military commanders from any criminal responsibility. In light of these events, jurisdiction was transferred from the military to the civilian courts and the Buenos Aires Federal Court of Appeals took over the case (Nino 2006, 124–139). Thus, the trials against the nine ex-commanders commenced in the civilian courts on 22 April 1985. The military considered that the trial was another episode of the "war against subversion" led by "former terrorists" associated with political parties and human rights organisations (Nino 2006, 171). For five months, more than 700 cases were presented with over 800 witnesses in the public hearings. On 9 December, the court handed down the sentences. The court gave two of the nine defendants, General Videla[3] and Admiral Massera,[4] life sentences. General Viola was sentenced to seventeen years, Admiral Lambruschini to eight years, and Brigadier Agosti to four and one-half years. The other four defendants, high-ranking members of the Juntas that ruled between 1979 and 1982 – Galtieri, Graffigna, Lami Dozo and Anaya – were acquitted since the judges considered there was insufficient evidence against them.

The trial of the military Juntas, known as "Case 13/84," provided the first example in Latin America of a trial conducted by a civilian court against a former dictatorial government. The trial largely succeeded in proving the systematic nature of the repression implemented by the military government. In the verdict, judges held that the Juntas had a systematic and organised plan of persecution and extermination that was carried out throughout Argentina, with the intention to economically and ideologically reorganise Argentine society. This was a judgment of lasting importance and influence for the current prosecutions. Furthermore, it created a factual record and helped to gather a great deal of information and evidence that made it possible to investigate other members of the security forces (Roht-Arriaza 2004, 97).

3.2 The promise of justice

The trial against the ex-commanders had a profound social impact and significance for Argentine society as well as for the victims. As Pilar Calveiro explains, the Juntas Trial set a limit on the power of the military, who until then believed themselves to be all-powerful and untouchable (1998, 103). As to the immediate outcome of the Juntas Trial, while restricted in scope, it meant a step towards justice. Since the court handed down the sentence, no one can say that the events did not happen, or that they did not know about them (Calveiro 1998, 104). Testimony of such events led to the immediate search for the traces and remains of the disappeared. The testimony of the survivors proved crucial; however, they had no evidence of the collective killings they were denouncing. The military had made every effort to hide the remains of their victims and make them disappear.

The fact that the prosecution was oral and public spread its deliberations into wider sectors of society. Some scholars stress that the public exposure of the state crimes during the Juntas Trial had a "pedagogical benefit" which remained etched in the memory of the victims, society and human rights organisations (Di Paolantonio 2004). According to Carlos Nino (2006), public inquiry into the truth is much more precise and much more dramatic when undertaken through a trial. In fact, according to him, the quality of narration in an adversarial trial cannot be fully replicated by any other means.

The "truth effects" of that trial were permeated by Bourdieu's symbolic effectiveness of law (1987) which provided those narratives with a powerful aura of authority and "objectivity" that questioned and uncovered the military's discourse of denial. According to Smulovitz (2002), the trial of the ex-commanders marked the beginning of a change in society's perception of the judiciary. It allowed judicial logic to transform historical information into legal evidence, producing in the process legitimate information about the past. The legal discourse ordered the past and lent credibility to the witnesses' stories. The political impact and high visibility of the sentencing began to transform the perceptions of the traditionally subordinate role of the judiciary. Judicial powers and abilities were re-examined (Smulovitz 2002, 252). However, a change in perceptions is a lengthy and gradual process that requires long-term policies. In this case, the fact that the prosecutions were halted by amnesty laws undermined such a process of change. However, according to Di Paolantonio (2004), the unfulfilled promises of the trial of the military helped to shape a legacy, a normative pedagogical resource, that he calls "a *nomos*," which was later utilised by human rights groups to contest legal restrictions on prosecution in the following phase of impunity.

3.3 Limitations of the Juntas Trial

3.3.1 The number of prosecutions

In spite of its huge social impact, the Juntas Trial had several legal and political limitations which prevented it from having a stronger reparative character for the victims. Among them was the fact that prosecutions were pursued only against the nine military leaders of the three military Juntas, which generated feelings of disappointment. Several interviewees have pointed to this fact as an important difference with the current trials. A survivor affirmed:

> it was not the trial one would expect, it was only against the Juntas members, who were not the ones that were in the camps.[5]
>
> (Int. 65, September 2012, Buenos Aires)

Similar was the statement of another plaintiff:

> It was positive for society at the time but it was not complete (. . .) because only two or three were convicted and all the others went unpunished.
>
> (Int. 23, March 2011, Rosario)

Against this background, many of the perpetrators were still active in the armed and police forces and they continued their careers as if nothing had happened. This had a profound impact on the victims who, while perpetrators were free, still felt at risk.

3.3.2 Testifying in fear

Despite the fact that there was a constitutional government in place, the social climate that surrounded the trial – though no longer one of terror – had the stamp of fear. One of the main differences between terror and fear is its intensity and extension in time. While terror has a paralysing effect and is usually circumscribed by the period of violence, the experience of fear does not disappear as soon as its causes have ceased to exist and allows some course of action (Kordon and Edelman 1986; Lechner 1992; Calveiro 2015). The legacy of terror can persist in the form of fear even after the authoritarian regime has ended, especially when perpetrators, though no longer in government, still have power and impunity. With the trial taking place less than two years after the transition, the presence of the military and the disappearances still haunted the victims. This climate of fear was mentioned by many interviewees, especially by survivors, many of whom gave testimony at the Juntas Trial. For many of them, their testimony at the trial was a way to resist the previously described effects of terror, to challenge the *mandate of silence* imposed by the military (Kordon and Edelman 1986). However, fear made it present in the courtroom and influenced the content of testimonies. As a witness in the Juntas Trial explained:

A[6]*:* [At that time] one was still very afraid of giving testimony about everything.
Q[7]*:* Afraid of what?
A: We had just returned to democracy, and "Turco Julián"[8] was out there walking in the streets, one was afraid but also had the commitment, in addition to the fear, the guilt. It took me a long time not to feel guilty for being alive.

(Int. 65, September 2012, Buenos Aires)

Testifying involved a mixture of strong emotions for survivors, "guilt" of having survived, "fear" but also "commitment." It was not an easy task. Fear had a real base. In the first place, many perpetrators were "out there walking in the streets," and in many cases they continued to threaten the victims so that they would not give testimony before CONADEP or at the trial. Furthermore, the perpetrators were feared because they could not be easily identified. Another survivor and witness in the Juntas Trial explained the difficulties of testifying due to fear and lack of information:

> It was very difficult. (. . .) We didn't know the names, surnames, [of the perpetrators] or what they looked like. Also, during the Juntas Trial there was a great deal of fear.
>
> (Int. 7, March 2011, Buenos Aires)

While some perpetrators were well known to everyone – this was the case of the military leaders – and others were well known to many survivors, there were many unidentified repressors. In many cases, the detainees in CDCs were blindfolded, and thus prevented from seeing the perpetrators' faces. In other cases, the victims saw the perpetrators, but they did not know their names. In addition, the perpetrators usually used aliases to refer to each other in front of the victims. This allowed the perpetrators to walk freely in the streets without fear of being identified and arrested, and caused the victims to feel constantly haunted and threatened. Anyone could be a torturer. They could be standing next to a perpetrator without knowing it or exposed to the perpetrators' threats in the street. There was still a great feeling of uncertainty. The fear that survivors felt in the streets was also perceived in the courtroom. One of the reasons for such fear was the intimidating presence of the police while testimony was being given. A plaintiff in the current trials and a child of disappeared parents from the city of Rosario narrated the experience of a person he knew:

> [In the 1980s] there were many people who did not dare [to testify]. They did not have the necessary guarantees. There is a [person] (. . .), he told me that when he testified, (. . .) he was surrounded by policemen for five hours, you had to testify in front of ten policemen.
>
> (Int. 23, March 2011, Rosario)

Similarly, another interviewee, who was a witness in the Juntas Trial, describes her experience as a difficult one:

> I was the last person to testify that night at 12 pm, [before that, I had been] surrounded by policemen in the waiting room. I remember a lot of cops telling me not to waste my time talking nonsense.
>
> (Int. 65, September 2012, Buenos Aires)

As the police forces had also been responsible for repression, the presence of potential perpetrators in that force was a factor of intimidation, a threat and a sign of power. As explained by the above interviewee, the intimidating presence of policemen considering her testimony as a "waste of time" and telling her not to talk "nonsense" did not provide an adequate and open environment in which to speak. The court was not perceived as a safe place. Testifying in that context meant a huge and tense challenge for survivors. It implied accusing and testifying before potential perpetrators who were also free and posed a real threat.

Indeed, in those years fear was still present and it had an intimidating effect on many victims and relatives of the disappeared, a fact which was reflected, for instance, in the number of reported cases before the provincial investigation commissions. In his analysis of the Bicameral Investigation Commission of Tucumán, the historian Ruben Kotler (2007) explains that the number of complaints received by that commission was lower than that presented to the human rights organisations in the province. The discrepancy was particularly remarkable in that the number of complaints of disappearances before the commission was much less. Kotler asserts that not only fear but even terror was still so alive in the province that many relatives of the victims could not make their accusations. On several occasions, victims and relatives appeared before the provincial commissions and expressed their reluctance to make reports about certain specific perpetrators who not only were still members of the police force but that in several cases had even been promoted and thus were in a higher position of power (Kotler 2007). In some places, especially in rural areas where there had been no purges of the security forces, the risk and terror of the victims was greater. In fact, many victims even doubted whether the investigation commission could provide them security when its own members were being threatened (Ibid.).

While the Juntas Trial – and the investigative commissions – had a crucial role in providing access to and making public State crimes, by themselves they were insufficient to provide adequate guarantees for the security and well-being of victims. The lack of such accompanying measures as effective purges reveals a "policy gap" that seriously hampered the reparation process. In particular, the continuity of personnel from the security forces of the dictatorship, which in several cases were even present in the court, undermined the reparative character of the trial. Fear was not, however, the only factors influencing testimonies in the 1980s.[9] Stigmatisation, and even the criminalisation of survivors, also played a significant role.

3.3.3 Silences in the testimonies: the reflection of stigmatisation on the judiciary

In the 1980s, the discourse that stigmatised the victims – both survivors and disappeared persons – that began with the dictatorship continued under the constitutional government of Raúl Alfonsín. Victims were made responsible for the violence they suffered under the "theory of the two demons," which constructed and supported an image of the disappeared that demonised them as "subversives" or "terrorists." This image ensured that their repression was legitimised. Some scholars, who analyse the construction of the victims during the trial of the Junta leaders in the 1980s, argue that the trials were conducted under this "theory" according to which the victims were portrayed as being guilty (members of armed groups) or innocent (Malamud-Goti 1996; Longoni 2007; Filippini 2010). Thus, the dominant social discourses in the years following the dictatorship – and which also emerged during the Juntas Trial – made it very difficult for the survivors to render accounts other than that of the horror experienced in the CDCs. The stigmatisation of prior militancy undermined testimonies in the 1980s. The survivors could not present themselves as political subjects of the 1970s without being stigmatised or even criminalised.

As previously noted, shortly after the transition, the Alfonsín administration passed Decree No. 157, which required that the leaders of the left-wing guerrilla organisations, the Peronist *Montoneros* and the ERP, also be brought to trial like the military leaders (Eliaschev 2011, 62). As a result, a legal correlation was created which legitimised the "theory of the two demons" in the judicial system. Thus, the repressive actions of the military and the actions of the armed organisations were made equivalent. Those who admitted having belonged to an armed organisation such as *Montoneros* or the ERP ran the risk of being arrested, just like the military. Thus, during the 1980s, this militancy became "invisible" or was concealed mainly behind the parallel prosecutions of the chief leaders of outlaw armed organisations (Filippini 2010, 26). As stated by two interviewees, both of them survivors of different CDCs in Buenos Aires and witnesses in the Juntas Trial:

> During the Juntas Trial (. . .) they applied the theory of the two demons. So, for example, I did not say that I had been a militant in an organisation.
> (Int 7, March 2011, Buenos Aires)

Another interviewee narrates the same experience. When asked if in her testimony in the Juntas Trial she had mentioned her militancy in the *Montoneros* organisation, the interviewee answered:

> I never said we were militants in the *Montoneros*, one felt fear at the time.
> (Int. 65, September 2012, Buenos Aires)

As explained by Ana Longoni, the hegemonic discourse of the "theory of the two demons" in the 1980s led the human rights movement to implement a legal strategy of concealing the political militancy of the disappeared (Longoni 2007, 25). Within this framework, the survivors and the disappeared were portrayed as depoliticised "innocent victims" and their history of militancy was thus denied (Ibid). Graciela Daleo, a survivor and ex-militant of the *Montoneros* organisation explained that at the beginning many survivors concealed their militancy for two reasons:

> In many cases because the family didn't know but in others because the disappeared were classified as "guilty" or "innocent." We had to conceal our revolutionary political militancy before the international organisations, since if you had been tortured and abducted because you were a *Montonero*, that was alright, but it was wrong if you were a member of the Peronist Youth.[10]
>
> (quoted in Longoni 2007, 17)

With this expression, Daleo stresses the difference that was made at that time – and even later – between political militants involved in armed groups and those who were not. She added: "(when) we had to testify in the trial against the Commanders, we couldn't speak about our militancy either because if we did so, we were arrested" (Ibid.). Daleo was indeed arrested after her testimony. The ideal of an innocent, depoliticised and passive victim prevailed in the 1980s. This was the ideal type into which the victims had to fit if they wanted their right to justice to be fulfilled as well as social acceptance and solidarity. This ideal can also be found in other kinds of victimisations in international law.[11] Thus, as explained by Daleo, survivors had to conceal their political condition when they sought help and support outside the country. It seemed as if political militancy stripped an individual of his or her condition as a victim and perpetrators were thus free to act as they liked. This displacement of responsibility towards political militants amounts to a denial of their victimhood.

As a result, the survivors continued to be perceived as suspects under the constitutional regime, and this was reflected in the treatment that many of them assert having received by the court in the Juntas Trial. For example, a survivor described the treatment afforded to her by the court in the 1980s in the following terms:

> I didn't feel comfortable in that trial. It seemed I was the guilty party rather than the victim, because of the questions, the way the judges treated you, they were really blunt.
>
> (Int. 65, September 2012, Buenos Aires)

The fact that the victims felt they were treated as if they were "the guilty ones" inhibited the broader testimony that is now emerging in the current trials. Furthermore, many interviewees who gave testimony in that trial stated they were constantly interrupted and not properly listened to. A witness stated:

> [In that trial] [t]he questions, the way in which they were put, the fact that they didn't let me finish speaking, I wanted to say something and [they said] "no, that's not important." And I told them: "it is important to me."
>
> (Ibid.)

Similarly, another interviewee affirmed:

> The trial of the Juntas was very limited, (. . .) because they virtually didn't let you speak (. . .). Every time I wanted to say something, they cut me off with questions, in-depth testimony was not encouraged, topics were dealt with quite superficially.
>
> (Int. 10, March 2011, Buenos Aires)

The mistreatment and social stigmatisation of the victims were also reflected in responses of apathy, indifference and even rejection, not only towards survivors but also towards relatives of the disappeared. An interviewee of the province of Tucumán stated that, during the dictatorship, she had to leave the country and was exiled for some years because as a political activist she was in danger. During that time her parents, a brother and a sister were made to disappear. With the restoration of democracy in 1983, she returned to live in her parents' house in 1984. However, she was strongly rejected by her neighbours:

> The neighbours didn't want me here. They collected signatures and submitted them to the judge so that I wouldn't be allowed to live here because I was a danger. This was 1984, you see.
>
> (Int. No. 70, October 2012, Tucumán).

The social rejection was an extra burden along with the pain of having lost her family. Another interviewee from the city of Córdoba, whose father is among the disappeared, also referred to the fact that the relatives of the disappeared felt very lonely in the first years of democracy in the 1980s:

> My mother says that when she testified at the Juntas Trial, it was much worse, she travelled alone [to Buenos Aires to give testimony], society was much more indifferent, she was not even accompanied by her family.
>
> (Int. 40, April 2011, Córdoba)

Unlike the current trials in which, as will be noted later, witnesses feel more supported and can give more extensive testimonies with references to their own social and political militancy in such historical context, in their testimonies in the 1980s, many survivors felt constrained to deliver an account of terror. Thus, they focused on the description of the crimes in the CDCs, the identification of other prisoners as well as perpetrators, and excluded aspects such as their social activism and political militancy. The reasons for this were manifold. Among them was the need to provide proof of the crimes committed by the military, which were just beginning to be spoken out loud, and some sectors were quite unaware of them. Yet another reason was the lack of a social and political context that allowed the victims' accounts of political activism to be "listened to" without the witnesses being turned into the guilty party. Thus, while the trial made it possible to convict the military leaders, it did not call into question the framework in which their actions took place, that is, the "anti-subversive fight," as described by the military themselves, thus contributing to a greater reproduction of the social and political discourse of the "theory of the two demons" (Crenzel 2001, 282–283). The exclusion of the historical context in which political militancy and social activism occurred hindered the reconstruction of the reasons underlying state repression. Only when such reconstruction and historical contextualisation are carried out can the victims be de-stigmatised and humanised rather than made responsible.

This limitation of the Juntas Trial was perceived by many interviewees as constituting an obstacle to the construction of historical truth. They were unable to make reference to the political identity of the disappeared and one's own political identity. According to a survivor and witness in the trials:

> [It] was a very, very significant limitation, I don't know if it limited the conduct of the trial or the conviction of those guilty of genocide,[12] but it did limit access to the historical truth of those years. The genocide was completely emptied of political and ideological contents.
>
> (Int. 28, March 2011, Rosario)

According to Pilar Calveiro, denying the disappeared their condition as political militants amounts to disappearing them again. The author emphasises that whether their political conceptions were right or wrong is an altogether different matter, but the truth is that the phenomenon of the disappeared is not that of the massacre of "innocent victims" but of the murder and attempt to make disappear and completely disintegrate a form of resistance and opposition (Calveiro 1998, 165). The Juntas Trial aimed to show an ideal victim which was supposed to be passive and, especially, depoliticised. However, the disappeared and the survivors did not fit that image of the "perfect victim." Such a discrepancy was punished on many occasions with criminalisation.

The historical and political context was not the only aspect missing in the testimonies of the 1980s. Sexualised violence was also invisible. Testimony given in the Juntas Trial was aimed at proving the existence of a systematic plan of repression and legally conceptualising the notion of disappearance (Balardini, Oberlín and Sobredo 2011, 107). The first testimonies in court – and also in the CONADEP – revolved around situations of systematic torture in the CDCs. Testimony focused on providing information relevant to the identification of other prisoners who had been killed or disappeared. The accusations against the perpetrators were based on offences under the Argentine Criminal Code,[13] which did not include charges for crimes against sexual integrity, even though multiple references had been made to such crimes in numerous testimonies (2011, 107). Evidence presented in court showed the systematic use of torture on detainees, including the type of abuse that is characteristic of gender-based violence; however, these incidents were not prosecuted as such. As a result, the accusations of sexualised violence – perpetrated against both women and men – were subsumed within the offence of torture and were thus displaced. In turn, as noted by Balardini, Oberlin and Sobredo, victims of sexualised violence have often not spoken about the ordeal they went through in order not to detract attention from "more important things," that is, uncovering the fate of their disappeared relatives, friends or partners (2011, 111). Women felt that testimony of what had happened to the disappeared had to be prioritised.

3.3.4 The capital-centric approach to justice

While the trial provided proof of the crimes committed, the fact that it was exclusively conducted in the capital city of Buenos Aires diminished its impact on other regions of the country, such as semi-rural and rural areas in the northern provinces of Tucumán and Santiago del Estero. In the rural areas of those provinces, the transition to constitutional rule and the pursuit of justice were perceived as distant concerns.

However, it is necessary to point out some important differences between these two Northern provinces. Tucumán was one of the provinces with the highest levels of repression, CDCs and number of disappeared nationwide, beginning even before the dictatorship with Operation Independence (1975) as explained in Chapter 2. In Santiago del Estero, the modality and extent of repression was a bit different since there were fewer disappeared people but many illegal detentions and political prisoners. Furthermore, in both provinces there was a provincial commission that investigated the human rights violations committed during the dictatorship with a final report. However, these reports had different fates.

Though finally both documents were incorporated in CONADEP' s "*Nunca Más*" report, in Santiago del Estero, the provincial original report mysteriously "disappeared." As an interviewee from Santiago del Estero, who is a former political prisoner, explained, the provincial government denied access to such a report, alleging that it had been lost. Fear precluded people from reacting to or challenging that "loss":

> [D]uring Juárez's governorship [1983–1987, 1995–2001], they [the authorities] told us that [the report] had gone missing, (. . .) [but] who was going to ask questions here in Santiago? You couldn't ask about that report with Musa[14] and the repressors walking past your house or giving you an anonymous call saying "keep your trap shut or you'll get wiped out." (. . .) It wasn't easy. They were often breathing down my neck.
>
> (Int. 52, April 2011, Santiago del Estero)

The intimidating presence and actions of repressors like the local former police chief, Musa Azar, in the institutions of the provincial government were overwhelming. This constant intimidation and harassment ("breathing down my neck") prevented the victims but also other sectors of society from gaining access to the report, and the wider diffusion of the latter's accusations and testimony. That made it easier for the local population to deny the report's content. Thus, in Santiago del Estero, the crimes of the dictatorship were often perceived as having been committed against others, somewhere else. As an attorney for the prosecution of the province of Santiago del Estero stated in connection with the attitude of society in his province in the 1980s:

> [People] said: "this happened in Buenos Aires," with respect to the grandchild of Estela Carlotto,[15] they said "this didn't happen in Santiago." They didn't understand the true scale of horror that had also occurred in Santiago del Estero.
>
> (Int. 60, April 2011, Santiago del Estero)

In the province of Tucumán, though the reports from the Bicameral Commission acquired higher visibility, there were also great internal differences between the capital city of the province (San Miguel de Tucumán) and the rural areas of the province. The difficulties in obtaining testimonies but also in making testimonies from other places available in the countryside were manifold. These included the extreme isolation of several rural communities due to lack of transportation and means of communication, and high rates of illiteracy.[16] People in the countryside had a different perception of the political transition and Junta Trial. A prosecutor from Tucumán described the differences between perceptions in town and the countryside as follows:

> [P]eople's accounts – or at least the accounts of the majority – [in the rural areas of the province] contain no reference to democracy or the dictatorship. People don't say: "Alfonsín came in in '83, then the trial happened," nothing changed for them in that regard.
>
> (Int. 50, April 2011, Tucumán)

However, while in both provinces geographical distance and the difficulties of access to information could in part account for society's lack of awareness of legal policy and the attempt to bring justice to the country, the failure to perceive the democratic transition was caused by the fact that in many provinces such a transition was formal rather than factual. The continuity of personnel from dictatorship to constitutional regime and the persistence of the repressive practices gave no sign of a transition.

In the case of Santiago del Estero, the repressive practices that had already taken place before the dictatorship continued under constitutional rule. In this connection, no clear distinction can be perceived between the constitutional government in office before the coup and the governments taking office after the military regime. As was the case in other provinces, such as Tucumán, there were already records of disappearances and killings prior to 24 March 1976.[17] As Ernesto Picco states, the atmosphere of persecution, repression and death, which ceased to exist in most of the country in 1983 with the return to democracy, pervaded life in Santiago del Estero for twenty more years (Picco 2012, 23). As the attorney for the prosecution of Santiago del Estero stated:

> [D]emocracy was restored in the Argentine Republic in 1983; in Santiago del Estero, it was restored in 2003,[18] this perverse repressive apparatus continued to operate until 2003.
>
> (Int. 60, April 2011, Santiago del Estero)

While 1983 saw an end to the military government and the beginning of a democratic regime at the national level, in the province of Santiago del Estero the rule of law was permeated by practices of state repression and persecution, such as spying on social and political organisations, torture and authoritarianism, along with the presence in the provincial government of officials having close ties with the dictatorship (Dargoltz, Gerez and Cao 2006, 62). In both the provinces of Tucumán and Santiago del Estero, the continuity of these repressive practices was also supported by some segments of the population, which elected governors accused of having committed crimes during the state terror.[19]

The Juntas Trial – and also CONADEP – were meaningful but had important limitations. On the one hand, the trial needed more time to reach across society and victims. Halted by the amnesty laws and the pardons, the process needed more time to mature, to become deeper and more comprehensive so as to address broader aspects of the repression – as the current trials do. An interviewee from Tucumán whose whole family was disappeared described that trial as a thwarted effort:

> [A]ll that which could have influenced the modes of understanding of what had happened in this country, which started with the Juntas Trial, was totally undermined by those damned [amnesty] laws.
>
> (Int. 70, October 2012, Tucumán)

Personal and social reparation is a long and gradual process, not a spontaneous and automatic change. The effectiveness of law in "influencing the modes of understanding," as the interviewee describes, requires time. The "discovery of law" produced by the Juntas Trial was no more than that – just a discovery. It did not have the necessary time to "mature" and to allow a reconfiguration of social ties which would have involved a change of social attitudes toward victims. The amnesty laws in 1986 and 1987 interrupted that process and undermined the reparative potential of the trial.

The Juntas Trial in the 1980s proved to be crucial in starting to address the crimes of state repression. However, it was constrained and influenced by various factors analysed in this chapter. Its implications and limitations also allow a glimpse of the social context and the relations of force prevailing at that time, in which the military still had enough power to influence the form of justice (i.e. only nine members of the military Juntas were prosecuted). In turn, the treatment of victims in court, including their stigmatisation and even criminalisation, was also the reflection or result of a socially hegemonic discourse that qualified the victims as "guilty or innocent" according to their previous history of political militancy. Finally, the analysis of the Juntas Trial allows a more appropriate understanding of the effects of current human rights trials for victims. As will be explained in the next chapters, most witnesses and survivors perceive the current trials as having a greater potential for reparative justice than that of the 1980s. In addition, the initiation of the current trials at a local level marks a turning point and increases their impact for society and the victims in the provinces of the country.

Notes

1 By virtue of Decree No. 157, well-known guerrilla leaders such as Mario Firmenich, Fernando Vaca, Enrique Gorriarán and Roberto Perdía were arrested and convicted (Eliaschev 2011).
2 They were Generals Jorge Videla, Roberto Viola and Leopoldo Galtieri; Brigadiers Orlando R. Agosti, Omar Rubens Graffigna and Basilio Lami Dozo; and Admirals Emilio Massera, Armando Lambruschini and Jorge Anaya. These former Junta members faced charges of illegal detention, murder and torture, among other crimes (Roehrig 2009, 730).
3 General Videla was found guilty of the following crimes committed by the army: eighty-three homicides, 594 illegal deprivations of freedom, 254 applications of torture, ninety-four aggravated robberies, 180 counts of ideological falsification of public documents, four usurpations of property, twenty-three counts of forced labours, one count of extortion, two extortive kidnappings, seven counts of child stealing and seven counts of torture resulting in death, in addition to the leadership role in the terror state (Nino 2006, 144).
4 Admiral Massera was found guilty of the following acts committed by the navy: eighty-three homicides, 523 illegal deprivations of freedom, 267 counts of torture, 102 aggravated robberies, 201 counts of ideological falsification of public documents, four usurpations of property, twenty-three counts of forced labours, two extortive kidnappings, eleven counts of child stealing and seven counts of torture resulting in death (Nino 2006, 144).
5 As mentioned in Chapter 2, many interviewees refer to the CDCs as concentrations camps since the captivity conditions were very similar to those of the concentrations camps during the Holocaust.
6 This letter refers to the "answer" of the interviewee.
7 This letter refers to the "question" of the interviewer.
8 "Turco Julián" is the alias of Julio Simón, a former member of the Federal Police who acted as a torturer in former CDC known as *El Olimpo* (Olympus) in the city of Buenos Aires during the dictatorship. In 2006 he was sentenced to twenty-five years in prison for crimes against humanity, for which he is currently under arrest.
9 In the specific case of Tucumán, Rubén Kotler points out that the access to testimonies in the countryside of the province was especially difficult not only because of the prevailing terror in those regions but because access was difficult for the rural population. This isolation was due to several factors such as lack of public transportation, illiteracy, lack of economic resources, etc. Moreover, repression in the rural areas was so high that in many cases entire family groups were made to disappear, leaving no records of them (Kotler 2007).

10 The *Montoneros* were one of the armed organisations of the political movement Peronist Youth.

11 This is similar to the case of the status of refugees in international law, according to which a person qualifies as a refugee if he/she is not involved in armed political groups (Adelman 1998, 50).

12 As explained in Chapter 2, many interviewees refer to the state repression as genocide. See the work Daniel Feierstein (2006) for more details on this.

13 The crimes tried were: unlawful deprivation of freedom, torture, torture followed by death, murder and theft.

14 Antonio Musa Azar is the emblematic figure of repression in Santiago del Estero before, during and after the military dictatorship. From 1975 Musa Azar was the head of the Police Information Department (DIP as per its acronym in Spanish), which is the police intelligence service of the province of Santiago del Estero (Rodriguez 2003). During the constitutional governments of governor Carlos Juárez in the 1990s and early 2000s, Musa Azar was the head of the provincial police. During that time, repressive practices continued to be applied which resembled the practices of the dictatorship. Musa Azar was finally sentenced to life imprisonment for crimes against humanity in three different trials since 2010 (Centro de Información Judicial 2013).

15 Estela de Carlotto is the president of the well-known human rights organisation Grandmothers of Plaza de Mayo. Her daughter Laura, who was pregnant, was kidnapped and disappeared by the military in the province of Buenos Aires in 1977. Laura Carlotto gave birth at the military hospital before being disappeared. Her captors absconded with the baby. After having looked for her grandson for over thirty years, Estela de Carlotto found him in 2014 (Capiello 2014).

16 This difference between the capital city and the interior of the province regarding access to testimonies and information can be seen even today, in trials carried out in Tucumán, for which it is difficult to find witnesses in rural areas.

17 For instance, in a trial conducted in the province of Santiago del Estero in 2012, fourteen disappearances and forty-five detentions were investigated which occurred before the military coup, during the constitutional governorship of Carlos Juárez (1973–1976).

18 When Néstor Kirchner's presidency began.

19 In the province of Tucumán, Antonio Domingo Bussi was elected as governor several times, as was Carlos Juárez, in Santiago del Estero. This will be explained in detail in Chapter 4 below.

Chapter 4

"As if nothing had happened." Legal impunity and its social implications for victims

Having analysed the important effects and constraints of the Juntas Trial, and the historical context in which it took place, in this chapter I address the implications that impunity, in the form of amnesty laws and pardons, had on the victims and on some segments of society. In doing so, I show how the implementation of amnesty laws and their consequences contributed to the deprivation of citizens' rights for the victims, to the reproduction of detrimental social attitudes towards them and to the benefit of the perpetrators, many of whom remained powerful in the 1990s.

The social harm caused by state violence – such as fear, isolation and destruction of social ties – does not automatically disappear with the end of an authoritarian regime (Kordon and Edelman 1986; Lechner 1992; Salimovich, Lira and Weinstein 1992; Feierstein 2011). The role of subsequent governments is crucial in either perpetuating or dismantling those effects over time. While in Argentina the years immediately after the end of the dictatorship saw on the one hand an attempt to deal with the consequences of state repression by means of the trial against the Juntas members, the creation of CONADEP and financial reparations for some groups of victims, the subsequent establishment of amnesty laws contributed, on the other hand, to the persistence of some of the effects of terror over time. An in-depth analysis of the serious implications of impunity for victims, a conceptual approach to the meaning of the amnesty laws as well as a review of the historical framework of the 1990s in Argentina are crucial to understanding why trials can have a reparative potential. To this end, this chapter is structured in four sections. In Section 1, I give an overview of the Argentine historical and political context in which the amnesty laws and pardons were put in place as well as an account of the struggle of the victims and human rights movement against impunity. In Section 2, I begin with a brief theoretical approach to the definition and meaning of impunity. I address some of the most difficult social implications of the amnesty laws for victims of state terror – fear, silence and indifference – not only in the big urban centres but also in semi-rural and conservative contexts, where authoritarian practices continued despite the restoration of the constitutional regime. In doing so, I show how impunity may also function as an instrument of social control. Section 3 shows how the persistence of older authoritarian figures and practices in the 1990s could rely on – to varying degrees – the support of the population, which again reflected more detrimental social attitudes towards the victims. Finally, in Section 4 I examine how impunity not only affected the relation of other segments of society towards victims but also how it undermined the latter's rights as citizens.

4.1 The era of impunity

The Juntas Trial in 1985 not only prosecuted the former commanders but also generated unexpected outcomes for the government of president Raúl Alfonsín. It led to further investigations fuelled by the discovery of new information that would allow the initiation of new trials and the prosecution of more officers. This posed a serious problem for the government's strategy, which had originally only aimed at prosecuting some of the leading figures in the military, and thus bringing the issue of human rights violations to a close. (Acuña and Smulovitz 1991, 16). However, despite Alfonsín's efforts to curtail the number of prosecutions, individuals continued to file indictments so that, by mid-1986, 3,000 cases were pending in Argentine military and civilian courts (Nino 2006). By then, it was clear that "the scope of the trials had already escaped the control of the executive and the judicial process had assumed a life of its own" (Brysk 1995, 80). Roehrig (2009) stresses that this second wave of trials resulted from two developments. First, in the convictions of the Junta leaders, the court included "Item 30," which maintained that lower level military personnel also shared responsibility for the atrocities (Roehrig 2009, 731). Consequently, the court was required to send evidence back to the military court that had acquitted these officers so that others could be brought to justice. A second reason for the wave of new trials was that Argentine judicial procedure allowed for civilians to file a case directly with the courts. The number of cases increased dramatically as individuals and human rights groups made extensive use of this provision (Ibid.). In response President Alfonsín and his legal team drafted a number of measures to decisively limit the number of trials. On 23 December 1986, Alfonsín passed Law No. 23.492, known as the *Ley de Punto Final* (Full Stop Law) which set a sixty-day deadline (23 February 1987) for the victims and relatives of the disappeared to file charges against members of the military and police suspected of human rights crimes. The Alfonsín government sought by means of this law to speed up and confine the filing of complaints to those sixty days. All those not accused within that period would be free of any prosecution. Despite the fact that the first thirty days of the period for submission fell within the traditional vacation period, a large number of indictments were brought forward. As military officers and personnel continued to be summoned before the law, the effect of consolidation that the Full Stop Law was intended to procure did not materialise as the government expected (Nino 2006, 148–150).

Some months after the Full Stop Law's deadline, on 15 April 1987, a serious military rebellion against the trials developed. Mid-ranking officers rebelled at the prospect of being held accountable alongside their commanders. A group of military personnel, the so-called *Carapintadas* ("painted faces" because of their use of face paint as camouflage), headed by Lieutenant Colonel Aldo Rico, staged a series of barrack uprisings demanding that the trials of those low- and mid-ranking officers be terminated so as to "restore the dignity and unity of the army" (Malamud-Goti 1996, 5). This "Easter rebellion" of the *Carapintadas* challenged the civilian government and its human rights prosecutions, which they considered to be a campaign to humiliate the armed forces.[1] After negotiations with President Alfonsín on 19 April, the mutineers were all seized (Nino 2006, 153, 154). However, as a result of this, and responding to the fear of future military rebellions, the Alfonsín administration passed Law No. 23.521, the second crucial law, also known as *Ley de Obediencia Debida* (Due Obedience Law) in June 1987. This law established that all those who, at the time when the acts in question were carried out, fulfilled a reviewing role as chief officers, subalterns and military personnel of the armed, security, police and prison forces were not responsible for acts otherwise punishable since they had acted out of "due obedience." It explicitly defined the notion of decision-making capacity and confined it to the higher military ranks. Subordinates were considered to have "acted in a state of coercion, under the subordination of to the higher authority, and of having carried out orders, without the power or possibility to examine, oppose or resist them" (Law No. 23.521 of 1987, Art. 1). This law put an end to most of the prosecutions. In line with his original intention to take a middle path, Alfonsín had now successfully confined the prosecutions to the high-ranking officers. However, offences involving rape and the abduction and concealment of minors, forgery of their identity and the extortive misappropriation of property were still prosecutable (Law No. 23.521, Art. 2).

Amidst a serious economic crisis, Alfonsín resigned in June 1989, five months short of completing his term. On 6 October, his successor, Peronist President Carlos Menem, enacted various decrees of pardon (numbers: 1002, 1003, 1004 and 1005 of 7 October 1989, and decrees No. 2741, 2745 and 2746 of 29 December 1990), which implied the end of all the then-existing criminal cases prosecuting the military Juntas. The pardons applied to three groups: 1) members of the security forces accused of human rights violations, which included thirty-nine senior officers who were facing charges in judicial processes and had already been sentenced; 2) members of guerrilla groups accused of "terrorist acts"; and 3) the military personnel who had revolted in 1987 (Nino 2006, 159). Menem justified these pardons in the name of "national reconciliation" (Druliolle 2013, 260). However, these decrees meant a major new reversal for the principle of justice and accountability. The measure was questioned by some parts of society. When President Menem's plans for pardons were announced in September 1989, thousands protested in the streets. Surveys showed that more than 68 per cent of the population opposed these pardons (Acuña and Smulovitz 1995, 81). A prominent journalist of the time captured the unpopularity of the pardons:

> You can imagine the indignation and outrage of those affected [by the violent repression] as they faced impunity and double standards of legality (. . .)

> If a citizen steals a chicken he goes to jail. If a member of the armed forces kills serially he stays home.
>
> (quoted in Roniger and Sznajder 1998, 148)

These double standards reveal the power relations underlying the institutions in charge of the creation and implementation of the law: the executive, the legislature and the judiciary. Impunity also meant the cancellation of many ongoing investigations started with the Juntas Trial and CONADEP as well as other provincial investigative commissions (such as those in Tucumán and Santiago del Estero).

In addition, during Menem's presidency, critical reforms in the judicial system of Argentina were undertaken. He expanded the number of judges on the Supreme Court from five to nine, arguing that the increment was necessary for the court to handle its growing workload. However a deeper reason may be that by appointing these new judges, Menem created an "automatic majority" that was loyal to him and to his efforts to protect the military from further prosecution (Roht-Arriaza 2004). The new judges were Menem's political allies. The Supreme Court was an unpopular institution that had already supported the Due Obedience Law and was viewed by many as a compliant supporter of Menem's economic policies during a period of corruption. The Supreme Court was also likely to block any attempts to reverse the two amnesty laws (Roehrig 2009).

Despite this bleak panorama for justice, there were some favourable changes in Argentine legislation during the 1990s due to the intense and continued fight of human rights organisations and victims. One of such changes was the constitutional reform of 1994, which added article 75, clause 22 to the national constitution. According to this article, international human rights treaties became part of the constitution and took precedence over national laws. Thereafter, if a domestic law conflicted with one of these treaties, the treaty trumped the law no matter which one was passed first (Roht-Arriaza 2004, 99). Furthermore, by means of Law No. 24.556 enacted in 1995, the Argentine National Congress approved the ratification of the Inter-American Convention on Forced Disappearance of Persons by the OAS. The government of Menem also passed important laws concerning economic reparation for relatives of disappeared persons, survivors and ex-political prisoners (Guembe 2008).

4.1.1 Partial justice: accountability for the theft of children and Truth Trials

Faced with the impossibility of initiating criminal cases, human rights organisations implemented different domestic and international legal strategies. A creative appropriation by civil society of the structures of legal opportunity started with the bringing of cases for crimes specifically excluded from the amnesty laws. Human rights organisations collected evidence and testimonies to demand justice in cases that involved the kidnapping of the babies of disappeared women born in captivity.[2] These demands led to arrests and prosecutions of former members of the military Juntas pardoned by Menem. In July 1998, Federal Judge Roberto Marquevich ordered the arrest of General Rafael Videla because of his responsibility for the theft of babies born in army CDCs at Campo de Mayo, El Pozo Banfield and Automotores Orletti in the province of Buenos Aires (Roht-Arriaza 2004, 106). The judge argued, furthermore, that the crimes were of such gravity that they should be considered crimes against humanity (Human Rights Watch 2006). In September 1999, Judge Adolfo Bagnasco indicted the other member of the first military Junta, Admiral Emilio Massera, on similar charges. During the 1985 to 2005 period, some thirty-eight defendants in total were indicted in criminal cases of child appropriation. In 84 per cent of these cases, the defendants were found guilty and sentenced (CELS 2012, 34).

As explained in Chapter 2, many of the judicial staff who held office during the 1980s, 1990s and 2000s, that is judges, public prosecutors and other members of the judicial system, had not only been in office during the dictatorship but had also actively contributed to human rights violations: for instance, by systematically rejecting *habeas corpus* or inquiries from those desperately in search of their disappeared family members, or by validating illegal detentions. The complicity of the majority of the judiciary enabled conditions for illegal repression during the military government. Thus, impunity not only meant the absence of prosecutions but also the continued presence of many employees in state institutions who had either contributed to or had deliberately ignored the illegal repression. Thus, the role of the judiciary was highly questionable not only during the dictatorship but also in the post-dictatorship decades in which the democratic governments upheld impunity by hindering claims to truth and justice. As described by Malamud-Goti, the request by relatives of the victims to exhume bodies discovered in secret mass graves was repeatedly denied by judges (1996, 163). Similar reluctance was to be found in cases for the identification of children who were thought to have been appropriated. The courts had almost unanimously dragged their feet about ordering the necessary measures to establish the identity of children of the disappeared (Ibid.).

In this way, the judiciary did not cooperate in the search for truth. With the support of NGOs, relatives of the disappeared brought complaints before the domestic courts, demanding to know the fate of the disappeared, where their bodies were and who was responsible – in addition to the possibility of obtaining criminal sanctions. They based their demands on the right (both of the relatives and of society as a whole) to know the truth, and the right of the relatives to bury and mourn their dead (Roht-Arriaza 2004, 101). The two cases first presented were those of Mónica Candelaria Mignone, the daughter of the human rights activist Emilio Mignone,[3] and of Alejandra Lapaco, the daughter of the co-founder of *Madres de Plaza de Mayo*, Carmen Aguiar de Lapaco.[4]

These judicial complaints, especially the Lapaco case,[5] gave birth to the so-called *Juicios por la Verdad* (Truth Trials) which consisted of judicial investigations and hearings before judges, however crucially, without criminal sanctions. The Truth Trials were first conducted in the city of La Plata and then expanded to several locations, including Bahía Blanca, Buenos Aires, Mar del Plata, Córdoba, Rosario, Mendoza, Misiones, Salta and Jujuy. Some trials had publicity, others very little.[6] In all cases the Army's cooperation was minimal (Human Rights Watch 2006). Army officers called to testify in these proceedings frequently refused to do so. The Army went as far as to provide legal and moral support to officers detained for contempt of court or perjury (Roht-Arriaza 2004).

While the Truth Trials contributed significantly to uncovering new evidence, the victims and human rights organisations were disappointed by the obstacles to the prosecution. An attorney from La Plata explained to me the contradictory feelings created by the fact that, despite all the information that was available, nothing could be done with it:

> [A]t the beginning there was a strong feeling of impotence when so many names of guilty people were mentioned, and there was nothing you could do.
>
> (Int. 17, March 2011, La Plata)

Many interviewees referred to this feeling of impotence due to the inadequacies of a trial without punishment. The contradiction created by judges hearing, in public, evidence of indictable crimes without the possibility of those responsible being prosecuted was unbearable for the victims. However, much of the information revealed in the Truth Trials would serve as evidence years later, for the (ongoing) criminal proceedings with the full prosecution of the perpetrators, thanks to the overturning and annulment of the amnesty laws between 2003 and 2005 (Maculan 2012).

4.2 Social and political implications of impunity for victims

Even though amnesty laws and pardons were an important factor of impunity in Argentina, the concept itself describes not only a juridical situation but also a phenomenon of social and political dimensions. In general terms, impunity can be defined as the "lack of punishment" (Zaffaroni 1983, 11). Diane Orentlicher defines impunity as:

> the impossibility, de jure or de facto, of bringing the perpetrators of violations to account – whether in criminal, civil, administrative or disciplinary proceedings – since they are not subject to any inquiry that might lead to their being accused, arrested, tried and, if found guilty, sentenced to appropriate penalties, and to making reparations to their victims.
>
> (2005, 6)

The right to justice, embodied in many international legal documents, appeals to states to investigate, prosecute and punish crimes against humanity. It implies that any victim can assert his or her rights and receive a fair and effective remedy, including the expectation that the person or persons responsible will be held accountable by judicial means (Guissé 1996). In this sense, according to human rights legislation, a state that does not sanction crimes committed by its agents also violates victims' rights, while at the same time denying, and in this way implicitly legitimising, previous violations. This means that systematic human rights violations occurred in Argentina not only during the period of the dictatorship but also under the following democratic governments in which legal impunity prevailed until 2003.

Impunity, as a political phenomenon, can take different forms. It may be *de jure* or *de facto*. *De jure* impunity arises directly or indirectly from laws or regulations, especially amnesties or presidential pardons. By contrast, *de facto* impunity is the result of the factual implementation of mechanisms or social and political constraints which impede criminal prosecution and punishment (Ambos 1999, 34). In Argentina both types of impunity co-existed. Formal impunity owed its existence to the amnesty laws, while *de facto* impunity existed because even though certain crimes were not covered by the amnesty laws, such as the kidnapping of children, theft and sexual abuse, many such crimes were still not prosecuted. In particular, cases of theft and sexual crimes were not reported and prosecuted.

To understand how impunity can affect victims and other sectors of society, it is useful to go back to some of the conceptualisations, outlined in Chapter 1, of the social functions of the law as an instrument of communication and regulation of behaviour. As stated by Bourdieu, the law operates as a powerful discourse that is coupled with the physical means to impose compliance on others (punishment), which might be understood as an instrument to normalise social behaviour (1987, 848). Laws are the product of historical, social and political processes and represent a system of rules and mandates, enforced through social and legal institutions, to shape public behaviour (Hollander 1978, 45; Tyler 2006, 16–19). According to Duff, criminal law, and the punishment it can imply in case of conviction, operates as an effective communicative process which aims to engage the addressee of the message as an active participant in the process who will receive and respond to the communication (2001, 80–81). The message(s) *received* by society is/are translated into social attitudes and behaviour. The most explicit of these attitudes is compliance with the explicit text of the law, as with "It is forbidden to kill." If, as Duff stresses, the law, or the groups of the society in whose name it speaks, is to mean what its written text says, it is committed to censuring those who violate the law's mandate. To remain silent in the face of serious crimes would be to deny that such conduct is wrong (Duff 2001, 27–28). The enforcement of amnesty laws is one of the most controversial forms of active legal silence and the clearest evidence of the power of perpetrators.

Now, as I described in Chapter 1, the message or instruction contained in criminal law can include implicit messages which yield a multiplicity of forms of conduct that go beyond the explicit mandate. In this sense, the enactment of the law not only communicates an explicit censure of or permission to do a certain act or crime but it also conveys underlying implicit messages to the direct victims, to perpetrators, to society and to state officials. In sending these messages – explicit and implicit – state institutions and regulations influence social perception and attitudes towards victims. Amnesty laws that deal with human rights violations form a special category of laws. These are not laws which prohibit a certain conduct such as torture or killing but, on the contrary, create a legal – and political – exception to those prohibitions for, initially, a specific group of people: the perpetrators, who were mainly – though not only – agents of the state. At the same time, this legal exception for perpetrators turns their victims into citizens exempted from rights which others in society enjoy.

Many scholars agree that the message that amnesty laws convey is one of denial (La Rue 1995; Cohen 2001). Denial of state crimes was, as shown in Chapter 2, a fundamental element of the repression as part of its regime of terror. However, during the constitutional governments that followed, denial did not cease but it took other forms. Indeed, there is a consensus that impunity, especially when it is legalised, involves an official denial by the state of its responsibility for human rights violations, since it means knowing but not acknowledging what happened. Impunity in Argentina entailed two forms of denial: by action and omission. On the one hand, even though the Argentine democratic governments knew in the late 1980s and 1990s that certain crimes committed during the dictatorship could be prosecuted (crimes such as sexual offences and the theft of babies were not amnestied), the state did nothing to investigate or prosecute. As Cohen puts it: "to know and not to act is not to know" (Cohen 2001, 23). On the other hand, amnesty laws are a strong and active form of official denial since even though the state knows what happened during the dictatorship, it not only refuses to act against the perpetrators (*de facto* impunity), but additionally it acts so as to formulate laws that prevent prosecution by others (victims and plaintiffs). The different governments in the 1980s and 1990s made an active political and legal effort to stop prosecutions that had already started with the trial of the military Juntas in 1985.

As discussed above, human rights organisations have been one of the most important opponents of impunity both under the dictatorship and in the subsequent thirty years. Because of its strength, and various contributions to bring justice, the struggle of the human rights movement is one of the most discussed in the literature on impunity in the 1990s in Argentina (Jelín 1995; Bosco 2004; Jacobs and Maldonado 2005; Humphrey and Valverde 2007; Van Drunnen 2010). Such analyses, while important, have neglected other aspects and serious social consequences of impunity for society and victims. Not all victims had the support, opportunities, and social and political resources – and in many cases the strength – to participate in the active struggle against impunity. Many of them lived in very adverse social and political contexts where political and social activism was not an option. That adversity, expressed in phenomena that will be discussed below – fear, silence, indifference, stigmatisation – was maintained by impunity. Analysing these contexts also involves going beyond the classical "capital city-centred approach" and looking at different locations in the country where struggle and resistance were much more difficult. In this sense, it is important not to confuse Buenos Aires and a few other important urban centres with Argentina as a whole and to assume that what happened in the capital city was the sum total of what was happening in the whole country. In this regard, I show that impunity had manifold consequences and that the victims do not belong to a homogeneous universe, but that they have had different experiences, possibilities and constraints. Understanding the impact of impunity on victims is crucial to seeing the relevance and possibility of reparative justice that comes with trials.

Given that the law operates as an instrument of communication which is able to influence social perceptions, the following questions arise: what kind of mandate and social attitudes do amnesty laws tend to promote? What impact do these social attitudes have on victims' lives? In what follows, the analysis of the information provided by the interviewees in different provinces of Argentina shows that just as regular criminal laws do, amnesty laws involve explicit and implicit mandates which yield social attitudes and perceptions that undermine the conditions of victims' lives and the possibilities of reparation.

4.2.1 Reproducing fear: victims at risk

In previous chapters I have described how the legacy and effects of terror can persist even after the end of an authoritarian regime if subsequent governments do not engage in a serious policy to combat them. Laws supporting impunity contribute to the extension of those consequences in time. The reproduction of fear – in some specific cases even terror – is one of them. Fear can have many sources but one of the most important is that impunity puts victims at risk by generating one of the main causes of this fear: the liberty of the perpetrators. This setting of permanent risk made itself evident in Argentina, where former officers of the armed forces or other members of the dictatorship were either free or, in the worst cases, continued to work in state institutions such as the security forces, public administration and the judicial system. An interviewee from the city of La Plata in the province of Buenos Aires, a young man whose parents were made to disappear and who had been active in the trials as a witness and plaintiff in 2010 and 2011, explained things as follows:

> Fear depends on the degree of impunity. (. . .) undoubtedly, the more impunity there is, the more afraid you get because the repressors are more free to do what they want, to call you up and threaten you, stop you on a street corner and scare the hell out of you, they can do whatever they want. If they were all in jail, as they should be, there wouldn't be so much impunity and there wouldn't be so much fear of the threats.
>
> (Int. 74, September 2012, La Plata)

In this sense, impunity involves denying the situation of risk in which the survivors, the relatives of the victims and even their supporters are placed. Impunity grants the victimisers freedom of action to do "whatever they want," while it leaves the victims defenceless. An ex-political prisoner from Santiago del Estero said in this regard:

> The effect of impunity on a person [a perpetrator] is dreadful, [he] thinks he's all-powerful, [he] can do anything, that he'll never be punished.
>
> (Int. 53, April 2011, Santiago del Estero)

This situation in which victimisers feel they are omnipotent and victims are defenceless is in turn reinforced by the continued presence of the perpetrators in public institutions. Several interviewees from different cities have referred to this situation, which is especially true of the security forces, and to the fact that they encountered the perpetrators regularly in the street. A survivor narrated:

> They were walking free here in the city of Rosario. And not so long ago, some 15 years ago, Lofiego[7] was a member of the police in Rosario (. . .) that is, long after the return to democracy (. . .) I have always lived in this area and I came across him regularly in the street.
>
> (Int. 28, March 2011, Rosario)

Being free and exempt from punishment places perpetrators at an advantage in relation to the victims and society at large. Furthermore, the perpetrators' positions of power within state institutions reinforce the asymmetry of power between them and the victims. As narrated by another interviewee from Tucumán whose family is disappeared:

> [Then there is] the case of a *compañera* [a fellow militant], who was held as a prisoner in Jefatura[8] (. . .) and she ran into her oppressor just around the corner, in the city centre. One had to bump into those sons of a bitch and, on top of that, they looked you in the eye, (. . .) as if saying "here I am."
>
> (Int. 70, October 2012, Tucumán)

Many victims had to live with perpetrators as neighbours and to tolerate their intimidations. The daily encounters with the repressors worked as a mechanism of control that revived fear and reminded the victims that state terror was over but they still had power. As psychologist Elina Aguiar argues, the impunity enjoyed by perpetrators resulted in the victims becoming an "at-risk population" (Aguiar 2006, 12). This oppressive social context was in some cases reinforced by the existence of repressive censorship and regulations that placed constraints on protests in public spaces and thus limited collective action and social mobilisation, especially in the north of the country. An interviewee explained that before 2003 in Santiago del Estero it was forbidden to carry pictures of the disappeared in marches in public spaces, this being a common practice in large urban centres such as La Plata, Buenos Aires and Rosario:

> [T]he pictures of the disappeared had never been publicly displayed before [2003]. (. . .) We couldn't meet in the square and march for the disappeared. (. . .) The use of the square for political reasons was forbidden. (. . .) What's more, we couldn't [use the square] because people made us feel so much pressure that it was very difficult to even leave home for the march.
>
> (Int. 52, April 2011, Santiago del Estero)

The provincial context was also clearly described by another interviewee in the following terms:

> [It is] a very complicated political context in Santiago del Estero because the governor was actively involved in repression before the coup [of 1976]. And the authorities who had been in power before and during the dictatorship remained responsible for the security and intelligence services in Santiago del Estero, like Musa Azar.
>
> (Int. 55, April 2011, Santiago Estero)

As perpetrators continued to serve in public institutions, they had the power to pass regulations – such as the prohibition on the public display of pictures of the local disappeared or placing restrictions on the use of public spaces and social protest – which served their interests. Such acts might threaten the official policy of denial of state crimes. Instead, prohibitions and regulations continued to maintain a social climate of fear and paralysis, undermining resistance and enabling the perpetrators to keep their positions of privilege. Impunity worked to reproduce their power. Consequently, it is no wonder that in provinces such as Santiago del Estero the phrase "here the dictatorship lasted until 2003" was frequently mentioned in interviews.

The context of fear was reproduced not only by the presence of officials from the dictatorship in the democratic state institutions but also by the persistence of dictatorial rhetoric and abusive violent practices in politics. As Malamud-Goti (1996) explains, the rhetoric of the logic of terror was quite common not only at the provincial level but even in national politics. As the author shows, a well-known example of this kind of *revival* took place in July 1992 when thousands of teachers, students and parents staged massive protests in Argentina's major cities against low wages and cuts in public funding for education. In response, President Menem startled the population by announcing that "subversion" was lurking behind the protests. He also claimed that students who rallied against the educational policies could soon be "disappeared" as thousands of dissidents had been during the military dictatorship (Malamud-Goti 1996) and warned that parents involved in the protest could "become Mothers of *Plaza de Mayo*." President Menem's words were the same as those used by the military dictatorship. The prevailing dictatorial rhetoric was imprinted on the memory of several interviewees. For instance, an interviewee, a son of disappeared parents and a member of the HIJOS organisation, recalls Menem's constant, intimidating messages every time the organisation held an "*escrache*"[9] protest:

> Those were the times of impunity (. . .), Menem said that if the *escraches* continued, people would disappear, I remember very well, (. . .) [Menem] said "don't complain if something happens." Things were very difficult for us.
>
> (Int. 23, March 2011, Rosario)

These intimidating official statements, incompatible with democratic respect for dissent and social protests, had a significant paralysing effect on protesters. Immediately after the president's speeches, demonstrations shrank to roughly a quarter of what they had been before (Malamud-Goti 1996, 7, 72). Impunity paved the path for such uses and abuses of dictatorial rhetoric reactivating fear and the sense of constant threat to those who attempted any collective act of resistance.

4.2.2 The silence and paralysis of society

The political and legal decision not to prosecute human rights violations, thus leaving the perpetrators at liberty and unpunished, conveys an explicit and implicit message to society, influencing feelings, perceptions and attitudes. In the 1980s many relatives of the disappeared and survivors in Argentina were actively taking part in protests and the search for information about their loved ones. But in the 1990s – while active participation did not come to an absolute standstill – the amnesty laws and pardons caused a breakdown in participation of many of those who had been very active before. As explained by a survivor:

> Above all in the 1980s. (. . .) we had a chance to go to the protests, the universities. But then came that breakdown that lasted twenty years and everything fell to pieces (. . .) Maybe people were tired or discouraged. Maybe we didn't take the initiative any longer.
>
> (Int. 68, September 2012, Tucumán)

That "breakdown" and subsequent discouragement in those years was to be seen in several locations of the country. Thus, and though, as shown above, human rights and victims' organisations implemented different judicial and non-judicial strategies to obtain justice in the 1990s, many other victims and relatives of the disappeared were discouraged from mobilisation. The feeling that justice could not be achieved reduced participation in social and political organisations. A daughter of disappeared parents from the city of Buenos Aires, who participated in the *Escuela de Mecánica de la Armada* (Navy Mechanics School, hereafter ESMA) trial of 2011 as a witness and plaintiff, recounted the experience of her aunt during the late 1980s and 1990s:

> My aunt was really active in that sense, [but] after the nullity of the laws, the pardons and the lack of information. Impunity was rampant, she gradually gave up, and (. . .) she stopped searching. (. . .) She stopped believing in the democratic system; she was rather sceptical.
>
> (Int. 62, September 2012, Buenos Aires)

Impunity in Argentina contributed to the continuity of certain practices of repression and intimidation, which in turn supported a social framework of fear, depolitisation, demobilisation and silence. According to Rawls, the law plays a fundamental role in that it defines a basic framework within which all other activities of life take place (1971, 236). Thus, the link between laws protecting perpetrators of serious crimes and the reproduction of fear in the social and political sphere becomes clear. In this way, fear anchored in impunity operated as a mechanism of social discipline that promoted social attitudes detrimental to the victims. The silence of society was one of the main expressions of these attitudes. The inability to speak in the years of impunity usually came up during most interviews. An interviewee, a former political prisoner from Santiago del Estero and a university professor at the time of the interview, emphasised this in the following terms:

> The two laws adopted by Menem and Alfonsín silenced, silenced speech.
>
> (Int. 53, April 2011, Santiago del Estero).

The law, through its mandates and consequences – freedom for perpetrators – operates as a mechanism for the authorisation of social speech and dictates what can or cannot be talked about. When asked about whether the trials in Santiago del Estero had been a turning point, the interviewee replied:

> Absolutely (. . .) Where do I see it? They have done away with all the gags, people can now name something which was said in whispers or not said at all. We can name people. We can name events, name things, this may sound ridiculous, but this city has been dominated by silence, (. . .) everything was silenced. It was not just the military coup and the Junta in its years of dictatorship, here we had a dictatorship which gagged us for fifty years.
>
> (Int. 53, April 2011, Santiago del Estero)

While different regions in the country experienced this fear of naming certain people and events, it was in the north where interviewees mentioned it the most. The same interviewee stressed:

> Naming Juárez was terrible, you couldn't name him because you thought that something . . . it's like some phantom, something oppressive. (. . .) you

> have no idea how strong it is. You can sense fear. I had classes [at university] in which you knew there were policemen present.
>
> (Int. 53, April 2011, Santiago del Estero)

Carlos Juárez served as governor of the province of Santiago del Estero for five terms under democratic rule. He and many of the officials under him were greatly feared because of the repressive and corrupt practices of the provincial police. In fact, in the current human rights trials, Juárez has been accused of involvement in the disappearance of several people. The presence of perpetrators in the security forces in a context in which they enjoyed total impunity worked as a threatening and inhibiting mechanism which reinforced silence and denial. Fear is not only a result of impunity but also of the social-psychological mechanism that helps to maintain it (Zur 1994). Victims of atrocities and their relatives dare not risk their personal safety by making accusations, especially when they fear retaliation.

Silence pervaded many public spaces and even permeated the private sphere of the victims' families, particularly of survivors and ex-political prisoners, where the experiences of political militancy prior to and during the dictatorship as well as having lived in captivity continued to be taboo topics. A former political prisoner told me:

> My in-laws wouldn't hear of that. They would say: "Forget about it, that's a topic we don't need to talk about, it's over, you have to get on with your life." I could never speak about it, and when I did, they isolated me. They only came over for Christmas and New Year.
>
> (Int. 52, April 2011, Santiago del Estero).

This kind of rejection led many victims to hide part of their experiences. Another interviewee said:

> Sometimes I lied, I made up stories. It was hard to say "I am a child of disappeared parents." I did not feel so free in the 1990s (. . .). I felt that I could not speak much about the topic, (. . .) I did speak about it with some of my best friends, but now it's completely different. (. . .) then I felt the impunity, and I couldn't speak about it.
>
> (Int. 62, September 2012, Buenos Aires)

A similar explanation was given by another child of disappeared parents from in La Plata:

> In the 1990s (. . .) people did not speak [about what had happened during the dictatorship]. If you said something, people gave you an odd look. My high school classmates didn't know that I was a child of disappeared parents. That was a very common thing at that time.
>
> (Int. 74, September 2012, La Plata)

The fear about the possible reaction of others was a significant obstacle to speaking about their stories. Such silence was also reinforced by stigmatisation. An interviewee from Rosario told how, as a child, his teachers at school blamed his parents for their having been disappeared:

> I always (. . .) knew that my parents were made to disappear, [when I was] in third grade my teacher asked me what had happened to my parents and I told her that they had been killed by the military, then the teacher answered "they must have done something," which is what everyone said at that time.
>
> (Int. 23, March 2011, Rosario)

It was difficult for the victims to tell their own story in a social context in which a likely reaction would be one of the victims themselves being blamed. The justice system sends an implicit message through impunity: it is the victims who are the guilty ones. This message is spread and legitimated through various means. One is by making use of explicit terms, which had formerly been used by the perpetrators, such as "antisubversive war," "dirty war" and "excesses." These terms continued to be used in the 1990s in official discourse and by the mass media to refer to the dictatorship and its crimes. Indeed, this language tends to create a perception of the world that serves the interests of those in power. Impunity thus gives criminal facts a different meaning by displacing and denying the responsibility of the perpetrators while it extends the tendency to blame the victims (Kordon 1997, 30).

4.2.3 Indifference and social impunity

In Argentina a process of internalisation and normalisation of impunity took place over the years which translated legal impunity into social impunity. In the 1980s and 1990s, it was quite common to see the repressors walking in the streets, attending public events and being greeted by their neighbours as if nothing had happened. A survivor from Santiago del Estero expressed her indignation when giving an example of how one of her neighbours talked to a well-known perpetrator in town with total normality:

> Ramiro López,[10] who has been convicted, the one who is supposed to have shot Kamenetzky,[11] was with an acquaintance of mine, a neighbour from my town, as if he was an ordinary, honourable person [as if] he wasn't a murderer. He was sitting, talking, I always walked past and said hello to that person from my town, but when I saw him with López, I walked past and didn't say hello, then he said to me "You know that I . . . " "Well, but you know who you are with," I told him. (. . .) That shows the degree of social impunity in which society becomes an accomplice, no one says anything to him, no one frowns at him, everyone says "hello" and invites him to have a seat.
>
> (Int. 53, April 2011, Santiago del Estero)

As the interviewee mentioned, legal impunity becomes "social impunity." While the relationship is not automatic, impunity contributes to the generation of social indifference in everyday relationships. The interviews show how legal denial generates a social denial of the differences between victims and perpetrators. The social naturalisation of impunity is reflected in the social treatment towards victims and perpetrators. In her analysis of the *escraches*, Susanna Kaiser describes the cultural context of impunity in Argentina as "the normalisation of living with major criminals" (Kaiser 2002, 501–503). This was a normalisation that, as Kaiser argues, revealed itself "in society's apparent adaptation, consciously or unconsciously, to the reality that torturers, assassins, and 'disappearers' (of people) have a place within streets, restaurants, coffee shops, television screens, magazines, holiday resorts, official ceremonies, and even significant public office" (Ibid). Impunity thus becomes naturalised, especially as far as the crimes of power are concerned. An interviewee from La Plata, a son of disappeared parents, described the situation as follows:

> The military were living in their houses and I, in mine, basically. It has always annoyed me, (. . .) and I felt that I couldn't rely on society because the majority of society is individualistic, it's not interested in what happens to the other, a repressor may be living next door to you and you don't mind.
>
> (Int. 74, September 2012, La Plata)

The naturalisation of these practices of indifference has an intense impact on victims' lives and their social integration since it exacerbates the lack of solidarity. During the interviews, many victims asserted that they felt they were living in a society of privileges and rewards for perpetrators while they themselves did not obtain any kind of help or acknowledgement from society and the state, a feeling that reinforced their sense of injustice. In fact, several interviewees described the decades of impunity as a period of "darkness," "frustration," "loneliness" and "lack of hope." Several respondents referred to how the absence of justice contributed to creating an image of society where it was "as if nothing had happened." This stressed the social normalisation of state crimes and their perpetrators' freedom, which led to feelings of loneliness and impotence. In this sense, Verwoerd argues that to know the criminal facts but not to acknowledge them inflicts a "second wound of silence" (2000, 158). A survivor from Tucumán, whose brother and sister were made to disappear, explained this feeling of loneliness in the following way:

> [W]e were alone for many years with our anguish and pain. It was devastating to go out into the street and see that life continued as if nothing had happened.
>
> (Int. 68, September 2012, Tucumán)

This was the message that, through the amnesty laws and pardons, was sent to society and conveyed to the victims and the victimisers. In Argentina no one seemed to care that people had been tortured, killed or disappeared. For many sectors of society, the victims seemed to be invisible, when not outright stigmatised. The indifference of society also contrasted with the boldness of perpetrators who went on with their everyday lives and even boasted of their past crimes in public. An interviewed survivor from the city of Buenos Aires explained:

> In the 1990s, these people [the perpetrators] (. . .) began to appear as if nothing had happened and to give interviews to the press. Or else we saw them acting as bodyguards for some politician.
>
> (Int. 7, March 2011, Buenos Aires)

The consequences of impunity are clearly very different for perpetrators. Impunity allowed them to lead a normal life. Most of them kept on working in the security forces and receiving a salary or pension. They had lost no relatives and did not undergo torture. They were not punished for the crimes they had committed. They enjoyed anonymity as long as nobody knew their faces and what they had done (especially because of the clandestine nature of the repression in Argentina and with regard to low-ranking officers). Using the same expression of "as if nothing had happened," another interviewee, a daughter of disappeared parents from Buenos Aires narrated her encounter with an oppressor in the 1990s:

> In the 1990s I was working in a coffee shop. In 1998 Astiz[12] came in to have a coffee at three in the morning. I was shocked, I found it so outrageous, it was so incomprehensible to me that this could happen, how a murderer could be having a coffee, as if nothing had happened. Someone who has killed so many people, (. . .) I got really worked up, very upset, I worked as a cashier and they had to give me some linden tea because I was really nervous. You feel like hitting him but you can't, because you say to yourself, "I'll hit him on the head with a frying pan" and you know how it will all end up. The police will come and put me in jail because I wanted to hit him, and all that. Impunity made me totally impotent.
>
> (Int. 62, September 2012, Buenos Aires)

Impunity alters the sense of how the law is applied: it blurs the distinction between the permitted and the forbidden, the licit and the illicit. The world seemed upside down. In times and political contexts like those, the sense of law is inverted since it is the victimisers who enjoy legal privileges denied not only to the victims but also to the rest of society. Any ordinary person, especially if he or she belongs to marginal neighbourhoods, could not escape justice after committing a crime. As an interviewee from Santiago del Estero explained, when society naturalises the situation where perpetrators and the victims live in the same community, support for the victims is often denied:

Q: Did other social sectors show solidarity towards you?
A: No, because we were made completely invisible, some people believed that the disappeared were people, perhaps from Santiago, that had disappeared somewhere else, for who knows what reasons. It was impossible to speak about human rights here.

(Int. 52, April 2011, Santiago del Estero)

Impunity imposes a model of interaction and naturalises indifference, which becomes an "affective anaesthesia" (Aguiar 1993, 4). This anaesthesia produces a social rift which makes the suffering of others invisible and undermines solidarity towards them. Consequently, social indifference also results in victims distrusting and lacking solidarity from their own community. A son of disappeared parents stressed the loneliness felt by many children of disappeared parents in the 1990s:

> It's complicated, there are guys who have been left isolated and were very bitter because of it. (. . .) They had support from nobody.
>
> (Int. 23, March 2011, Rosario)

Impunity was central to this isolation of the victims which in turn impeded the creation of bonds of support and trust within society. The isolation and the lack of solidarity were more profound in the northern areas of the country, where the presence of human rights organisations was much less significant[13] than in the large urban centres such as the city of Buenos Aires. Several of the interviewees, who are also human rights activists, explained how they had to face rejection and indifference in their efforts to obtain the support of other social sectors in their mobilisations and demands for truth and justice. In Santiago del Estero, well into the new millennium, prejudice against ex-political prisoners and the relatives of the disappeared discouraged support from other social organisations. An ex-political prisoner and human rights activist explained:

> [M]any social organisations were very reluctant to accept us (. . .). Some sectors said: "here come the zurdos"[14] [the lefties], (. . .) "That's your problem."
>
> (Int. 55, April 2011, Santiago del Estero)

Many people were unconcerned about the impunity enjoyed by perpetrators, not considering it their own problem but rather someone else's ("the *zurdos*"), the victims' problem. Many people did not identify with the victims, nor did they assume responsibility for the repressive crimes of the dictatorship. These social sectors wanted nothing to do with the matter. They did not question their own role in the period of state terror or in the 1990s. Consequently, the potential solidarity towards the victims, which had already been undermined by state terror (Lechner 1992; Malamud-Goti 1996; Feierstein 2006), continued to be disrupted under democracy. In fact, many of the interviewees saw the two terms of Carlos Menem in the 1990s as a continuation of the neoliberal model set up by the dictatorship. As explained in Chapter 2, the military government wanted to liberalise markets and reduce state intervention in the economy. The Menem administrations further pursued that economic project. Therefore, many interviewees considered that the elites who had supported repression in the 1970s were those who were rewarded in the 1990s. By reproducing fear, silence and indifference, impunity was useful to deter any potential resistance to that economic model. As pointed out by a plaintiff from Tucumán:

> Unfortunately, the liberalism of the 1990s marked the culmination of what the dictatorship had begun at the cultural level. People said "don't get involved,"[15] (. . .) such was the relentless radical individualism that pervaded social life in the 1990s.
>
> (Int. 70, October 2012, Tucumán)

As explained by the interviewee, this attitude of indifference – "don't get involved" – under democracy not only applied to victims of the dictatorship but extended to other types of state abuses such as police violence, which in the 1990s increased considerably in the 1990s. In those years, torture by the police was becoming more and more common (Malamud-Goti 1996, 148). However, there was a generalised indifference towards the use and abuse of violence by the police. Several scholars agree that impunity contributes to a large portion of the citizenry accepting institutional violence and seeing it as normal (Gingold 1991; Aguiar 1993). According to Malamud-Goti, the continued perpetration of abuses by the police and the widespread support of these abuses by sectors of the middle classes were reminiscent of the dictatorship (1996, 161). The author asserts that there is a tight relationship between popular support for police violence or indifference and the institutional neglect of and contempt for victims of repression. According to Laura Gingold, many members of the community showed themselves indifferent to the numerous cases of police murders of lower class teenagers. Gingold points out that there are opposing perceptions about the role of police violence in the 1990s: for many neighbours of the victims, it was a continuation of the dictatorship in another form, while for others "the victim must have done something" to deserve that violence (1991).

Society becomes accustomed to living with impunity, but not with all kinds of impunity, since the regular criminal system continues to operate within society against ordinary crimes. There is a naturalisation of impunity, but only for crimes of powerful actors. In that sense, impunity is always selective. Some are punished by the criminal law and others not. As a result, two parallel systems of justice with designated crimes, punishments and rights implicitly coexist within the same society. These legal dualities – or unequal application of the law – generate disbelief, helplessness and impotence for victims while also impacting the perceptions and social attitudes of others towards them. All the examples above show how impunity fostered a detrimental "social framework" with serious consequences for victims of human rights violations. Fear, indifference, stigmatisation, apathy and lack of solidarity with the victims are all different expressions of that social framework. These attitudes, which in some regions were stronger than in others, ended up assuming a function of social control undermining the strengthening of social bonds and with it the creation of collective identities and acts of resistance or opposition.

4.3 Public support for perpetrators

This social context of silence and indifference was not only the result of fear but also of the explicit support given by certain social sectors to individuals and political parties whose members had had a highly active role in the repression during the dictatorship. One survivor gave a very lucid explanation of the social messages conveyed by this lack of accountability:

> A crime that goes unpunished is often not seen as a crime, but as an excess on the part of well-intended persons or a legitimate action that got out of control.
>
> (Int. 68, September 2012, Tucumán)

Thus, once the law, through amnesty laws and pardons, exonerated the criminal actions of perpetrators, the latter were supported by many sectors of society. This support for well-known perpetrators was reflected in several provincial and district elections. In the 1990s gubernatorial and congressional candidates with extremely authoritarian records and views obtained high levels of support. Some of these candidates had represented the military dictatorship (in the same constituencies where they were running for elections in the 1990s). Many of them were emblematic of and responsible for the dictatorship's human rights violations. But nonetheless they later regained political positions and power in several cities in Argentina. As briefly mentioned in Chapter 3, two paradigmatic cases were the provinces of Tucumán and Santiago del Estero, in which elected governors were notorious for having participated in cases of enforced disappearances. Antonio Domingo Bussi was elected governor of the province of Tucumán and Carlos Juárez, of Santiago del Estero.

In the first case, General Domingo Bussi, who during the dictatorship had been installed as governor of the province of Tucumán, was an emblematic figure in the 1990s. Bussi's dictatorial governorship between April 1976 and December 1977 had committed crimes that ranged from summary executions to the systematic torture and disappearance of many people. In spite of this, under democracy he was electorally successful in the very province he had governed during the dictatorship. After benefiting from the amnesty laws passed in 1987, Bussi won eight elections, among them the governorship of the province of

Tucumán for the legislative period of 1995–1999. In 2008, Bussi was sentenced to life imprisonment for the murder of politician Vargas Aignasse, considered a crime against humanity. Bussi died in 2011.

In Santiago del Estero, after the dictatorship Carlos Juárez served three terms as governor of the province (1983–1987, 1995–1999 and 1999–2001). During the Juárez administrations, the rule of law was permeated by state repression and persecution, such as torture and illegal and arbitrary detentions (Picco 2012). The climate of tension in the province reached its peak with the well-known *La Dársena* crimes in early 2003. The disappearance and murder of Leyla Bshier Nazar and Patricia Villalba, two young women who had been tortured and killed with the aid of members of the provincial political establishment and some of their relatives, triggered outrage and engendered a full-scale social mobilisation in the province (Carbajal 2003). Silent marches were held demanding truth and justice until the national government intervened in the province in 2004 and a criminal investigation was initiated. After long years of silence and impunity, the protests that started in 2003 after the *Dársena* crimes acted as a catalyst for other mass protests against human rights violations in the province (including disappearances, murders and persecutions by the security forces of the province under the control of Juárez). The impact was so strong that it marked the end of the "*Juarista* era" in Santiago del Estero. In 2004, Carlos Juárez and his wife (who was governor at the time) were arrested and prosecuted for multiple corruption-related crimes and crimes against humanity. Carlos Juárez ended his days under house arrest on charges relating to the disappearance of several persons and finally died in 2010 while awaiting trial (Dandan 2010).

In the province of Buenos Aires, there were also candidates in smaller towns with authoritarian leanings and a past in the dictatorship. A relevant example was former military Aldo Rico, famous for his role in the above-mentioned "Easter rebellion" of 1987 and 1988 (the Monte Caseros mutiny) where sectors of the armed forces staged open revolts to protest against the judicial policies of President Alfonsín. Rico was pardoned by president Carlos Menem in October 1989 and later launched a political party known as MODIN (as per its acronym in Spanish for "*Movimiento por la Dignidad Nacional*," in English "Movement for National Dignity"). He contested several elections in the province until he was elected mayor of the district of San Miguel (1997–2003) and was minister of security for the Buenos Aires province for a short period in 1999 (Malamud-Goti 1996; Yapur 1999). Another paradigmatic case in the province of Buenos Aires is the one of former senior police officer Luis Patti, who was also involved in the repression of the dictatorship as a low-ranking police officer. He is even mentioned as a torturer in the CONADEP report. Despite all the many accusations against him, Patti was elected mayor of the district of Escobar in 1995 with 73 per cent of the votes (Malamud-Goti 1996, 149).[16] In 2011 Patti was finally convicted of murder and sentenced to life imprisonment (La Nación 2011).

Therefore, in all these locations, the continuity of repressive police practices was largely supported by the population, and figures involved in or having close ties with the state repression of the 1970s were also elected as provincial governors and mayors. Society's support in democratic times for those figures from the dictatorship sends a clear signal of lack of support for the victims. As stated by a survivor from Tucumán:

> When Bussi was elected governor, we felt that half of the people in Tucumán didn't care about his crimes.
>
> (Int. 68, September 2012, Tucumán)

4.4 Victims as second-class citizens

Against this background, the relation of victims to the state had clearly deteriorated. The legal deprivation of citizens' rights for the victims (such as the access to justice) broke the principle according to which to be a citizen is to possess the same legal status and rights as other members of the same community. Through amnesty laws, victims belonged to a special category: that of citizens legally excluded from the justice system. As shown above, when legal impunity is established, victims can claim neither the same rights nor the same treatment from the state – and society – as other citizens.

In turn, impunity not only involves the denial of the right to justice but also the failure to adopt other social policies to address the serious health, social, psychological and economic consequences resulting from the violence suffered. In the case of Argentina, even though there were some reparation laws, the state provided no form of medical or psychological support to the survivors and families of disappeared persons. An interviewee from Tucumán, who is a survivor, referred to the precarious situation of the victims in the country. Based on the conclusions of a nationwide census conducted to find out the situation of the survivors and ex-political prisoners, the interviewee stated that:

> [Many are] in a very bad condition, all around the country. (. . .) some of our fellow victims are now homeless, beggars, and the provincial state has never taken responsibility. (. . .) For this reason, we asked for compensation from the national government for the situation we've gone through, in many cases we've lost our identity, our belongings, our freedom, our expectations, because we were detained when we were very young. We lost our chance to study, to realise our potential, many people lost their jobs and were never able to get them back. We've lost many things. The tortures, disappearances and rapes (. . .) left psychological wounds that will never heal, that burden will always be on us. This means that the state has to take responsibility.
>
> (Int. 73, October 2012, Tucumán)

The violence the victims experienced has left them in a precarious position. The experience of having been *disappeared* (i.e. of detention in a CDC), in which torture was constant, inflicted physical and psychological damage on the survivors and the effects lingered on after they were set free. In many cases, this experience of terror interrupted the life plans of the survivors. For instance, a survivor explained to me how her life perspectives changed radically after being kidnapped for months in a CDC:

> [Before the kidnapping] I was a medical student (. . .) [but] I never took up my studies again. (. . .) My life as a student finished after the CDC.
>
> (Int. 63, September 2012, Buenos Aires)

The consequences of the dictatorship affected not only the direct victims but also their relatives and the people connected with them, who all had to learn to live with those injuries. These wounds often required clinical and psychological treatment, but during the period of impunity – and sometimes even today – the state provided no response. In fact, some NGOs, such as the *Equipo Argentino de Trabajo e Investigación Psicosocial* (Argentine Work Group for Psychosocial Research, hereafter EATIP), were the ones who assumed the task of providing psychological support for many victims and relatives of the disappeared (Guglielmucci 2015, 29). A child of disappeared parents explained to me that, while he was granted economic compensation in the late 1990s, like other relatives of the disappeared and people who had been unlawfully detained, this policy failed to effectively grapple with the consequences of state terror and to integrate the victims into society:

> [W]e got compensation many years ago, but the state should have given us a different type of assistance, it should have integrated us. When I was involved in drugs, I had no assistance at all.
>
> (Int. 23, March 2011, Rosario)

The negligence of the state towards the sequels of the dictatorship on the victims had in many cases a devastating impact on them. According to psychologist Elina Aguiar (1993), many of the victims face difficulties getting back to work or reintegrating into society. Aguiar explains that in many cases the victims feel that they do not belong in a state and society that are unable to provide an efficient response to the traumatic experiences they suffered (1993, 4). Impunity only deepens the wounds caused by violence. It reaffirms and reproduces violence by denying it.

While according to the concept of citizenship all members of the state have equal rights as individuals, social, political and economic constraints and limitations show that often this is not the case and that citizenship does not apply to all so-called citizens in the same way. In this sense, scholars such as Charles Black and, later, Kenneth Karst employed the concept of citizenship to refer to the rights necessary to achieve "full and equal membership" (cited in Bosniak 2000, 464). For Judith Shklar and Roger Smith, citizenship refers to an individual's "standing" in society, and each focuses on how the law has been used historically to structure and reproduce that standing in society (Shklar 1991; Smith 1998). Focusing on US society, this group of scholars is concerned with exclusion and second-class citizenship, and the ways in which economic-, ethnic- or gender-based subordination has distorted formally egalitarian polities. For the Latin American context, Guillermo O'Donnell (1993) states that citizens' rights are not equally effective throughout the national territory and across existing social and economic stratifications (O'Donnell 1993, 5). O'Donnell uses the concept of "low intensity citizenship" to refer specifically to the formal and informal legal precariousness of some groups in the population (such as peasants, slum-dwellers, indigenous people, women, et al.), who often do not receive fair treatment from judges, the courts or from other state agents.

The differentiated access to citizens' rights affects not only those individuals who belong to certain ethnic, economic and social groups. It also affects the quality of citizenship of those groups whose rights were violated by the state if it later supports impunity policies. The legal impediment to the prosecution of perpetrators of human rights violations automatically converts their victims into a different kind of citizen: low-intensity citizens who are legally deprived of access to justice with the deleterious consequences discussed above. Legal impunity is the maximal expression of inequality before the law since it is applied differentially to the members of the same state. In the case of those whose rights have been violated, the state has an obligation to re-establish such rights. As will be shown in the following chapters, human rights trials operate in the opposite way to impunity laws in that they recognise individuals as victims *and* as citizens. The annulment of amnesty laws entitles individuals to some of the rights they were denied (not all of them), such as the right of accusation and of access to justice, to have judicial investigations carried out and to be heard in court. This restitution of rights works as a catalyst for other dimensions of what here is considered a framework for reparation.

Notes

1 Military revolts were not over. The Easter rebellion was followed by three other military revolts, the last and most violent of which, in early December 1990, claimed twenty-one lives (Malamud-Goti 1996, 67, 68; Roehrig 2009, 733).

2 Regarding this specific crime, the Menem administration supported the creation of a national genetic data bank, set up by President Alfonsín, to identify the disappeared children. A National Commission for the Right to Identity (CONADI) was set up in 1992, which included the Association of Grandmothers of Plaza de Mayo. The Commission centralised and coordinated the search for appropriated children. Out of 400 cases of disappeared children, more than 100 children have been found. Some have been reunited with their grandparents; others, who were handed over to couples acting in good faith, remain with the couples that raised them. By dint of this patient legal work, many of the couples who received the babies and lied about their identity were arrested and sentenced to prison terms.

3 Mónica Mignone disappeared after being abducted in May 1976 and taken to former navy CDC ESMA.
4 Alejandra Lapaco and her mother were detained in March 1977 and held in the "Athletic Club," an army detention centre in Buenos Aires. Her mother was released two days later. Alejandra was never seen again.
5 In the "Lapaco case," the court accepted the petition by the relatives and ordered the Ministry of Defence to provide all the information the Army possessed on the fate of Alejandra Lapaco and other prisoners who had disappeared while in the custody of the First Army Corps between 1976 and 1983. However, the Army denied having any information. This led Carmen Aguiar de Lapaco to file an appeal with the Supreme Court. The Court took three years to deny Lapaco's appeal (Roht-Arriaza 2004, 102). In response, in November 1998, Lapaco lodged a complaint with the Inter-American Commission on Human Rights. In November 1999, it finally brokered a mutual settlement of the dispute, by which the state agreed to guarantee the right to truth and obtain clarification of what happened to disappeared persons. The agreement, therefore, made it an official obligation on the part of the state to deploy all means to obtain information of the whereabouts of the disappeared (Roht-Arriaza 2004, 102–103). The Truth Trials were the result of that.
6 The Truth Trials took a different form in different locations. While in La Plata there were public hearings, in Córdoba and Mendoza the hearings were held behind closed doors (Roht-Arriaza 2004, 103). Up to now La Plata has been the only city where Truth Trials hearings continue parallel to criminal proceedings.
7 José Rubén Lofiego or Lo Fiego, alias "the blind man," was a frequently interrogated police chief of the province of Santa Fe. In 2012 he was prosecuted and sentenced to life imprisonment for crimes against humanity in the city of Rosario (province of Santa Fe).
8 The term *"Jefatura"* refers to the "Jefatura de Policía de Tucumán," the Tucumán Police Station. The *Jefatura* in San Miguel de Tucumán operated as a CDC during the dictatorship.
9 The human rights organisation HIJOS started in the mid-1990s with the practice of "*escraches*," which were a type of public demonstration in front of the homes and workplaces of perpetrators that indicated and made visible their presence in that neighbourhood, and made their crimes explicit. One of the intentions of the *escrache* was to break with the normalisation of repression that consisted of patterns "revealing a distortion of public values that has to be considered as a legacy of terror in the public sphere" (Kaiser 2002, 500).
10 Ramiro López Veloso is another of the most notorious perpetrators in the city. He was a policeman and also served in the Police Investigation Department in the province of Santiago del Estero during the dictatorship. He was sentenced to life imprisonment for crimes against humanity in three different trials (Judicial Information Centre 2013).
11 Cecilio Kamenetzky was a law student and a militant in the Guevarist Youth.
12 Alfredo Ignacio Astiz was a naval commando, marine and intelligence officer during the military dictatorship. He was known as *El Ángel Rubio de la Muerte* (the Blond Angel of Death) and had a reputation as a notorious torturer.
13 Unlike other more urbanised areas, Santiago del Estero did not see the formation of organisations such as *Madres de Plaza de Mayo* or *Abuelas de Plaza de Mayo*, which have a great capacity for mobilisation. The HIJOS organisation was set up in Santiago del Estero much later than in other provinces.
14 Pejorative term used in Argentina to describe people who have a left-wing political position.

15 In Spanish, "No te metas."

16 Patti launched a new party in 1999, *Unidad Bonaerense*, now called *Partido Unidad Federalista* (PA.U.FE). He was re-elected as mayor in Escobar that year and stood for election as governor of Buenos Aires province, in which he came in second. In addition, he was elected to a seat in the Argentine Chamber of Deputies in 2005. However, he was prevented from taking his seat because of allegations against him in torture and murder cases, which were re-opened that year (Ventura 2008).

Part III

Reparation through domestic human rights trials

Chapter 5

An introduction to human rights trials in Argentina: dynamics, advances and challenges

While in the previous sections I have analysed the seriously damaging consequences of state terror and impunity for the victims of human rights violations, in this chapter I give an account of the specificities of human rights trials and of the political and legal conjuncture in which they emerged. A general overview of the main actors, advances and difficulties that these prosecutions have faced over the last ten years is essential for a proper understanding of the reparative effects the trials have on the victims.

This chapter is divided into four sections. Section 1 offers a historical account of the political and legal steps which led to the amnesty laws being overturned between 2003 and 2005. This includes a brief overview of the Kirchner administration and its human rights policies towards the crimes of the dictatorship. Section 2 provides a detailed description of the criminal court system in Argentina. Understanding the workings of the local judicial criminal system helps to identify the positive features and the difficulties in the conduct of the trials. Section 3 gives an account of the main actors participating in the trials. Section 4 analyses the dynamics and developments of the trials between 2006 and 2015, including the advances but also the challenges and the main obstacles mentioned by many actors participating in them. Finally, I briefly summarise the new developments and risks of the trials under the new administration of Mauricio Macri, whose priorities do not seem to be centred on human rights.

5.1 The path towards justice

In Chapter 4 I described how the intense and continuing struggle of the civil society – principally victims, relatives and human rights organisations – were a crucial factor in the repeal of the amnesty laws. The possibilities for accountability gradually changed between 1995 and 2003. By 1998 Menem's power over the judiciary was loosening, and neither he nor the military had the same power as before.[1] Additionally, international pressure against the Full Stop and Due Obedience Laws by human rights bodies was gradually increasing. Under the human rights treaties ratified by Argentina in the years after the dictatorship, the country was under a duty to investigate and punish grave human rights violations.[2] This was a duty that had been repeatedly stressed by the Inter-American Court of Human Rights for more than a decade.[3] Simultaneously, events such as the arrest of Chilean dictator Augusto Pinochet in London in October 1998 and the requests for the extradition of military officers by judge Baltazar Garzón in Spain began to show that crimes against humanity committed in Argentina could be prosecuted anywhere in the world (Capdepon 2015). Thus, in the late 1990s the legal impossibility of prosecutions in Argentina gave way to the intervention of domestic courts in other countries, such as Spain, Germany, Italy and France, which under the doctrine of universal jurisdiction helped to lay siege to the state of impunity in Argentina (Roehrig 2009, 734–736). Thus, through the activities of different domestic courts in other countries, these convictions had an enormous impact on the public awareness of the possibility of prosecuting gross human rights violations. However, successive Argentine governments, such as the ones of Carlos Menem and Fernando de la Rua (1999–2001),[4] refused to cooperate with foreign legal processes in these prosecutions. At the same time, Argentina's Supreme Court dismissed foreign claims and was uncooperative in its response to requests for the detention and extradition of Argentine citizens wanted for human rights violations. However, by 2001 some federal judges gradually started to enforce some important obligations contained in human rights treaties and to declare that the Final Stop and Due Obedience Laws were null and void in specific cases. Along with the struggle of NGOs, this had a profound influence on the subsequent decisions of the Congress and the Supreme Court.

The first court ruling to declare the laws null and void was issued in the so-called Poblete/Hlaczik case, concerning the theft of a child, abducted together with her parents. In 1978, a police task force kidnapped José Poblete Roa, a Chilean citizen, and his wife, Gertrudis Hlaczik, along with their eight-month-old daughter, Claudia Victoria.[5] During their captivity, the baby was taken away from her parents, who were later disappeared. After a long investigation assisted by the Grandmothers of Plaza de Mayo, the child Claudia Poblete was found in the late 1990s living with a retired police lieutenant colonel and his wife, who had hidden her real identity for twenty-two years (Roht Arriaza 2004, 112–113). Judge Gabriel Cavallo indicted police officers Juan Antonio del Cerro (alias "Colours") and Julio Simón (alias "Julian the Turk") for stealing and giving the baby to the couple, and charged them with concealing her and hiding her true identity. The case would have progressed like any other child theft case prosecuted in the 1990s, were it not for a legal action brought by human rights organisation CELS in October 2000, asking for the amnesty laws to be invalidated and for the two defendants to be charged with the torture and disappearance of the child's parents. Consequently, in March 2001, federal Judge Cavallo set aside as unconstitutional the two amnesty laws protecting junior and mid-level officers from prosecution and charged Simón with the couple's illegal arrest and torture.[6] This decision dealt a severe blow to the wall of impunity in Argentina and was followed by others.[7] Judge Cavallo's landmark ruling was thus the first to declare the amnesty laws unconstitutional as they were incompatible with Argentina's international obligations under human rights treaties (Roht-Arriaza 2004, 114–115). The wider social significance of the ruling can be discerned in how it opened the way for other courts to pursue charges against military personnel accused of similar crimes. In August 2003, the National Congress, both the lower house of Deputies and the Senate, enacted Law No. 25,779 and declared the amnesty laws null and void. Finally, the Supreme Court affirmed Judge Cavallo's decision in the "Poblete/Hlaczik case"[8] and declared the amnesty laws null and void/invalid.[9] Significantly, the Supreme Court also labelled all crimes committed by the last military dictatorship as crimes against humanity, turning them also into criminal acts exempt from the statutes of limitations (CELS 2005).[10] Since then, former military officers are being systematically prosecuted in federal courts all across Argentina. The declaration of unconstitutionality of the amnesty laws was supported by the left-leaning Peronist President Néstor Kirchner (2003–2007), elected in 2003, who spoke out strongly against the dictatorship. Soon after he came to office, President Kirchner called for the amnesty laws to be made unconstitutional. Thus, the current trials are perceived by many interviewees as the result of a struggle over many years on behalf of human right movements which finally found some resonance in the Kirchner administration.

In fact, several changes started to become evident in different ways under the Kirchner administration. Even though the Supreme Court had still not decided on the constitutionality of the amnesty laws, its composition changed substantially after the election in 2003. Several judges retired or were ousted on corruption charges and some of the new judges have a more pro-human rights background (Roht-Arriaza 2004, 116). Another relevant measure, which Kirchner took after only five days in office, was to purge many top-ranking officers from the military. This measure cemented civilian control of the military. Roberto Bendini, a relatively junior officer, was appointed to the post of Army Chief-of-Staff. By Army custom, when a general is appointed to this top post, all officers above that rank who are bypassed for promotion are expected to retire. Thus, Kirchner's move required the retirement of almost half of the top generals (Roehrig 2009, 737). The Kirchner administration also deployed a multiplicity of symbolic measures including the creation of a memorial wall of victims' names and the transformation of several ex-CDCs, such as the former ESMA, into museums and memorials for the disappeared victims (Schindel 2012). An important symbolic act showing disapproval of the crimes of the dictatorship occurred in 2004, when Kirchner ordered the removal of portraits of General Jorge Videla and General Reynaldo Bignone, both former members of the Junta, from the gallery of presidential pictures in the military college base in the outskirts of Buenos Aires (Telam 2013). The ceremony itself lasted seconds, but its symbolism was a very strong message for the victims. Indeed, several interviewees mentioned this event as something they would never forget. The act gave the victims confidence in the new government's intention to take human rights seriously and the struggle to end impunity (Seidel 2014, 130). Against this background, the human rights trials became a central piece. In order to understand their dynamics and effects, I provide below an overview of their procedural characteristics.

5.2 Prosecuting human rights violations in the domestic legal system

It is significant that the trials in Argentina are not being conducted by temporary international or hybrid tribunals or special laws, but by regular and domestic criminal laws and institutions. These prosecutions – which are oral and public – are, at first sight, conducted like any other criminal trial. According to Argentina's Criminal Code, oral and public proceedings are instituted only in cases of trials for criminal offences. In the Argentine justice system, these trials are divided into two stages: an investigative stage and one of an oral and public trial before a three-judge court. Each stage has its own judges and prosecutors, which means that the investigative judges and prosecutors are usually different from those of the oral trial stage. In the first stage – known as *etapa de instrucción* (investigative phase) – documentary evidence is collected, witnesses are examined, and expert reports are prepared. At that point, if witnesses are summoned by the plaintiff's attorney, the attorney may be present during their testimony and, depending on the features of the case (i.e. whether there is a defendant or not), defence attorneys may or may not be summoned. Neither the defendant nor the public attend hearings during this phase, as these hearings are private (Varsky 2011, 32). As lawyer Carolina Varsky explains, during this investigative phase, if witnesses are also survivors, as most of the witnesses in the current human rights trials in Argentina are, they are examined about what they remember and are asked to testify about the time during which they were held in captivity. If they witnessed a kidnapping, they are asked about that specific event. Everyone is asked if they have been witnesses at previous points of the trial, whether in judicial or administrative proceedings, in order to spare them from having to repeat their testimony. If they have previously testified, they are asked to ratify their testimony and the public official then proceeds to ask questions about the facts that have already been stated and to invite them to add any additional information (Ibid.). Based on the information collected, the prosecutor and judge make formal charges against the accused. These charges will then be evaluated by the court in the second phase of the judicial process, the oral and public trial. This second phase works as a "debate" between the prosecutor and the defence attorney with whom an agreement is reached regarding the evidence and testimony to be presented at the oral trial. Oral and public hearings are then held in which the witnesses from both sides, the plaintiffs and the accused, are interrogated. Then, the defence and the prosecution make their closing arguments and, following an evaluation of the different elements, the court proceeds to read its judgment, which may provide for the acquittal or conviction of the accused. The different actors of the criminal process have the possibility of filing an appeal against the judgment with the Criminal Court of Appeals, which may affirm or reverse the judgment.

As Varsky (2011) explains, in accordance with Argentina's procedural law, the testimony that is admitted as evidence is that provided during this debate phase (as opposed to that provided in the investigative hearings). As to those witnesses who are deceased or somehow unable to testify during this phase, the testimony from their investigative hearings is admitted into evidence and read aloud after the submission of certificates of applicability. Nevertheless, if they are alive or able to testify but still fail to appear before the court, their testimony cannot be submitted as evidence in the trial. Varsky, who acted as an attorney for the plaintiffs in the trials for several years, stresses that this has caused serious problems in current trials because most survivors and families of the disappeared are tired of these proceedings (2011, 32–33). Many of them have been subpoenaed repeatedly to testify in cases that do not concern them directly and, over the years, many people have testified numerous times both in court and out of court. In addition, in the case of elderly people who wish to submit their testimony before the trial commences, courts have often allowed them to provide an early testimony and have resorted to video conferences for witnesses who live abroad or far from the jurisdiction in which the trial is being held.

Moreover, as a consequence of the fragmentation of the criminal proceedings, the judges of the oral court who will try the accused and the prosecutors acting in this phase do not know what the case is about until they read the statements of the case prepared by the defence and the prosecutor who acted at the investigative stage. Thus, the investigative stage is of the utmost importance in the judicial process, given that the exclusion of some aspect – such as omitting charges for a number of crimes or charges against the accused – is very difficult to modify (although not impossible) at the oral trial stage and can cause obstructions and delays. Thus, this stage usually takes more time than the oral trial. In view of this situation, different strategies are adopted by the prosecution or by the victims' attorneys. Prosecutions can be initiated either by the government itself or by individuals or groups. Survivors and groups representing victims can act as "*querellas*" ("private plaintiffs") and may initiate criminal proceedings either directly or indirectly. From a managerial perspective, prosecutions and judgments are carried out by federal prosecutors and courts, whose decisions are revised by two nationwide appeals courts: the national court of cassation, and the Supreme Court of Justice, the head of the judiciary and the ultimate interpreter of federal law (Filippini 2009).

5.3 The constellation of actors in the trials

There is a wide range of activities and actors involved in the conduct of the trials. For an accurate analysis of the dynamics, functions and effects of domestic prosecutions in Argentina, it is crucial to take a look at the role played by the different actors in these processes.

The country's government between 2003 and 2015, with its many institutions, had an important role in the implementation of these trials. As the trials advanced, new and unforeseen factors such as the growing number of cases, security risks to witnesses and the emotional burden for the victims who have to give testimony evidenced the need to create new supporting institutions. Thus, the Kirchner administration deployed diverse special agencies and programmes, unusual in ordinary criminal trials, in order to support these prosecutions. As will be explained below, all these programmes showed that there were serious difficulties in the effective implementation of the trials.

In 2007 the government created the *Programa de Verdad y Justicia* (Truth and Justice Programme) within the sphere of the Ministry of Justice as well as an *Unidad Fiscal de Coordinación y Seguimiento de las Causas por Violaciones a los Derechos Humanos cometidas durante el Terrorismo de Estado* (Prosecution Unit for the Coordination and Monitoring of Cases Involving Human Rights Violations Committed During the Period of State Terrorism, hereinafter, Prosecution Unit), established within the ambit of the Public Prosecution Ministry. This special unit was created in order to assist, coordinate and monitor these legal processes and is responsible for carrying out investigations, analysing strategic problems and issuing general guidelines for all public federal prosecutors for advancing these cases in the trials throughout the country (Procuración General de la Nación 2013). The Public Ministry, which operates as the state attorneys' office, defined a national strategy for dealing with the legal aspects of the crimes of state repression (Filippini 2009). This Prosecution Unit was replaced in July 2013 by the *Procuraduría de Crímenes contra la Humanidad* (hereafter Office of Crimes against Humanity) with a similar mandate within the Public Prosecution Ministry, but with more personnel and a wider spectrum of concerns, including following up cases of sexualised violence and prosecutions that include civilians such as business people (Procuración General de la Nación 2013).

Another important actor is the *Secretaría de Derechos Humanos de la Nación* (National Human Rights Secretariat). Its main objective is to collaborate with the Ministry of Justice, Security and Human Rights in the promotion of policies and programmes for the protection of human rights. The Secretariat took an active role in the judicial processes after a reform of the Criminal Procedural Code in 2009 that enabled not only those directly affected but also associations and institutions representing larger sectors of society to appear in court as plaintiffs. Under this reform, the National Human Rights Secretariat filed charges itself as plaintiff, in many trials in the country, but not in all of them. The criterion for becoming a plaintiff in some trials and not in others, however, is unclear. According to the Secretariat, its participation in the trials aimed to strengthen the judicial process and give the trials more visibility. In turn, it is a political and symbolic strategy to provide society with a sign that the national state takes a stance in these trials. As a prosecutor asserted: "The state of today confronts the state of the dictatorship" (e.g. Int. 50, April 2011, Tucumán). However, the adoption of the role of plaintiff by the state has also generated some controversy among different actors participating in the trials. While some believe that the Secretariat's participation is only a symbolic and rhetorical strategy that is contradicted by the lack of resources allocated to the conduct of the trials – a problem that will be addressed below and that has been stressed by many interviewees – others support this "state engagement." It is also argued that the presence of the Secretariat would not be legally proper since the prosecutor has already accused the defendants on behalf of the state. Some victims have also voiced their discontent, saying that the state was not the victim of the dictatorship and therefore cannot occupy the victims' place and act as plaintiff. In this sense, the stance, whether positive or negative, towards the role of the Human Rights Secretariat is highly influenced by the conception that different actors have of the state and of the current government. Those persons or organisations with a more favourable stance towards the government supported the role of the Human Rights Secretariat as a plaintiff, whereas those who were more critical only saw it as a demagogic position.

Furthermore, the Human Rights Secretariat created the *Plan Nacional de Acompañamiento y Asistencia Integral a los Querellantes y Testigos Víctimas del Terrorismo de Estado* (National Plan for the Accompaniment and Integral Assistance to Plaintiffs and Victim–Witnesses of State Terrorism), which aims to unify, strengthen and make more effective efforts to support the victims when attending the trials. The psychological support offered to the victims consists of plaintiffs and witnesses being accompanied by psychologists over the course of the trials and in particular when they are called to testify. This Plan has also been coordinated with the Office of the Prosecution Unit, the judiciary, and human rights bodies so that victim–witnesses are assisted, accompanied and protected. In addition, in 2009 the Ministry of Justice, Security and Human Rights set up the *Centro de Asistencia a Víctimas del Terrorismo de Estado "Dr. Fernando Ulloa"* (Centre for the Assistance of Victims of State Terrorism "Dr. Fernando Ulloa"), whose function is the integral attention of individuals who have suffered human rights violations and of their relatives. The Ulloa Centre has a broad mandate since it assists not only victims of the time of the dictatorship but also of other human rights violations during the subsequent constitutional regimes.

The importance of these programmes lies in the specific characteristics of the witnesses giving testimony in the trials. Within the framework of the trials, the victims participate mainly as witnesses and thereby acquire a new status: "victim-witness." Witnesses who testify in such trials are compelled to speak from the standpoint of a victim. This implies both the experience of incarceration in the detention centres and ultimately of survival, as well as that of being a relative of one of the disappeared victims. Indeed, the Plan of Psychological Accompaniment distinguishes between a "survivor-witness" and a "relative-witness" (Tumini, Plaza and others 2008, 43). Because these individuals were themselves victims, they are fundamental actors in the current trials. In regular criminal trials, witnesses are not necessarily also victims. This is a peculiarity of these judicial proceedings that implies that the treatment of witnesses requires more care and support than in ordinary cases. This was also stressed in the interviews with psychologists supporting witnesses and plaintiffs. Finally, the national government also implemented the *Programa Nacional de Protección de Testigos* (National

Programme for the Protection of Witnesses) for those witnesses and victims who participate in the trials. The protection of witnesses and victims is crucial in any efficient investigation and prosecution of perpetrators of human rights violations, especially when many perpetrators are still free, as in Argentina. The programme consists of the accompaniment of plaintiffs and witnesses by police members as well as other security measures, such as providing witnesses with a so-called anti-panic button, which sends an alert to the authorities in cases of impending threat. However, due to the distrust many victims have of the security forces, many witnesses have refused to avail themselves of these measures. Furthermore, several interviewees have complained about the low effectiveness of the security measures considering the constant intimidation of witnesses.

The participation of victims is one of the main characteristics of these trials. In Argentina, the active role of survivors and relatives of disappeared people in the struggle against impunity and now in the human rights trials challenges the predominant view in the literature of victims as passive individuals without agency. They belong to what Cath Collins calls "accountability actors" (2010), that is to say, entities or groups, domestic, external or international, which promote measures for judicial accountability in either criminal or civil form. It means that along with the state bodies there is a wide range of non-state actors who have accessed or attempted to access judicial settings and contributed to the conduct of these trials. Such actors include survivors, relatives of disappeared people, human rights organisations (new and old, national and international) and independent human rights lawyers, among others. Many human rights organisations are in fact comprised of survivors and relatives of disappeared people. The main human rights organisations participating in the trials are: HIJOS, *Justicia Ya!* (Justice Now!), CELS, APDH, ANDHES, *Abuelas de Plaza de Mayo* and so on. Their activism and work have been essential for the implementation of the trials, and in some cases these organisations even seem to replace the role of the state. It is possible to distinguish different types of engagement and participation:

Suing: The world of the plaintiffs is varied. As discussed above, following the reform of the Criminal Procedural Code in 2009, it is not only those directly affected that can appear as plaintiffs in the trials but also associations and institutions representing wider sectors of society. Thus, along with the direct victims, human rights organisations can also bring charges. Notably, in many cases those victims that are qualified lawyers act as legal counsel for other victims. This is the case, for example, in the trials concerning the children of the disappeared taking place in Tucumán, Córdoba, Rosario and Buenos Aires. Many – but not all – of them are members of the organisation HIJOS, mostly formed by children of disappeared people. While there are exceptions, they do not usually act as legal counsel in the cases of their own parents.

Testifying is a key form of participation. Through their testimonies, survivors are the centrepiece of these trials since they are the essential witnesses of the crimes committed by the military. However, the survivors are not the only ones providing testimony. According to psychologist Fabiana Rousseaux (2014), it is possible to identify different types of witnesses: a) historical witnesses: those survivors who testified immediately after their release of the CDCs in the 1980s. They have provided information about what they experienced in their captivity and have given testimony in innumerable opportunities; b) relatives of disappeared persons: those who suffered such terrible loss also became victim-witnesses and they have given testimony of their experience at the time of the disappearance and of the consequences in their lives; c) militant fellows, work colleagues, neighbours or friends of the disappeared; d) witnesses who, having forcibly integrated some of the CDC circuits as conscripts, nurses or employees of morgues and cemeteries, describe what they saw and heard at that time; e) survivor-witnesses or direct relatives who have never testified before and do so for the first time, after more than three decades.

Accompanying victim-witnesses is another fundamental activity carried out by human rights organisations. This is the case of EATIP, an organisation that supports victim-witnesses and plaintiffs. Even though the state set up the above-mentioned National Plan for the Accompaniment and Integral Assistance of Victims and Witnesses, it earned criticism as the initiative is considered to be insufficient. As explained below, the lack of resources and staff is one of the reasons for that. However, according to many interviewees, there is also a lack of adequate training and psychological strategies. Here also several human rights organisations have made their own arrangements to provide psychological support to plaintiffs and victim-witnesses participating in the trials, especially when they have to appear in court and give testimony. It is important for these organisations as well as for those testifying not to be alone.

Investigating and providing evidence is another of the activities conducted by the victims, especially those in collective and human rights organisations. Many of them, such as *HIJOS* and *Justicia Ya*, have internal commissions that carry out investigations and search for legal evidence to be delivered to the judges and public prosecutors. In fact, some organisations have stated that they are often called on and consulted by the prosecution and judges in order to obtain more information. As with the other activities, a huge part of all this work is usually done for free by people who also have to attend to their own regular jobs and activities.

The *publicity and information* about the trials, the testimony provided and the judgments handed down by the courts is crucial for their social impact. Along with the media, NGOs are one of the main promotors of these trials. The trials are publicised through a variety of channels: radio programmes, events organised in the streets, at universities and demonstrations, through leaflets and brochures and internet blogs.

Other key actors in these processes are the perpetrators and their defence attorneys. In most cases, the defendants do not cooperate with the processes or provide any information. Indeed, many of the defendants' attorneys have used legal manoeuvres to delay and obstruct the trials.[11] They justify their actions by arguing that they were fighting a "war against subversion." The defendants are often excused from attending the trials on account of ill health. Some interviewees have distinguished between the more "technical" or "political" defences deployed by the defendants' attorneys. Political defences are used by those defence attorneys who are particularly engaged with the cause of the accused and are convinced that the actions of their clients were appropriate. The more technical defences are used by attorneys provided by the state (i.e. public defenders): while in many cases these may have some empathy with the military regime and thus with their clients' ideology, it is not necessarily a condition for taking on their defence. Hence, when closing arguments in the public hearings, these attorneys do not usually necessarily base their defence on political explanations but use more technical legal arguments. However, the line between political and technical defences is a very thin one and is often crossed, as explained by many attorneys interviewed.

5.4 The dynamics of the trials

Following the Supreme Court's decision annulling the amnesty laws in 2005, many new cases have been brought to trial and prosecutions for crimes against humanity have been pursued systematically in many provinces of the country. Hundreds of survivors and other witnesses give their testimony and turn their memories and suffering into legally valid evidence. Unlike the 1980s Juntas Trial, current prosecutions include not only key leaders, but also mid and low-ranking perpetrators, and although the focus of the prosecutions is still on military and police personnel, they are progressively including civilians who contributed in diverse ways to the crimes, including a priest, judges, and business people, among others. Moreover, current prosecutions also include atrocities committed by state-sponsored security agencies prior to the coup d'état of 1976. This reinforces the idea of state responsibilities beyond the limits of the military rule, and illuminates another face of state terrorism, which was arguably overlooked by justice in the 1980s.

According to information issued by the Office of Crimes against Humanity of the Public Prosecution Ministry in its December 2016 report on the current state of the trials, between January 2006 and December 2016, 174 judgments were handed down by different federal courts in almost every province of the country (Página 12 2016b). On the one hand, as Figure 5.1 shows, there was a remarkable acceleration of the criminal processes from 2010 onwards. While between 2006 and 2009 only twenty-three decisions were issued, the number rose to 151 between 2010 and 2016. This increase can be attributed to the gradual overcoming of both legal and political obstacles as well as the increasing experience in this kind of litigation.

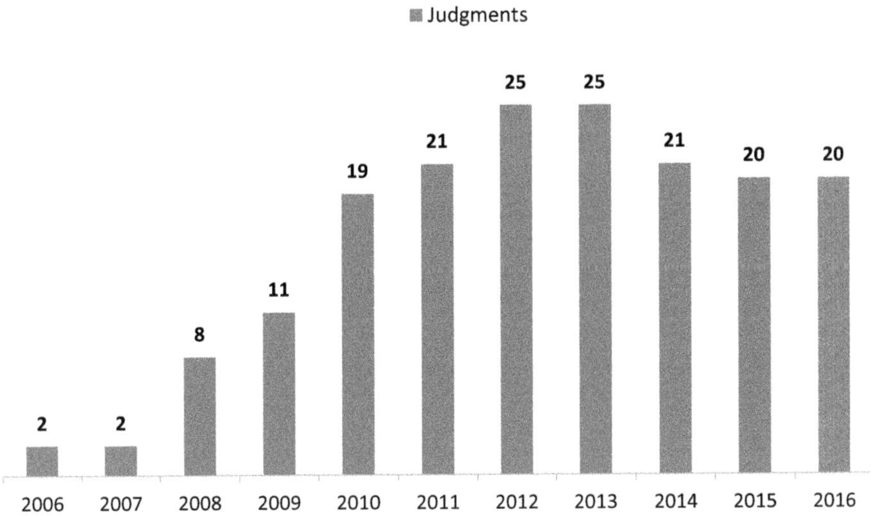

Figure 5.1 Number of judgments per year between January 2006 and December 2016

Source: Table prepared by Office of Crimes against Humanity (Procuraduría de Crímenes contra la Humanidad 2016, 16).

On the other hand, there was a slow reduction in the number of judgments issued in the last three years. One of the reasons for this is the change in the way in which the trials are being organised. Beginning in 2006, and particularly the first three years, only a few trials (two per year) were held in which, in most cases, a single individual was prosecuted.[12] This was in stark contrast with the human rights organisations' goal to hold larger trials with multiple perpetrators, victims and facts. Thus, in order to reverse this trend, the government sought to achieve the highest number of trials in the shortest period of time possible. To such end, in 2010 the Prosecution Unit introduced some logistical and legal strategies in order to turn these fragmented processes into fewer and larger trials that incorporated many victims, perpetrators and offences. Thus, many trials began to be held that dealt with a number of cases involving more accused individuals and more victims who give testimony. This gave rise to the so-called Megacausas (mega-cases),[13] that is, prosecutions which maximise the number of defendants and victims in order to minimise the number of trials. The larger number of offences, defendants and victims involved in the mega-cases meant that both phases of the trials lasted much longer than the earlier versions. It was this process of rationalisation of the judicial process that reduced the number of judgments issued in recent years. For instance, in 2016 the courts hearing two of the mega-cases that had been underway for several years – the trial for the crimes committed in the CDC La Perla in Córdoba[14] and the one for the so-called Plan Cóndor[15] – handed down their judgments.

The accumulation of cases in the mega-cases also led to a significant increase in the number of defendants involved in every trial. The report by the Public Prosecution Ministry shows that 813 former military personnel, police members and civilians were convicted between 2006 and December 2016, while eighty-seven obtained acquittals (Ibid.).

Another aspect to consider is that the crimes under investigation in the trials were committed forty years ago. As time goes by, the number of defendants that die increases considerably, particularly because most of them are elderly.[16] Similarly, due to ill health, many others had to be removed from the trials. According to the Public Prosecution Ministry, as of 2015, while sixty defendants died after being convicted, another 239 passed away during the trial, either in the investigative stage or during the oral hearings (Procuraduría de Crímenes contra la Humanidad 2015b, 16). Moreover, by June 2015, fifty-four individuals were on the run from justice, including two after being convicted (Procuraduría de Crímenes contra la Humanidad 2015a, 12). Figure 5.2 shows the changes in trends in the number of individuals convicted and acquitted per year between 2006 and 2016.

The yearly increase in convictions and cases is remarkable. Up to 2009, the convictions secured did not outnumber seventy-five, whereas in 2010 alone nineteen trials were concluded and ninety-nine individuals were convicted, more than in the previous four years. In 2016, 142 more were convicted, while by the end of that year the total number of acquittals significantly rose to twenty-five – the highest number since the trials started in 2006.

Furthermore, from a comparative historical perspective, the current trials intensify the erosion of impunity in a very significant manner. Figure 5.3, prepared by

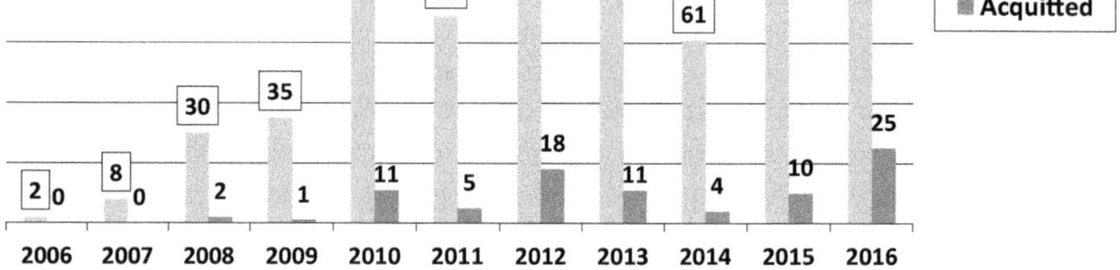

Figure 5.2 Convictions and acquittals per year between January 2006 and December 2016

Source: Table prepared with information provided by reports of the Office of Crimes against Humanity (Procuraduría de Crímenes contra la Humanidad 2016, 16; 2015b, 10) and newspaper Página 12 (2016b).

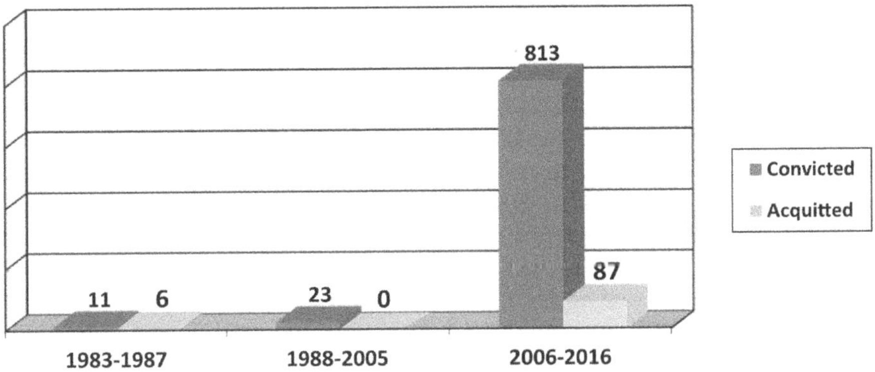

Figure 5.3 Individuals convicted between 1983 and 2016

Source: Table prepared with information provided by reports of the Office of Crimes against Humanity (Procuraduría de Crímenes contra la Humanidad 2016, 16, 2015b, 1) and newspaper Página 12 (2016b).

the Public Prosecution Ministry, shows the number of individuals tried (convicted or acquitted) in three periods. During the first period in the 1980s, only two trials took place, the Juntas Trial and the trial for crimes committed in La Plata, in which the former head of the Buenos Aires provincial police, Ramón Camps, and members of his task force were prosecuted. Of the seventeen defendants prosecuted in both cases, eleven were convicted and six acquitted. In 1987 the enactment of the Due Obedience Law precluded the progression of more than 300 cases that were registered across the country. In the second period, spanning from the 1990s to the early 2000s, only cases of child appropriation were brought to justice. There was a total of twenty-three convictions (Procuraduría de Crímenes contra la Humanidad 2015a, 2). Cases of theft and sexual crimes, which were excluded in the amnesty laws, were barely reported (CELS 2012, 34). The numbers in both periods are very low compared to the number of convictions secured following the Supreme Court's decision to repeal the Final Stop and Due Obedience Laws in 2005.

As Figure 5.3 shows, the repeal of the amnesty laws brought about a quantitative and qualitative change with respect to the period before 2006. In quantitative terms, many more alleged perpetrators were investigated and brought to justice. In qualitative terms, the nature of the crimes prosecuted changed after 2006 to include, among others, homicide, sexual abuses, torture and unlawful deprivation of liberty. Before 2006, these crimes were non-prosecutable.

5.4.1 Political and bureaucratic challenges

Despite the advances made in the new trials, some important problems emerged. One significant obstacle to the proper functioning of the prosecutions is the "slowness" of the judicial system, a concern that has been repeatedly voiced by many interviewees. Although the lack of experience in this kind of case in Argentina was one factor adversely affecting the rapid development of the trials, especially in the first three years (2006–2009), legal and political constraints have also played an important role. As sociologist Ines Izaguirre states (2009), this slowness can be attributed to various bureaucratic and political factors. Political factors include the lack of specific measures, including insufficient funding, to support the trials in those first years. However, there is also the controversial role of many juridical agents such as judges who in many cases remain sympathetic to the military regime and have acted accordingly, delaying the advance of cases (Roehrig 2009). The bureaucratic factor involves the juridical system's own dynamics in prosecuting individual cases. As explained above, individual cases were prosecuted in each trial in the initial years, as opposed to the subsequent consolidated trials involving numerous perpetrators and victims.

What is more, as pointed out by many interviewees, the trials are further slowed by the lack of sufficient resources. The number of crimes committed during the dictatorship is such that more human and material resources are required from the government. At present, the courts are understaffed, and there are not enough judges and prosecutors to cover all cases. Added to this is the basic lack of federal courtrooms in which to conduct trial proceedings. This was a very significant factor that delayed the beginning of oral trials (Dandan 2011). Even when a few creative attempts have been made to rectify this situation – for instance, one criminal trial was conducted in a football stadium[17] and another in a theatre[18] due to a lack of courtrooms – the problem still persists. The successive governments since 2003 have been slow to provide the funding, investigating magistrates and judges for a multitude of new cases. In a court system that is already notorious for its slow pace, the lack of necessary resources only prolongs the process. In addition, the courts are not well organised. If the courts were staffed with personnel who worked exclusively on the complex cases of human rights violations, the workload would be reduced, judgments would be made in a reasonable time frame and, importantly, the demands of effective legal protection of victims and culprits according to due process standards would be satisfied. In this sense, the state contradicts itself when it institutes a judicial policy but does not provide the necessary infrastructure to properly carry out these trials. These contradictions in state policy can also be found in the above-mentioned programmes and institutions set up to support the trials. As stated above, many prosecutors must work on these new trials in addition to their normal caseload, which in many cases reduces the possibility to conduct effective investigations. According to some NGOs and victims, the lack of investigative results leads many judges to reject cases. Thus, perpetrators are not identified, and hence remain free without having to stand trial (FIDH 2009, 33). This is particularly troubling in light of the large amount of information that remains unavailable about the whereabouts of forcibly disappeared victims.

The National Programme for the Protection of Witnesses and Victims suffers from similar flaws. According to a UN report, the programme contains important deficiencies, such as inadequate laws, an insufficient budget, poorly trained security personnel and a lack of coordination between national agencies in providing protection for witnesses (Borello 2010). In this sense, the problem of witness protection is another aspect which reveals the political struggles and contradictions within the state, especially since the disappearance of Jorge Julio López, one of the primary witnesses and joint plaintiffs in the trial of a former police commander in the province of Buenos Aires in 2006. After López identified the defendant as one of the men who had tortured him in 1976, he was made to "disappear" days before the ruling was issued in the case. Human rights organisations have voiced their concern that, eleven years after Julio López's disappearance, the investigation has not progressed significantly. What happened to him is not an isolated incident. Indeed, there have been several cases of witnesses being kidnapped and released within days. This, as shown in Chapter 7, had a powerful impact on other victims participating in the trials. NGOs contend that those responsible for such threats have connections with state security forces, the secret service and security firms (CELS 2010, 21). The fact that all these cases of murder, abductions and threats to witnesses have taken place with the participation or knowledge of active-duty security forces, as some human rights groups allege, would indicate that the national state does not have complete control over the state security apparatus, which still employs members of the former repressive regime. Thus, even though these attacks on victims or witnesses seem to come from within the state, it is extremely difficult to prevent them and to carry out serious investigations to clarify them.

Similar obstacles arise from the staff structure of the judicial system. Although several judges were appointed after a legal reform in 2003, enabling positive human rights policies, many others as well as prosecutors and other members of the judicial system who were not only in office during the dictatorship but also actively contributed to human rights violations still hold positions within the judiciary.[19] The complicity of most of the judiciary was an enabling condition for illegal repression under the rule of the military Junta. As many of the interviewees have asserted, this judicial complicity has concrete effects on the development of the trials today. This is clearly reflected in the use of legal manoeuvres to delay and obstruct the trials, and in the lack of investigations that need to be undertaken to advance the cases. To have current criminal trials run by some judges and prosecutors who were also members of the judiciary in times of the dictatorship is an obvious impediment to the progress of the trials, for it fails to inspire confidence among the plaintiffs and the witnesses.

5.4.2 The criminal responsibility of civil actors

One of the main current challenges facing the trials is the prosecution of civilians responsible for the commission of crimes against humanity. Of the 2821 individuals charged with this type of crime since the process was re-opened, 343 are not military personnel or police officers (CELS 2016, 32). The possibility of establishing in court the truth about the links between the military government and sectors of the economic, ecclesiastical and judicial sectors depends on how much progress is made in these cases (CELS 2016, 29). The involvement of public servants shows that the military was the visible face of the dictatorship, but it was not the only one. The civilians played an important role in state repression, supporting what is today considered to be a civil-military regime.

As part of a very slow and gradual process, several judges and prosecutors have been removed from their positions in different provinces of the country for their alleged involvement in human rights violations (CELS 2011, 51). As a matter of fact, as of 2015, a total of fifty-four officials of the judiciary had been charged for their involvement in crimes against humanity (Procuraduría de Crímenes contra la Humanidad 2015b, 14). Almost fifty per cent of them were judges at the time in which the events occurred, while the rest held different positions within the courts or acted as prosecutors. The criminal investigations in these cases are still slow: between 2009 and 2016 there were only five convictions for this kind of case.[20]

With respect to the prosecution of members of the Catholic Church for their involvement in the commission of crimes against humanity, there was only one conviction.[21] No significant progress has been made despite the abundant information provided in academic and media research and the testimony given by witnesses of the links between the church and the dictatorship (CELS 2016, 33). The involvement of the business sectors with the dictatorship is another of the major challenges in the trials. In December 2015, the Ministry of Justice and civil society organisations issued a joint report entitled: "*Corporate Responsibility in Crimes Against Humanity: Repression of Workers during State Terrorism*" (Ministerio de Justicia y Derechos Humanos 2015). The report provides evidence of the responsibility of part of the local and foreign corporate sector for human rights violations committed against workers during the dictatorship. The report contains an initial list of over 100 companies whose workers were victims of repression under state terror, in different business sectors and regions of the country.[22] The investigation leading to the report identified in only twenty-five of these companies almost 900 victims, 354 of whom are still disappeared, sixty-five were killed and more than 450 were abducted and subsequently released. Most of the victims were workers of such companies that had taken part in the conflict and worker organisation processes before the coup d'état in 1976 (Ministry of Justice and Human Rights 2015, 407).

Such businesses provided their assistance to the dictatorship through employees with a hierarchical position, including members of the boards of directors, shareholders or owners of the companies. The report shows that such actions must be analysed within the framework of the general militarisation process of working establishments, which led to the set-up of clandestine detention and torture centres in such establishments.[23] The set-up of these clandestine centres was the most extreme form of militarisation. Other more common forms, especially since the coup d'état, included operations with a large-scale deployment of military and police personnel in factories. In addition, different corporate practices took place that included explicit calls for military intervention and the provision of materials for such purpose. Corporate contributions to repressive logistics included the supply of different resources, such as economic assistance for the maintenance of soldiers, financial assistance to cover expenses, the provision of vehicles for the transportation of troops and abducted individuals, and the supply of information for repressive purposes (Ministry of Justice and Human Rights 2015, 415). In the past few years, the courts have opened up investigations concerning the responsibility of the owners and/or top officers of companies in the repression of workers. However, the cases have progressed at a very slow pace. While different investigations have been ongoing for several years now, as at December 2016, only one businessman had been convicted of crimes against humanity.[24]

5.4.3 The trials "in the provinces"

As Figure 5.4 shows, the number of trials held varies significantly from province to province. While in some cities such as Buenos Aires, Tucumán and La Plata more trials were held in the period from 2006 to 2014, there were considerably fewer judicial processes in other provinces.

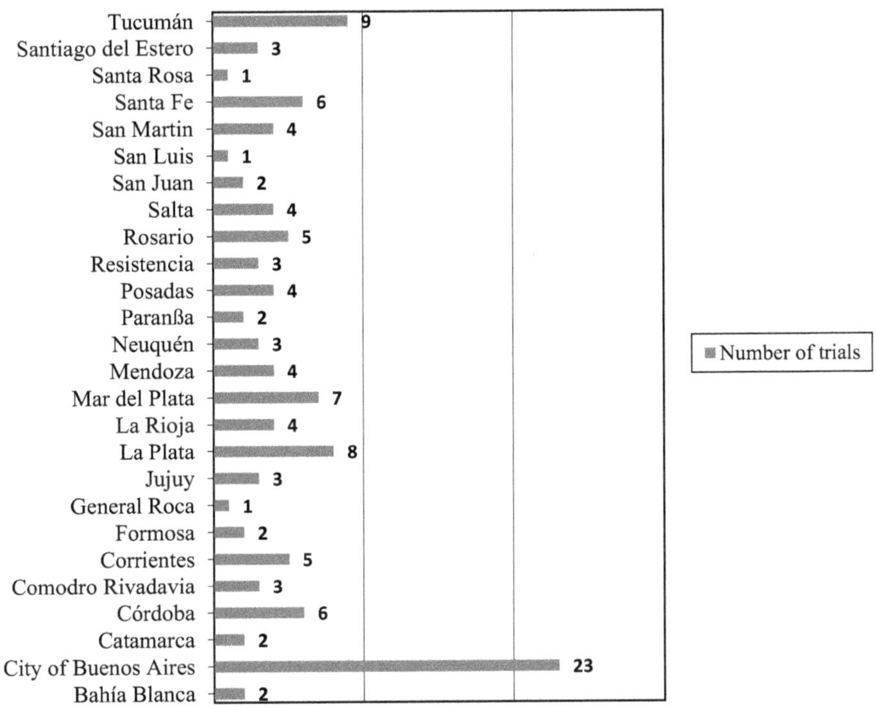

Figure 5.4 Number of trials held per regional jurisdiction between 2006 to 2014

Source: Public Prosecution Ministry 2014.

The existing political and social disparities between rural and urban regions are reflected in the implementation of the trials. Here again the lack of resources and of local government support, along with the slowness of justice, have resulted in only a small number of trials being held in small towns or even provincial capital cities. The above-mentioned problem of the shortage of judges to hear the cases has a greater impact in the provinces, with the consequent delays in the conduct of the trials (Procuraduría de Crímenes contra la Humanidad 2016, 19). In contrast, the city of Buenos Aires is the jurisdiction in which the most trials were conducted between 2006 and 2014, with a total of twenty-three oral and public trials and court decisions. This is due to the larger availability of resources, both material (more federal courts and judges than in all other provinces) and political since, being the capital city of the country and its largest urban centre, it has more visibility. However, it should be noted that the political support for the trials in the capital city does not come from the local government. Indeed, the former (now president) twice-elected mayor of Buenos Aires, Mauricio Macri (2007–2011; 2011–2015), as well as the current mayor, Horacio Rodriguez Larreta (2015-ongoing), have never focused on or shown interest in human rights policies.

The speed of judicial processes and the effectiveness of accompanying programmes (witness protection and psychological support programmes) also vary from province to province. Coordination between national and local governments, and their degree of participation in and commitment to these trials, have played a crucial role. Whereas the programmes in provinces such as Córdoba and Santa Fe work relatively well, they have been particularly unsatisfactory in the provinces of Santiago del Estero and Tucumán (Clarín 2011). According to many interviewees, this can be attributed to the unwillingness of the provincial governments to cooperate.

5.4.4 Human rights policies in times of the Macri administration: trials at risk?

While this research focuses on the trends identified in the first nine years of the trials – during which the Kirchners were in office (2006–2015), thus giving rise to the so-called *kirchnerismo* period – it is important to briefly point out some of the many new worrying developments regarding human rights policies in Argentina since the right-wing government of Mauricio Macri took office in December 2015. Already since his years as mayor of the city of Buenos Aires, Macri's position has always been one of reluctance and disparagement towards the human rights policies promoted by the previous governments of Néstor Kirchner and Cristina Fernández. As an example of this, when running for the presidency in 2014, Mauricio Macri referred to state-sponsored human rights policies as a "*curro*"[25] and to current prosecutions against the military as "revanchist" (Pertot 2014), thus arousing the outrage of national and international organisations, and showing what his position would be if he was elected president. Indeed, since

Macri took office, many human rights organisations have voiced their concern about the continuity of the trials, especially in light of the measures adopted in 2016. Such measures include, among others, a reduction in the already insufficient budget for the carrying out of investigations for the trials, increased delays in the conduct of public hearings, the appointment to government positions of individuals who are supportive of the military, and the repeated gestures and expressions of disinterest and even contempt for human rights organisations and human rights violations committed during the dictatorship (Verbitsky 2017; Calloni 2016; Ginzberg 2016a).

Budget cuts for the trials are one of the most worrying measures and a sign of the new government's position towards the prosecutions. Though, as described above, the trials had serious financing and resources problems during the previous administrations, the situation worsened during 2016. Massive layoffs of state employees have touched on human rights areas such as the above-mentioned *Ulloa Centre*, the Truth and Justice Programme and the Human Rights Secretariat (CELS 2016, 28).[26] By the end of January 2016, only one month after Mauricio Macri took office, the number of dismissals in different human rights areas and offices amounted to 489 (Página 12 2016a). The recruitment of controversial individuals, linked to the military, in key positions in governmental human rights areas, has also become a cause for concern among human rights organisations and victims. One of the most paradigmatic cases is the one of the new director of the National Witness Protection Programme, former military officer Francisco Lagos, son of retired colonel Luis Hilario Lagos, who taught at the military School of the Americas in the years of the dictatorship (Ginzberg 2016b). Survivor Enrique Fukman refers to the inadequacy of and disrespect shown by the adoption of such measures in the following terms: "Appointing an individual that was a member of the Army to be the head of Witness Protection policies is an in-security measure for all of us" (quoted by Dandan 2016). When analysing these developments, it is important to consider the topicality of the prosecutions, which are still ongoing. While long-term outcomes are yet to be seen, significant changes for the victims and society have already taken place. Thus, in the next chapter I analyse how, despite several obstacles, the human rights trials are having gradual but important reparative effects on the victims, re-establishing their rights, acknowledging their voices and generating new social attitudes towards them.

Notes

1 Roht-Arriaza stresses that the widespread perception of Menem's government and the judiciary as corrupt institutions was even scaring away potential foreign investors (2004, 99).

2 The duty to prosecute and punish those responsible for grave violations of human rights has its legal basis in the International Covenant on Civil and Political Rights (Article 2); the Convention against Torture and Other Cruel, Inhuman and Degrading Treatment or Punishment (Articles 4, 5, and 7); the American

Convention on Human Rights (Article 1); the Inter-American Convention to Prevent and Punish Torture (Articles 1 and 6); the Inter-American Convention on the Enforced Disappearance of Persons (Articles 1 and 4).

3 See, for example, the judgment rendered in the case of *Velásquez Rodríguez* (24 July 1989).

4 For instance, in August 2001 president De La Rúa refused to extradite naval intelligence officer Alfredo Astiz – protected by amnesty laws in Argentina – who was charged with numerous cases of forced disappearance (Human Rights Watch 2006).

5 They were held and tortured in the CDC known as "El Olimpo" in the neighbourhood of Floresta in the city of Buenos Aires.

6 Only his ill-health prevented the other defendant, Del Cerro, from being indicted as well. The two accused filed an appeal in 2001, but the Federal Court of Appeals unanimously affirmed Judge Cavallo's decision both in regard to the charges – which the court of appeals deemed to be crimes against humanity – and to the amnesty laws, which it agreed were unconstitutional and without legal effect.

7 On 2 October 2001, another federal judge, Claudio Bonadío, issued a second decision declaring the Full Stop and Due Obedience Laws unconstitutional and null and void. Judge Bonadío was investigating the theft of property belonging to Conrado Gómez, who was made to disappear after his abduction in January 1977 (Roht Arriaza 2004, 115). His captors, members of an ESMA task force, made off with the contents of his apartment and safe, including the deeds of properties worth almost USD 20 million (Human Rights Watch 2006). They then allegedly transferred ownership of the assets to themselves using fictitious names and a realty company owned by Navy Adm. Emilio Massera and his son. Thus, the investigation began with crimes that were excluded from the amnesty laws, in this case criminal association and plunder. As in the Poblete case, however, the defendants were immune from prosecution for much more serious crimes, such as Gómez's abduction and murder. Declaring the Full Stop and Due Obedience Laws to be without legal effect on the basis of arguments similar to those put forth by Judge Cavallo, Judge Bonadío indicted Adm. Emilio Massera as the leader of a criminal association and four members of the task force not only for criminal association, but also for illegal arrest aggravated by violence and threats (Viau and Ginzberg 2001).

8 Accused Simon and Del Cerro had also filed an appeal with the Supreme Court.

9 In Argentina the repeal of a law, once confirmed by the Supreme Court, not only invalidates the application of that law to the case at issue, but also overturns decisions taken when the law was in force.

10 In September 2006, an appellate court also declared unconstitutional the earlier pardons of the Junta members convicted in 1985, and the decision was followed by a 2007 ruling of the Supreme Court, which also declared a presidential pardon invalid. As a result of the ruling, around 3,000 officers, of whom 300 were still serving in the military, could be called for questioning in any future prosecutions (Roehrig 2009, 739).

11 The defence strategies include continuous requests for disqualification of judges, intimidation of witnesses and constant interruptions and procedural manoeuvres to delay, confuse and obstruct the trial. Their disrespectful and aggressive attitudes in the oral and public hearings cause discomfort and the re-victimisation of witnesses.

12 Indeed the first trials in many locations such as the city of Buenos Aires (the Poblete/Hlackzik case in 2006), La Plata (the Etchecolatz case in 2006), Mar del Plata (the Labollita case in 2010), Córdoba (the Brandalisis case in 2008), Misiones (the Caggiano Tedesco case in 2008), Tucumán (the Vargas Aignasse case

in 2008), Corrientes (the Regimiento 9 case in 2008), Formosa (the Colombo case in 2009), Mendoza (the Guevare case in 2010) and Santiago del Estero (the Kamentezky case in 2010) were for just a small number of victims and perpetrators.

13 Among the mega-cases are the trials for the crimes committed in the largest CDCs in the country, such as the ESMA in the city of Buenos Aires, La Perla in the province of Córdoba and Arsenales in the province of Tucumán.

14 The trial, which lasted more than four years and was finally decided in August 2016, addressed the kidnappings, tortures and murders of 716 victims since March 1974 in Córdoba. Out of the forty-three defendants under prosecution, thirty-eight were convicted and five acquitted (La Izquierda Diario 2016).

15 In this trial, in which a decision was delivered in May 2016, fifteen former military personnel were convicted and two acquitted for the abduction and murder of 105 victims, forty-five of whom were Uruguayan, twenty-two Chilean, thirteen Paraguayan, eleven Bolivian and fourteen Argentinian (Clarin 2016).

16 For instance, in the trial for the Plan Cóndor, of the initial thirty-two defendants, only seventeen were alive to hear the judgment in May 2016 (Clarín 2016).

17 This is the case of the trial conducted in 2009 in connection with the crimes committed in the former CDC Campo de Mayo in the province of Buenos Aires (Página 12 2009).

18 Due to the lack of courtrooms, for the trial of former repressor Luis Patti in 2010 and 2011, a municipal auditorium was used in the district of San Martín in the province of Buenos Aires (Dandan 2011).

19 Many judges systematically rejected *habeas corpus* or inquiries from those desperately in search of their disappeared family members or validated illegal detentions, as shown in Chapter 2.

20 The first was the case of Judge Victor Brusa in 2009 in the province of Santa Fe. It was followed by the case of former Judge Manilo Mattinez in the province of Tucumán in June 2015 (La Gaceta 2015). The latest three convictions were issued in 2016 against former federal Judges Luis María Vera Candioti in Santa Fe, Roberto Catalán in the province of La Rioja and former federal prosecutor Gustavo Demarchi in the city of Mar del Plata.

21 In the city of La Plata in October 2007 the Catholic priest Christian von Wernich was sentenced to life imprisonment. It had been proved that during his time as chaplain of the Buenos Aires province police force, Von Wernich relayed information he received from inmates to the police. He had participated in seven murders, thirty-one tortures and forty-two abductions during the military dictatorship (Judgment Von Wernich 2007, 344–353).

22 The list of such companies includes, among others, mining company *Minera Aguilar*, transport company *La Veloz del Norte*, textile company *Grafanor* and sugar companies *Ledesma*, *La Fronterita* and *Concepción* (Northwest of Argentina); textile company *Alpargatas*, food companies *Molinos Río de la Plata* and *Swift*, steel manufacturer *Propulsora Siderúrgica*, shipyard *Astillero Río Santiago* and petrochemical company *Petroquímica Sudamericana* (south of Buenos Aires); textile company *Grafa*, car makers Ford and Mercedes Benz, china manufacturer *Lozadur*, shipyards *Astarsa* and *Mestrina*, steel manufacturers *Dálmine-Siderca* and *Acindar* (north and west of the province of Buenos Aires and south of Santa Fe); car maker FIAT (centre of the country); yerba mate producer *Las Marías* (north east of Argentina); and cement producer *Loma Negra* (Buenos Aires) (CELS 2016, 40).

23 The report found that five of the companies investigated had confinement areas where the victims were illegally detained and subjected to ill treatment and

tortures. In addition, in some of the cases, the top officers of the companies took part in the abduction, captivity and torture of the workers (Ministerio de Justicia y Derechos Humanos 2015, 407).

24 This is the case of businessman Marcos Levín in the province of Salta, who is the owner of the transport company *La Veloz del Norte*. Levín was sentenced to twelve years' imprisonment on charges of unlawful deprivation of liberty and tortures sustained by the then-union leader Víctor Manuel Cobos. The victim was abducted by the police along with other fourteen workers. This is the first time a business person has been convicted of crimes against humanity committed against workers under his charge.

25 "*Curro*" is a colloquial derogatory term used in Argentina to refer to a robbery or fraud.

26 An example of this situation was the dismissal of fifteen employees of the thirty-three who worked in the Human Rights Office of the Ministry of Security. In that context, the body in charge of analysing the archives of the dictatorship and assisting the federal courts with evidence known as *Grupo Especial de Relevamiento Documental* (Documentary Investigations Special Group) was also dismantled (Ginzberg 2016b).

Chapter 6

Towards legal and civic reparation

In Chapters 2 and 4, I analysed how systematic human rights violations, state-orchestrated terror and the subsequent impunity laws left serious scars on the victims of those crimes and Argentine society more generally. Against this background, legal prosecutions can have an important role in helping to overcome – at least partially and under certain conditions – some of those consequences. The experience in Argentina can help to better understand what prosecutions can achieve in terms of reparation, which goes beyond the traditional narrow concept of monetary compensation. For such purpose, it is crucial to distinguish between the different types of reparation which domestic human rights trials, when properly held, may provide for victims. As outlined in Chapter 1, reparation can be civic–legal, personal and social. This expanded multidimensional notion of reparation takes into account the impact of trials not only on the legal and personal sphere but also on the social context, since changes in society are echoed in turn in the victims' feelings and everyday lives. In this sense, reparation is understood here as a change in the legal, political and social conditions that reproduce the damage caused by violence to the victims. The trials bring changes and redress for the victims inside and outside the court. Indeed, their mere implementation already implies a change, at least but not only, of the legal conditions supporting re-victimisation. How profound that change and the ensuing reparation can be will depend on several other factors discussed below. For a more detailed analysis of the three types of reparation, in this chapter I focus on the first form of redress – civic and legal – while in the next chapters I delve into the personal and social types of reparation. In what follows I describe some of the most relevant changes these processes have *started* to bring about, such as the restitution of rights and access to new information, which are all massively important for the victims. By using the words "have started," I aim to point out the contemporaneity of these prosecutions. Long-term outcomes are yet to be seen. Thus, the current analysis treats these findings not as a final outcome, but rather as a partial result.

The chapter is divided into three sections. In Section 1, I focus on the more formal type of reparation that the trials provide for the victims: the restitution of the rights of which they were deprived before. I also give an account of how the enjoyment of these rights, such as the right to justice, also echoes in their feelings of inclusion in the state as full citizens. In Section 2, I analyse how the access to the legal system is also linked to the right to a judicial investigation that allows knowing what happened. I examine the progress made by the prosecutions in the prosecutions in uncovering the past and the value of knowing the truth as an essential condition for reparation, especially for the families of the disappeared. In addition, I address the serious limitations faced by the trials in allowing access to information, particularly when the perpetrators do not cooperate and the crimes concerned were committed forty years ago. Finally, in Section 3, I discuss the role of the trials in acknowledging and legitimising the victims' voice, allocating clear responsibilities and defining what kind of violence took place – all crucial elements in a reparative process.

6.1 Civic and legal reparation: towards the restitutions of rights

The notion of civic and legal reparation refers to the formal restitution of the relation between the state and the victims of human rights violations understood as citizens. As soon as the military took power, the most basic civil and political rights were suppressed in Argentina. While the dictatorship deprived victims of all their rights, the following period of legal impunity, albeit under formally democratic governments, turned survivors and relatives of the disappeared into second-class citizens.

As discussed in Chapter 4, the decades of impunity were described by many interviewees as a period of "frustration" and "lack of hope." Many survivors and relatives of the disappeared were discouraged from undertaking mobilisations. The feeling that justice could not be achieved reduced participation in social and political organisations. Indeed, before the trials, the judicial system was perceived as a remote and even unattainable sphere, only the privilege of others. As several interviewees stated, during the period of impunity justice seemed a distant, unachievable goal. A witness from Rosario stated:

> In the Menem period, I saw [justice] as a distant thing, I thought we would never see it happening.
>
> (Int. 23, March 2011, Rosario)

Another interviewee said in a tone of irony:

> If in 2001, 2002, someone had told me that they [the perpetrators] would go to prison, would get punished, I would have laughed.
>
> (Int. 28, March 2011, Rosario).

Similarly, a plaintiff from Buenos Aires stated:

> At that time [in the 1990s] I couldn't foresee what justice was, I didn't think that [the trials] would happen.
>
> (Int. 62, September 2012, Buenos Aires).

Those who were previously excluded perceive access to justice almost as an extraordinary experience. When exclusions prevail for decades, they carry the risk of normalisation and resignation. The normalisation of exclusion may lead to its acceptance and to the loss of prospects of obtaining justice, all of which can result in social demobilisation and paralysis. On the contrary, access to justice has the potential to encourage participation and a feeling of belonging. As some scholars state, citizens' rights function as a mechanism of inclusion in or exclusion from a particular social, legal and political sphere (Brubaker 1992, Bosniak 2000). If citizens' rights imply formal membership in a specific community, the victims' legal deprivation of rights also results in their partial exclusion from that community. The victims become a marginalised group of citizens legally deprived of rights enjoyed by others in society. The impunity of perpetrators of human rights violations automatically converts their victims into a different kind of citizen who is legally deprived of access to justice, of the right to be safe in their daily lives without having to come across perpetrators in the streets and being threatened by them, the right to have judicial investigations and the right to know the truth. By contrast, human rights trials operate in the opposite way in that they recognise individuals as citizens by bringing them back into the legal system. In fact, many interviewees have said that they felt the state was including them through their participation in the prosecutions. As stated by one of the plaintiffs, a daughter of disappeared parents from Buenos Aires, when describing her feelings as she gave testimony:

> It's the first time the state has listened to what I have to say. It listens to me as a victim of genocide (. . .). The state listens to my family history. For me it was an important moment.
>
> (Int. 62, September 2012, Buenos Aires)

As can be seen, the trials mark an important change by including victims as citizens and members of the state and society. They are no longer invisible. The trials legally entitle the victims to their rights. This inclusion, reflected for instance in the possibility of giving testimony and being heard by the state, has been described as a very important and reparative experience by many interviewees. As recounted by a son of disappeared parents from Buenos Aires when he heard the sentence that was passed in 2010 in connection with the crimes committed against his mother:

> To me it was a celebration. (. . .). First, it has an effect (. . .), which is to put things in the right place.
>
> (Int. 15, April 2011, Buenos Aires)

Whereas the amnesty laws created an exception from the legal system with serious consequences for the victims, the trials reinforce the principle that everyone is equal – at least formally[1] – before the courts and the law. Of course, absolute equality before the law is an ideal difficult to reach in any society since the interpretation and application of the law is usually influenced by the social and political power relations in each specific context as well as by the judges' points of view. However, the legal establishment of a differentiated access to justice through the impunity laws clearly evinces a political decision to privilege perpetrators of crimes against humanity and to exclude the victims from the justice system. In this sense, human rights trials put an end to that legal asymmetry and parallel systems of justice and rights within a society. The trials have given hope to many plaintiffs and witnesses in Argentina that the prosecution of human rights violations can gradually become the norm in the criminal justice system and no longer the exception. An interviewee described her feelings when recalling the conviction of the perpetrators for the disappearance of her parents:

> [Y]ou have the feeling that justice does exist. You don't have your parents any more (. . .), but well, the justice system is working, and you can believe a little more. (. . .) [I]t gave me hope, belief in justice and in the democratic system.
>
> (Int. 63, September 2012, Buenos Aires)

Thus, civic reparation is, according to several plaintiffs, a fundamental element for their inclusion in the institutional, legal and political system. As a matter of fact, many interviewees have stated that the trials provided them with their first opportunity to access the justice system.

6.2 The right to the truth: reconstructing the puzzle of the past

The enforcement of the right to justice through the prosecution of human rights violations also implies access to the right to the truth. Both rights are linked and reinforce each other, as can be seen in the Argentine experience. Thus, in addition to their retributive character, the trials can operate as truth-seeking mechanisms as they allow the victims to make accusations and thus enable investigations of human rights violations. Judicial investigations contribute to reconstructing the past – in the relevant literature usually described as "knowing the truth" – which in cases of enforced disappearance becomes a means of reparation for the family of disappeared victims. For them, the reality of loss and victimisation may continue to be a daily event, even after many years. It then is essential to know what has happened in a concrete, clear way – to learn the factual circumstances of the death or disappearance of relatives (Parlevliet 1998, Robben 2007). From a legal perspective, knowing what happened is considered to be a fundamental human right, especially in cases of enforced disappearance, as established in the UN Convention (United Nations 2006, art 32). The right to know the truth is an emerging principle contained in several legal documents. International law entitles the families of disappeared persons to know the totality of circumstances surrounding the fate of their relatives and imposes an obligation of investigation on states.

The need to know what happened is an urgent demand from the relatives of disappeared victims, especially after generations of cover-ups and evasions, as in Argentina. Human rights trials make it possible to reconstruct what several interviewees have described as the "puzzle of the past." This puzzle is constructed from various mechanisms such as witness testimonies, police raids, search warrants, access to classified documents and excavations in search of the bodies of the disappeared. Through investigation and testimony, the trials seek to articulate causal links and meanings and thus serve to build a story by putting together the fragmented elements of the puzzle. Search warrants allow access to evidence hidden in the homes of the accused, as well as other potential actors involved. Without trials all these investigations would not take place.

Access to the truth can in itself have a strong reparative effect. Indeed, part of the ongoing suffering of many relatives of the disappeared is caused by a lack of knowledge of what happened to their children, parents, brothers or sisters. In this sense, one of the main expectations the survivors and relatives have from these trials is to access new information about the whereabouts of their loved ones. In the interviews, the victims and other actors such as lawyers and judges voiced different opinions about the contribution of the trials to further knowledge of the past. Some said that the trials have so far contributed to important findings about facts and persons for whom there was previously no information. They claimed to have learned during the trial new facts about disappeared persons, relatives or the identity of perpetrators involved. As stated by a survivor who testified at one of the trials in the city of Rosario:

> [At the trials] the murders of some *compañeros*[2] [fellow militants] who are disappeared are now coming to light, and (. . .) we are just now beginning to find out what happened to them.
>
> (Int. 28, March 2011, Rosario)

Similarly, a survivor who gave testimony in a trial in the city of Buenos Aires pointed out:

> A great deal of new information is coming up in the course of these trials, because of new witnesses.
>
> (Int. 10, March 2011, Buenos Aires)

The interviewee emphasised how the trial led to the identification of a perpetrator who was only known by his alias: "We all knew him as 'the Frenchman' but nobody knew his real name, now [due to the trial] it was possible to arrest him and identify him completely" (Int. 10, March 2011, Buenos Aires). Several interviewees have mentioned the link between reparation and access to the truth about what happened to their own relatives. For instance, an interviewee from the city of Córdoba, whose father was murdered in the prison known as *Unidad*

Penitenciaria Número 1 (Prison Unit Number 1, hereinafter UP1) during the dictatorship, explained this link in the following terms:

> *A:* The mere fact that a trial was held has a clear reparative effect. And I'll tell you why. During the trial, we [my family and I] were able to learn exactly what happened at [prison] UP1. Everything was described in detail by the persons that were detained there.
>
> *Q:* And didn't you know all of this before?
>
> *A:* I did, but after having heard all those testimonies, I can say that I realised I knew less than half of it.
>
> (Int. 37, March 2011, Córdoba)

Similarly, another interviewee from Tucumán whose father is disappeared explained to me why it was important for her to attend all the hearings in the trials, even though her father's case was not being prosecuted yet:

> It is important because if you attend the trial, you can begin to piece together your own story. When a witness testifies to having seen a disappeared person during the trial, you get to know who saw him or her and what happened to him or her. This was my experience in [the trial for the crimes committed in the former CDC of] *Jefatura*. My father's case was not part of [that trial], but I was able to find out who saw him [when he was illegally detained there].
>
> (Int. 72, October 2012, Tucumán)

Many victims have stated in the interviews that the judicial process has a reparative effect on them, since it comprises investigations into the past that provide them with new relevant information about their relatives, friends or colleagues. At this point, it should be stressed that access to the truth has also been made possible by the efforts of the victims. Thus, new information is available in the trials thanks to the testimony of witnesses, the results of judicial investigations, the exhumations of common graves carried out in the course of the trials, but also due to the contributions of informal inquiries conducted by the survivors, the relatives of the disappeared, the victims themselves and human rights organisations, as described in Chapter 5. They have carried out a wide range of activities with the goal of collecting information to reconstruct that puzzle. Within this framework, they have held meetings to share and exchange their stories in order to discover new data; they have sought new witnesses and have spread their campaigns in search of testimony and evidence for the trials. As can be seen, the reconstruction of the past that takes place in the trials is also the result of a previous collective process of data collection in which the relatives of the disappeared and the survivors have a crucial role. A survivor, whose mother is disappeared, described such process of historical reconstruction as follows:

> At the beginning people gave testimony and said: "I don't know where I was but I heard noises," for example of planes or metal blinds. And then someone

> else would come forward with more data, and then someone else, and he or she would say, for example: "I saw a girl who was pregnant, but I don't know her name." And then one of the girl's relatives filed a deposition and so we got to know who she was. So, reconstructing the list of the disappeared seen in the CDCs, the list of the repressors, was a task carried out by many people.
>
> (Int. 65, October 2012, Buenos Aires)

Therefore, the reconstruction of the past in court not only hinges on judicial and forensic investigations but also on a collective historical process of searching, gathering and making sense of the different pieces of the puzzle. At the same time, this informal reconstruction is strengthened, legitimised and disseminated to a broader sector of the population through the trials.

6.2.1 The incomplete puzzle

An analysis of the reparative function and the effects of the trials also reveals their shortcomings and contradictions. Indeed, not all the information about the past is accessible. As shown below, access to the truth – especially in cases of enforced disappearances which occurred almost forty years ago – suffers from significant constraints. Such situation has been accurately described by a survivor and plaintiff in the trials as: "[It's] a jigsaw puzzle with many missing pieces" (Int. 65, October 2012, Buenos Aires). Another survivor and witness in the trial for the crimes committed in the ex-CDC known as *El Vesubio* in Buenos Aires shared this view:

> We have data for only about 10 per cent of the cases (. . .) we've been working since 1978. We have a commission made up of victims, survivors and relatives, among others, that has held meetings every seven or fifteen days for almost thirty years. I think the *Vesubio* is the most thoroughly investigated CDC in Argentina, and even though we have identified some 300 *compañeros*, that's not even 15 per cent of the victims who were detained there. And in some cases, we only have a nickname, a name, the physical description, we don't even know the surname.
>
> (Int. 10, March 2011, Buenos Aires)

After more than thirty years since human rights violations took place in Argentina, there are relevant aspects of the past which are still not accessible. Many pieces of this puzzle are still missing. As a consequence, in many cases the initial optimism about gaining access to unknown facts has been tempered by several factors.

The first and most fundamental obstacle is the very nature of enforced disappearance, a repressive clandestine practice aimed to guarantee the impunity of the perpetrators. Without the body of the murdered person, perpetrators leave no evidence of the crimes. Added to this, the identification of victims and perpetrators is hindered by other factors such as the existence of clandestine torture centres, the state's denial of the detentions, the use of nicknames by perpetrators and the fact that detainees-disappeared were blindfolded and not called by their names but by identification codes consisting of a number or letter. Even though the survivors provide evidence of the existence of the CDCs and of the disappeared persons detained in them before being killed, they cannot give testimony of the death of the disappeared. Enforced disappearance is a crime without a body and without direct eyewitnesses to the murder. Once prisoners were transferred from the CDCs, their whereabouts became unknown and none of those transferred returned from the so-called *traslados* (transfers)[3] or death flights. Thus, the disappearance of people has a core effect as a strategy of terror: the uncertainty caused by the lack of information about how the person died, who exactly killed them, where it happened and where the body is now. Even though exhumations of mass graves carried out by the NGO Argentine Forensic Anthropology Team have been a key element in finding and identifying the remains of disappeared victims, a range of questions still await answers. The analysis of the remains of dead bodies has enabled forensic experts to determine in many cases how the victims were murdered. However, most of the victims or, to be more precise, their bodies, have not yet been found.

A second factor limiting access to the truth is the lack of cooperation from the accused, which poses a significant challenge to finding more information through other means in the trials. Most of the perpetrators on trial maintain a so-called pact of silence. Even in those cases where perpetrators have already been convicted and sent to prison – and thus, their confessions cannot change their current situation – they have made a decision not to talk. This pact of silence also tends to guarantee the impunity of those accused who have not yet been convicted. Thus, many of the survivors and former political prisoners who testified at the trials stated that they did not discover much new in court. They all stressed that access to new information would only be possible if the perpetrators confessed. Asked if she had learned something new at the trial, a survivor and witness in the trials in Buenos Aires explained and lamented:

> No. The trials were based on what I testified. New information for me would mean finding out what they did to my partner (. . .) [who until today remains disappeared] and no one has told me that. No one has contributed information about that.

And she stressed:

> [The information] is always [provided] by witnesses, but nothing from the other side, [from] the accused, they didn't speak, they didn't say anything.
>
> (Int. 63, September 2012, Buenos Aires)

Similarly, a plaintiff from Buenos Aires, whose parents are disappeared, explained:

> You expect other witnesses to contribute some information (. . .). Yes, new contributions are made, you discover new things, but I didn't find out anything very important, because the military didn't speak.
>
> (Int. 62, September 2012, Buenos Aires)

Another child of disappeared parents from La Plata voiced similar concerns. He admitted that initially he had hopes of gaining more information about his parents' disappearance. His expectations did not last long:

Q: What were your expectations about the trial?
A: One of the things I expected – I was very naive, I soon realised it was a kind of dream – was to find out what had happened to my parents.
Q: Did you think you would find it out through the trial?
A: Yes, but my expectations only lasted for two days.
Q: Why?
A: Because I knew the military wouldn't say anything, not in this trial or in any other, save for very rare exceptions. (. . .) I didn't find out anything new.
(Int. 74, September 2012, La Plata)

Even though the relatives of the disappeared are certain that their relatives have died, in many cases their suffering has not diminished since the disappearances occurred. Not knowing what happened to their loved ones is a form of continued torture. In turn, the "pact of silence" also hides not only the location of the bodies of the disappeared but also that of the "living disappeared," that is, of all the children who were stolen after being born during the captivity of their mothers, and then deprived of their biological family and delivered to other families with a different identity. According to the human rights organisation *Abuelas de Plaza de Mayo*, more than 350 individuals currently live under a false identity without knowledge of who their parents really were (Ginzberg 2002).[4]

Another factor affecting access to the truth-finding process is the role of the state at the national and provincial levels. As described in Chapter 5, a general problem undermining investigations and the trials themselves is the lack of sufficient material and human resources. For example, many human rights organisations and victims have pointed to the understaffing of the Prosecution Unit created in 2008 to prosecute cases of human rights violations. This has meant that many public prosecutors, especially in the first five years, had to work on these "new" trials in addition to their normal caseload. In a number of Argentine provinces, such as Santiago del Estero and Córdoba, many of the victims I interviewed complained that public prosecutors were overwhelmed by the large amount of work. Despite the fact that more staff has been retained and special units have been set up in some provincial courts, the amount of work is still very high, and thus many victims see the lack of resources for the judicial investigations as a crucial problem. While this is a general problem, the financial and political support of the government in each province can make a difference and thus speed up or slow down judicial investigations. In those provinces with a stronger local government backing the investigations, the prosecution and judges have more support and resources to conduct their inquiries.

A fourth factor constraining the uncovering of the past is the passage of time and its impact on the trials. This is compounded by the above-discussed clandestine nature of state repression in Argentina, as the systematic enforced disappearance of people leaves no documentary or written evidence of those crimes. In this sense, it is the surviving victims who have the most information about the period of repression. Because of their captivity in the CDCs, they are the ones who were able to see and identify other prisoners as well as perpetrators. Survivors are thus crucial witnesses of what happened. However, after thirty years, the death of witnesses becomes an imminent threat to the judicial investigations. As explained by the above interviewee:

> After thirty years, it's very difficult to reconstruct what happened. In some cases, there are no relatives alive, (. . .) after twenty or twenty-five years, they've all died. When the trials began, twenty-seven years had passed with respect to some facts. (. . .) Unfortunately, protracted impunity has inevitable consequences. For all the good will, some things cannot be rebuilt after thirty years. And if we let more time go by, we will have no more witnesses.
>
> (Int. 10, March 2011, Buenos Aires)

In addition, the surviving witnesses' recollections can change or even fade away as time goes by. This situation adds to the pressure on and vulnerability of the survivors in an expectant court. Several psychologists assisting the victims have explained that the passage of time also builds pressure on survivor-witnesses. Many of them are deeply afraid of not remembering all the details after such a long time and feel burdened with a great responsibility for their own testimony and for their disappeared fellows and their families. The sacralisation of an intact memory that judicial logic demands from witnesses – which memory will be put to the test with harshness and even with cruelty by the defence attorneys – becomes an extremely heavy burden for the survivors as the day for them to appear in court and give testimony approaches (Rousseaux 2014). As stated by a survivor:

> One week before [I have to give testimony in court] I can't get to sleep, I get a stomach-ache, many things happen to me, I read my [previous] testimony so that I won't forget my prior statements. I gave testimony before CONADEP and the investigative criminal court. I begin to repeat the names of the *compañeros* I saw [in the CDC] so that I won't forget anyone.
>
> (Int. 63, September 2012, Buenos Aires)

The witnesses feel imprisoned between the duty to recall facts with a judicial and historical logic and their own memories, which sometimes become irreparably altered and follow a temporal and subjective logic that differs completely from the historical events as they occurred (Rousseaux 2014). Thus, access to the truth through the judiciary is not a black-and-white process but presents many nuances and difficulties for all the actors involved.

In general terms, everyone in Argentina knows something about past state terror, its practices and the disappearances. The gains in knowledge produced by the trials vary and are determined by the different social, political and personal conditions of those seeking to access that information. The historical and political context of every locality in which the trials take place has relevant implications on the access to the truth and what is perceived as new knowledge about the past. While many interviewees, especially in the north-central provinces of the country, said that they had discovered important new aspects of the past through the prosecutions, many others, especially in the large urban centres such as Buenos Aires and La Plata, described the new information offered by the trials as "just details." It should be recalled that, as discussed in Chapters 3 and 4, a significant portion of society, especially in provinces such as Tucumán and Santiago del Estero, lived under social regimes where silence, fear and indifference were the norm during the period of impunity. The refusal of many people to know what happened in more detail was an expression either of fear or of support for the perpetrators. In these places then the facts presented at trial seem to have had more of an impact not only on the victims but also locally.

In addition, those who have been somehow involved in victims' and/or human rights organisations have more knowledge of the past than those who have not. Informal networks and human rights organisations play a key role in allowing the victims to have contact with others with whom they may have exchanged and shared experiences. For that reason, in those provinces in the north of the country with a weaker presence of human rights organisations and more conservative and semi-authoritarian provincial governments, talking about state crimes and acquiring more information through informal networks was a less likely occurrence than in cities such as La Plata and Buenos Aires with a stronger human rights movement. Thus, all these factors have also generated different layers of access to the puzzle of the past. The function of the trials is not only the mere gathering and public presentation of data of the past, as explained below, but also putting all the pieces together within a historical and political framework. Indeed, all current criminal rulings in Argentina dealing with the crimes of the dictatorship, starting with the important judgment known as "case 13/84" to try the military Juntas in the 1980s, devote a considerable part of their content to reconstructing the historical period of the dictatorship,[5] and thus fulfill a reparative function for the victim.

6.3 Acknowledging and legitimating the victims' voices

Criminal trials in human rights cases not only rely upon the presentation of facts, but they also express and legitimise an interpretation of those facts. By evaluating and interpreting all the evidence presented in court, judges make a selection between competing historical explanations of the past and acknowledge it as official (Wilson 2005, 918). Almost all court decisions so far have held that state repression in Argentina was part of a systematic plan of extermination against all those considered to be opponents and that the crimes committed by the state within that framework are regarded as crimes against humanity.[6] In this way, reparation is not only provided by human rights trials through the access to new information but also by the official acknowledgement of the crimes committed by state agents.

Several scholars stress the importance of defining truth not only as knowledge of what happened, but also as acknowledgement: the determination of facts about the past, and a full, public and official acknowledgement thereof (Weschler 1990). This distinction between knowledge and acknowledgement was originally made by philosopher Thomas Nagel in the late 1980s, and has since been an important conceptual reference. According to him, the difference between knowledge and acknowledgment "is what happens and can only happen to knowledge when it becomes officially sanctioned, when it is made part of the public cognitive scene" (quoted by Molesworth 2007, 939). The basic facts of what happened are often already known to some extent, in which case establishing the truth comes down to confirming what is already widely known but denied. As Parlevliet (1998) asserts, the "added value" of truth-telling is therefore considered to reside in this aspect of acknowledgement: what was private becomes public knowledge, shared amongst the wider population, and bearing the official sanction. This is vital for the victims, especially for the survivors who, as shown above, did not obtain much new knowledge through the trials – since they were the knowledge providers – and were condemned to silence for years. Thanks to the trials, they can finally have their knowledge officially acknowledged.

The acknowledgment function of the trials has been underscored in one way or another by many interviewees. A survivor from Tucumán, whose brother was made to disappear, explained how shocking it was for him, even knowing that his brother had been murdered, to hear the testimony of an eyewitness confirming the kidnapping of his brother for the first time in thirty years. The interviewee also remarked how important it is to prove that his brother's disappearance was a crime and not a voluntary action, as many people had suggested:

> In 2013[7] an eyewitness to my brother's kidnapping appeared in court to testify for the first time. (. . .) It was very shocking. It's one thing to have grounds to believe that my brother was not a deserter[8] and disappeared in [the CDC called] *Arsenales* and another to hear this witness – a fellow military conscript – say: "I saw his abduction." This story made us shudder.
>
> (Int. 68, September 2012, Tucumán)

New testimonies provide certainty about crimes that went unacknowledged for years. Many plaintiffs find a reparative effect in hearing testimonies and evidence that officially confirm the commission of a crime against their relatives or themselves. The symbolic effectiveness of law (Bourdieu 1987), with an apparently neutral and universalising rhetoric, operates as a criterion for acknowledgement and for truth (Foucault 2007). The judiciary's recognition of victimisation weakens other explanations circulating in society that deny the crimes and devalue the victims, for instance that the disappeared were abroad or responsible for their own disappearance. As the interviewee stressed, testimony in court confirming the kidnapping of his brother publicly destroys the idea that his disappearance was voluntary. The trials contribute to the official admission that crimes which had been reported by the victims for years had indeed taken place. Thus, many plaintiffs expect the judicial system to officially acknowledge that the "disappeared" were murdered and provide an explanation for the disappearance of their relatives. Indeed, the judicial account and reconstruction of the past allocating clear responsibilities was described by several victims as being reparative and even healing. A son of disappeared parents from Buenos Aires recounted that when he heard the judgment that was passed in 2010 in connection with the crimes committed against his mother:

> To me it was a celebration. (. . .) I felt healthier, better. First, it has an effect (. . .) we no longer have to discuss who is the victim and who the victimiser. Justice defines boundaries and puts things in the right place. And then suddenly you take the role that you are supposed to take, which is that of a victim, whether or not you are a militant. So, that does have a reparative effect. The state is taking responsibility for an issue. (. . .) If that didn't happen, what would be the victim's fate when the state was absent, when the state served the interests of impunity? You'd be totally unprotected. The violence you once suffered would keep coming back. So, a trial has a reparative effect. It's the state's recognition, not [only] the recognition of the victim but also of a state that acted as a victimiser. The state is acknowledging its own acts.
>
> (Int. 15, April 2011, Buenos Aires)

Acknowledgment through the trials symbolises the state taking responsibility for past violations. The reparative effects of the trials derive in part from their power to construct and define identities where major crimes were committed. In addition, many survivors and human rights activists consider that these judicial processes contribute to the state's validation and legitimation of the victims' testimonies. As stressed by a plaintiff in the trials in Tucumán:

Q: Do you think the trials have a reparative effect?
A: Yes.
Q: Where do you see it?
A: A truth is revealed, (. . .) and part of that truth becomes institutionalised through the trials (. . .). So, the trials not only have a cathartic role for us, because we can sit there and say what perhaps we cannot say in other spaces, [but also] the community can see us as the victims that we were (. . .) so that this perception that we were the bad guys of the movie can be reversed.

(Int. 73, October 2012, Tucumán)

In contrast to the period of impunity, the current trials are simultaneously an official expression of the disapproval of state crimes and the recognition of the victims' status, which is crucial to the reparation process. As shown in Chapter 4, the previous denial and lack of acknowledgement generated by impunity made the survivors feel invisible, or be treated with suspicion. These trials provide the survivors and the relatives of the disappeared with the credibility that impunity had taken away from them. Several interviewees referred to the legitimising power of the justice system. A survivor stated:

A: What happens in [the trial for the CDC] Arsenal is proof of the crimes. It wasn't something made up by the families [of the disappeared]. What we said was true, and now the evidence for that has come up. (. . .) There's a big difference between a person telling the truth in the form of an accusation and the judiciary, as a branch of the state, confirming that truth, considering it to have been duly proven. Then, the information provided by the relatives becomes official and has a value of objectivity and truth that would otherwise be non-existent.

Q: Do you feel that when you don't give testimony in court but in other places . . .

A: . . . then it's the mere accusation by a relative of a disappeared person, but here it's the justice system which gives the same account another hierarchy. (. . .) [Because of the trial] there's been a recognition that heinous crimes were committed, that [people] were hunted, kidnapped, tortured and disappeared, on such a large scale, (. . .) and it is the justice system which is saying it now.

(Int. 68, September 2012, Tucumán)

As explained by the interviewee, the trials make the victims' truth official by confirming what they affirmed for years. Due to a widespread acceptance of the judicial methodology and state character of judicial institutions, criminal trials confer heightened legitimacy on the facts and crimes as contained in the judicial record. The state legitimises the accusations and accounts made by the survivors and relatives, and gives them "another hierarchy." Such "value of objectivity and truth" mentioned by the interviewee derives from what Bourdieu calls the neutralisation and universalisation effects of law, which aim to mark the impersonality of normative utterances and to establish the law's decisions as the result of consensus, impartiality and objectivity (1987, 820). Bourdieu stresses that rational rhetoric as a methodology and the professionalisation of the juridical field increase the separation between legal judgments based on the law and others. As stated by the interviewee, there is a huge difference in terms of impact and legitimacy between a single individual telling the truth in the form of an accusation and the judiciary confirming that truth. Unlike other social narratives of the past, the significance of judicial narratives produced in the course of human rights trials is to a large extent based on the legitimating force that the judicial system as a state institution has in society (Diaz 1980, 11–12). This shows that it does matter how, where and by whom the truth is delivered. The apparently unbiased logic and rhetoric of rationalisation is what provides the law with authority and legitimacy to effectively communicate specific explicit and implicit messages, giving them a higher social impact, different from that of the survivors and the relatives of the disappeared alone. Juan Mendez, a human rights scholar and lawyer, argues that

> knowledge that is officially sanctioned and thereby made part of the public cognitive scene, (. . .) acquires a mysterious quality that is not there when it is merely "truth." Official acknowledgement at least begins to heal the wounds.
>
> (quoted in Hayner 2002, 26)

An interviewee, daughter of disappeared parents and a plaintiff in the trials for the crimes committed in the ex-CDC of ESMA in the city of Buenos Aires, referred to this greater legitimacy of the justice system as follows:

> [The trial] gave me more strength, because it's no longer just me saying something, now it's the judiciary, a branch of the state, saying it. All that becomes collective, it no longer belongs only to me and the ESMA victims and their relatives; it belongs to society as a whole.
>
> (Int. 62, September 2012, Buenos Aires)

Many victims feel that their accounts become official and that they are no longer "only" their own accounts. The justice system as a state-sponsored institution enables such accounts to "become collective" or, in Bourdieu's words, to "become universal." In turn, the state's ratification of the accounts gives the victims strength along with a sense of reparation, given that the crimes can no longer be officially denied. The trials have also brought more awareness to large sections of society and have made the victims' accusations more visible. This is confirmed by several interviewees acting as plaintiffs in the trials:

> There's quite a difference between meeting with two *compañeros* and saying "Roberto was taken away" and feeling accompanied in testimony of that kind by three federal judges and all the people.
>
> (Int. 40, April 2011, Córdoba)

> The trials allowed me to reach out to a wider part of society, so that as many people as possible might become aware of what happened here (. . .). [The trial] gives [the accounts about state crimes] an increased significance and hierarchy. [Now] that's undeniable. Added to that is the imposition of a penalty. A crime that goes unpunished is as if it hadn't been proved, as if it didn't exist. It's only an accusation by the victim, but here it is the judiciary

saying that the events have been proven and imposing punishment. It's no longer possible to have doubts about this.

(Int. 68, September 2012, Tucumán)

Thus, the trials fulfil one of their most meaningful and reparative functions when the state publicly recognises its own responsibility in previous human rights violations and legitimises those voices which in the past it had ignored and underestimated. The three aspects discussed in this chapter – inclusion of the victims in the justice system, access to judicial investigations and the public acknowledgement of state responsibility for the violence endured by the victims – reflect an institutional change that is not only of great importance for the survivors and relatives of disappeared victims, but also for society and the national democratic system. The prosecution of perpetrators of crimes against humanity in domestic courts reveals a process of incorporation of human rights rules into the local judicial system, which is an essential institutional condition for the protection of human rights violations in the future. In order to provide a more comprehensive picture of the reparation afforded by the trials, I examine in the next chapter how since the beginning of the trials, many victims have started to experience concrete changes and new forms of freedom that translate into new possibilities of action and expression.

Notes

1 As already mentioned in Chapter 4, there are also important differences in the application of the law among ordinary citizens and in the enjoyment of citizens' rights, especially in the most marginal sectors. However, these differences are more informally applied in contrast to the legal status of the impunity laws.

2 I keep the Spanish term because it has a very special connotation in Argentina. While it could be translated as comrades or fellows in English, the meaning of this word goes beyond that. As sociologist Estela Schindel (2014) explains, "*compañero*" is a keyword deeply rooted in the tradition of the Peronist movement, but also used more broadly to denote social and political activists: "a compañero is one of our own, a figure at once anonymous and yet closely related and affectively charged" (Schindel 2014, 248). The author stresses that speaking about the disappeared as *compañeros* is an explicit acknowledgment of the political engagement of the victims of state terror and at the same time a declaration of one's own political activism. The term is commonly used by the interviewees to refer either to the disappeared or to other survivors or human rights activists.

3 This is a euphemism for the transfer of prisoners who were taken away from the clandestine centres in cars or lorries and never seen again.

4 From the 500 estimated cases of appropriated children, 117 individuals have already been identified in the past decades (Ginzberg 2015).

5 All the judgments contain a reference to the historical reconstruction. Many of them include a specific section under the heading of "historical context" or "recitals." See for example Judgment Julián Simon 2006, 16–38, Judgment for the massacre of Fatima 2008, 45–65, Judgment Mansión Seré 2008, 198–215, Judgment Vargas Aignasse 2008, 77–84.

6 See for example Judgment Julián Simon, 2006; Judgment Vargas Aignasse 2008.

7 Though the original interview was conducted in 2012, the interviewee updated his interview when, during a trial in Tucumán one year later, he obtained new information regarding the disappearance of his brother.
8 When he was made to disappear, the interviewee's brother was doing military service, which at that time was mandatory for all young men.

Chapter 7

Reparation as empowerment

In order to give an account of the different ways in which prosecutions can be reparative, in this chapter I examine how human rights trials may also bring concrete changes and redress for the victims not only at the legal level but also in other personal aspects of their lives. The whole judicial process – from the detention of perpetrators, the investigation of crimes, the access to the truth, to the possibility of participating and being heard in public hearings – contributes to creating new social and institutional conditions with reparative effects. By "personal" I do not mean an isolated or merely individual process of reparation, but rather a process through which an individual, as result of changes in his/her institutional context, is able to undertake and confront situations that were out of his/her reach before. Reparation means empowerment and concrete changes which bring about new possibilities of action and expression for victims in their social environment. However, in accounting for the reparative processes generated by the trials, it is also important to consider the difficulties that they involve. While some of these limitations can be overcome with political will, especially those related to legal, bureaucratic and financial obstacles, others cannot. There always remains something irreparable which is linked to the survivors' experience of captivity and torture, the interruption of personal life projects and the loss of their loved ones in the case of relatives of disappeared persons.

This chapter is divided into two main sections. Section 1 examines the meaning of personal reparation and its different dimensions, including the link between the trials and the possibility of facing fear. I explain how the trials as a state-sponsored mechanism can help to lessen fear, allowing new practices to arise inside and outside the court and thus empowering victims. Section 2 addresses one of the main consequences of fear being dispelled: the breaking of the victims' silence. Even after more than thirty years since the crimes occurred, new testimonies make possible the discussion of previously silenced topics such as sexualised violence and the political militancy of the victims. In doing so, this section also considers the difficulties and challenges posed by these new possibilities and the need to address them in order to sustain this process of reparation in time.

7.1 Dealing with fear

As shown in Chapter 4, legal impunity served, to a greater or lesser degree, to reproduce and maintain fear in different segments of the population, especially in many victims. During that period, the perpetrators continued to threaten and intimidate the victims. Thus, an important change in the local context takes place when the perpetrators who were once free are now in prison. Indeed, many interviewees have stressed that the conduct of trials in their own cities helped to reduce fear. Incarcerating the perpetrators removes them not only from the social sphere, but also from their positions in public institutions such as the security forces. This enables the victims to enjoy a new form of freedom. The latent risk the victims felt before gradually decreases, giving them a wider scope for action and speech. In the course of the trials, the survivors and relatives of the disappeared tell their stories, assigning names to events and people (most of them perpetrators) who had been unmentionable before. A plaintiff's attorney from the province of Santiago del Estero explained how she perceived new attitudes among the local people after the first human rights trial took place in 2010. According to her, many people started to give public accounts of their disappeared relatives and visit public monuments dedicated to the disappeared, which they had previously avoided:

> With the trial, people became less afraid. Less afraid to speak, less afraid to participate [in political activities] (. . .)[less] afraid to go to the monument of the disappeared here in the city square and to bring a flower or just visit it because they have a brother who was disappeared, for example.
>
> (Int. 57, April 2011, Santiago del Estero)

Such examples illustrate a gradual process of change in the social and institutional conditions. As shown in Chapter 4, during the period of impunity, severe restrictions were placed on social protests against state repression. By contrast, the trials and decisions handed down by the courts have given the victims the strength – and the legitimacy – to confront the fear of speaking out in public about the crimes of the military. An ex-political prisoner from Santiago del Estero referred to this in the following way:

> The judgment [passed in the first trial] gave us some sort of legitimacy and helped us overcome our fears (. . .); we dared to do more things. It gave us more strength, it encouraged us to do open radio programmes in the square and speak in the square, which had always been an alien territory, because we couldn't speak about these issues. Ten years ago, nobody would have thought that I could be standing [there] with a microphone. I wouldn't even have been allowed to finish a single sentence; (. . .) a cop would have kicked me out. All the things we've managed to say now (. . .) were unthinkable in the past.
>
> (Int. 52, April 2011, Santiago del Estero)

Unlike the impunity laws that reproduce fear as a mechanism of social control, the trials send a clear message with concrete consequences: by prosecuting those responsible for human rights violations, the justice system rejects state repression and enables the emergence of new practices and attitudes by and towards the victims. The explicit – and implicit – prohibitions imposed by legal impunity are no longer officially supported. As a survivor from Tucumán said:

> We feel supported by the state policy now in place, and the military are no longer what they were back then, they've lost power and influence, so in most cases people begin to dare to speak out.
>
> (Int. 68, September 2012, Tucumán)

This was also made possible by the fact that several of the perpetrators who were still in power in the public administration were removed from their positions in order to allow for their prosecution. However, fear, built up over the years, does not disappear from one day to the next, and for some it may never do so altogether. When asked if he thought the trials were helping to dissipate the fear still prevailing in many sectors of society, particularly in Tucumán, the above interviewee replied as follows:

> I think people feel less afraid. Being heard by the justice system helps overcome fear. Overcoming fear does not mean not feeling it but, despite feeling it, going on to testify. I have some examples. A neighbour, whose house my dad looked after when they kidnapped me, is willing to testify now. However, another neighbour who I asked to tell what he had seen and heard the night of my kidnapping, said "no, please no." Despite the years, I saw the fear in his face.
>
> (Ibid.)

The persistence of certain levels of fear has multiple sources. Overcoming fear is a very slow and hard process, involving institutional, social and personal conditions. Changes in those conditions can help to dispel fear. While human rights trials have contributed to this, they are not sufficient. Trials are also long bureaucratic processes, which require time to yield results. Therefore, not all the perpetrators can be accused and arrested at once. Judicial investigations and trials can take many years in Argentina. Thus, while some of the accused are already detained or on trial, others still await trial in freedom and some even continue to hold positions in the security forces. This seriously affects the security of the victims participating in the trials. As explained in Chapter 5, one of the main witnesses in a trial in the city of La Plata, Jorge Julio López, was even made to "disappear" in 2006 after having identified a defendant as one of the men who had tortured him in 1976. The lack of progress in the investigation eleven years after López's disappearance is an alarming sign for human rights organisations.

This case left profound marks on many of the victims that have taken part in the trials. As stated by many interviewees:

> One still feels fear. Well, not fear, but we are aware of what happened to Julio López, who is still disappeared. [Besides,] other witnesses in several trials have suffered violence or been threatened. Then we are very aware of it.
>
> (Int. 62, September 2012, Buenos Aires)

> We know that these guys [the perpetrators] are still operating. Otherwise, Julio López wouldn't have been made to disappear.
>
> (Int. 63, September 2012, Buenos Aires)

Indeed, what happened to Julio López is not an isolated incident. Threats and intimidations of witnesses, human rights defenders, lawyers and even judges are commonplace (Nizkor 2013). There have been several cases of witnesses being attacked and even kidnapped. Many interviewees, not only in the city of La Plata – where López was made to disappear – but in nearly all the cities where the trials are taking place, have stated that they were threatened or that they heard of others being threatened. When asked about the threats she had received, a survivor and plaintiff in the trials in Buenos Aires stated:

Q: When did you receive threats, was it before or after the trial?
A: Before and after. (. . .) Someone called me at 3 a.m. and just breathed down the phone. And this year they left a message on my answer machine playing back the meeting I had had [with the lawyers] the day before.

(Int. 63, September 2012, Buenos Aires)

Similarly, another interviewee, a witness in the trials, stated:

> Fortunately, I didn't receive any threats, but there were some colleagues from [the organisation] HIJOS that did.
>
> (Int. 74, September 2012, La Plata)

Almost all the interviewees reported either having experienced threats themselves or having heard of others being threatened. Despite the witness protection programme set up by the national government, many witnesses and lawyers continue to experience intimidation, especially while hearings are being prepared (Telam 2014). These are also attempts to intimidate potential witnesses from testifying in other trials. Human rights organisations have repeatedly criticised the fact that no proper investigations are being conducted of those individuals who use intimidation and violence to obstruct the prosecutions. NGOs assume that those responsible for such threats have connections with state security forces, the secret service and security firms (CELS 2010, 21).

In turn, the fact that many of the accused have been released from prison even though their trials are still pending tends to increase the likelihood of encounters between victims and perpetrators, generating a form of social coincidence – which is typical of impunity – with one added feature: the fact that the perpetrators face legal charges. They are no longer untouchable. Against this background, the perpetrators intimidate both victims and their lawyers, so that the latter have also become subject to threats, acts of aggression and robberies. A lawyer in Santiago del Estero gave his experience:

> [I got] many calls saying "we know where your daughter is now," meaning that we were being followed, that they knew all our movements.
>
> (Int. 60, April 2011, Santiago del Estero)

The lawyer went on to explain that he felt defenceless and at risk when he ran into the accused, as they would see him as responsible for their future convictions:

> We bump into [the accused] in public spaces every day. (. . .) They are at liberty and they know, for example, that "there goes the little lawyer (. . .) who can get me a life sentence in a couple of months."
>
> (Ibid.)

Furthermore, the links between the accused and state or private security forces have still not been dismantled. The interviewees are well aware of these links and point to them as one of the main reasons for the threats surrounding the trials. An interviewee, who is acting as a plaintiff in the trials in Santiago del Estero, spoke about the robberies that took place at the offices of the human rights organisation of which he is a member:

Q: Have you suffered any attacks or threats?

A: Robberies, we had the computer stolen. After that incident, we asked for security because it was the third time we'd been burgled.

Q: The third time during the course of the trial or had it started before?

A: Before and after the trial. And we know where this comes from (. . .) It's from one of the accused, D'Amico,[1] an ex-Army major, (. . .) who was Secretary of Security under the administration of [former governor] Carlos Juárez and who, oddly enough, runs one of the largest security agencies in the province that is in charge of the security at the National University. And he has been released from prison pending trial.

(Int. 55, April 2011, Santiago del Estero)

Within this context, the interviewee noted the asymmetry between the accused and the victims and lawyers, describing the situation as one of "unequal social coexistence," where in many cases, such as that of D'Amico, the accused continue either intimidating or exercising power:

> We are faced with situations in which one of the accused [such as D'Amico] was a member of intelligence in the Army, and nowadays owns two private security agencies, that is, some sixty armed men, operating 24/7, as opposed to this little lawyer (. . .) who is on his own, unprotected, having a coffee in the same coffee store as this guy. Social co-existence in this city is unequal, (. . .) and we feel rather defenceless.
>
> (Int. 60, April 2011, Santiago del Estero)

Another interviewee, a plaintiff in the trials in Tucumán, stated that one of the accused continued to live opposite her house when the trials commenced and – knowing who she was – behaved in an intimidating manner:

> You come across them [the accused] all the time. (. . .) One of the accused lived opposite me until two weeks ago, (. . .) Now they've taken him to the prison in Villa Urquiza (. . .). The guy would stop in the street and stare at me; I've never felt anything so strongly as this guy's stare. Impunity is so widespread in this province that this man lived in a house given to him by the police, retired on a pension from the police and his son is a cop. The guy has been accused in [the trial for the crimes committed in the former CDC known as] *Jefatura* on charges of kidnapping, torture followed by death and homicide.
>
> (Int. 72, October 2012, Tucumán)

The sustained, defiant and harsh stare of the perpetrators has been described by several interviewees as one of the typical acts of intimidation that the perpetrators used as a sign of power every time they came across the victims in the street during the period of impunity. Thus, the incarceration of the perpetrators brings relief to the relatives of the disappeared and the survivors.

> It's a relief for me to know that the forty-two people accused [in this trial] are now in jail.
>
> (Ibid.)

As outlined in Chapter 5, although the national government created a nationwide programme for the protection of witnesses, it suffers from glaring deficiencies, such as an insufficient budget, poorly trained security personnel and a lack of coordination between national and provincial agencies in providing effective protection for witnesses (Borello 2010). Indeed, in many cases, when the interviewees were asked how they evaluated the witness protection programme in their towns, many of them answered ironically:

> What Witness Protection Programme? There isn't one.
>
> (Int. 55, April 2011, Santiago del Estero)

One of the main contradictions of the witness protection programme that has been highlighted by many interviewees is that the protection is afforded by members of the police, some of whom might be connected with the old repressive system. How can the witnesses feel protected under those circumstances? As explained by several interviewees in Santiago del Estero:

> The witnesses [at the trial] are under the protection of members of the provincial police that, in many cases, were designated and trained by Musa Azar, the main accused in all the human rights cases.
>
> (Int. 60, April 2011, Santiago del Estero)

> There was a group of police officers that were at your disposal but they offered no guarantees at all. [In the current trial] you bring a lawsuit against the police and you are protected by policemen.
>
> (Int. 55, April 2011, Santiago del Estero)

In this regard, many victims and attorneys have highlighted the need for a purge of those who were active during the military government and their removal from training the new generations of police officers. A survivor from Buenos Aires stated:

> [It is necessary] to clean up the security forces, purge all those forces. To remove all those who were active at the time of the dictatorship. They shouldn't teach [the new generations]. Because the new kids in the police think they are Rambo.
>
> (Int. 63, September 2012, Buenos Aires)

The actions of the security forces during the dictatorship and the continued presence of many agents in subsequent constitutional governments contribute to feelings of mistrust, fear and rejection that remain with the victims until today. However, while López's disappearance and the attacks and threats suffered by other witnesses send an intimidating message, in most cases such circumstances have not deterred the survivors and the relatives of the disappeared from taking part in the trials. In some cases, this even allowed them to summon the strength to go on in spite of all the difficulties. This is explained by an attorney of one of the plaintiffs who participated in the trial during which López was made to disappear:

Q: Did [López's disappearance] stop witnesses from giving testimony in other trials?

A: For many people that called into question whether it made sense to hold the trials, López's disappearance showed that it did. The ones on trial are not poor old men with no money and no power, as [the accused] Etchecolatz

> argued. These are guys that have a real power of action. Far from stopping people, López's disappearance generated more commitment.
>
> (Int. 17, March 2011, La Plata)

Similarly, other interviewees asserted that, in spite of these feelings of insecurity, they went on testifying and participating in the trials.

> We're not afraid and we assume the risk of what may happen to us. For many of these issues the state is still absent. (. . .) Judges don't fully understand that in the face of certain crimes, the accused cannot be at liberty whilst the trial is still pending. A way of protecting witnesses is to put those that committed genocide in prison.
>
> (Int. 60, April 2011, Santiago del Estero)

Many human rights organisations have demanded that those accused of crimes against humanity be held in preventive detention while their trials are pending in order to prevent them from going on intimidating witnesses and lawyers. Now, although many plaintiffs and witnesses have stated that they feel "defenceless" and "at risk," fear no longer deters them from acting and giving testimony. Nonetheless, most of them, especially in the provincial cities, have claimed that more support is needed not only from the national state, but also from the provincial authorities.

7.1.1 Facing fear in court

The struggle against fear takes place inside and outside the courtroom. The face-to-face encounter with perpetrators requires a great deal of courage from the survivors who testify. Indeed, several interviewees have said that they felt intimidated while providing testimony. For instance, a survivor and witness from the city of Buenos Aires explained how one of the accused showed her with hand gestures that he would break her neck if she went on talking (Int. 63). Another plaintiff also revealed the acts of intimidations carried out by another of the accused in the trials for the crimes committed in the ex-CDC ESMA and the way judges failed to intervene:

> It was very shocking to see one of the accused, Alfredo Astiz, at the trial holding a book titled *Volver a matar* ["To kill again"] (. . .). That made me angry with the court. Why didn't they take the book away from him? That was a provocation, because he showed it to all of us who were in the courtroom.
>
> (Int. 62, September 2012, Buenos Aires)

This kind of behaviour is often threatening for the witnesses and, in many cases, judges and prosecutors fail to take appropriate measures to stop it. These constant intimidations serve as a symbol of power while at the same time indicate that a certain level of impunity is still prevalent in court. The perpetrators seem to forget that their power is not the same as in the past and that they are now facing charges. Thus, while providing testimony before one's own torturer is a situation of intense emotional stress and anguish, in many cases, it has also been shown to be a means of empowerment. A survivor who has testified in several cases explained her experience of overcoming fear in the following way:

> [When I went in to testify] I did not look at them [the accused], I was really scared. During my testimony, I looked at the floor. I said to myself: "I'm not going to look at them" (. . .). Suddenly, I don't know why, or at what point exactly during my testimony, I thought, "Why am I not looking at them? If I'm testifying and they're handcuffed, why should I do them the favour of showing that I can't look at them, that I'm afraid?" And then I took courage (. . .) and I started to look at them and point to them (. . .) and I finally managed to name them and talk to them and look at them without fear (. . .) I said with gestures: "you see, I'm also looking at you."
>
> (Int. 63, September 2012, Buenos Aires)

The ability to defy or return the perpetrators' intimidating stares is an act of courage and empowerment. As the interviewee explained the difficulty yet importance for her to be able to face her fear of the perpetrators (her torturers), other survivors and relatives of disappeared people also mentioned that it was very important for them to be able to look the repressors in the eyes and accuse them publicly in court. This process of overcoming fear inside the court is extremely challenging for most of the victims, but also a reparative experience for many of them. As the interviewee explains, being able to look directly in the eyes of those who had tortured her and wanted her to remain submissive reflects an act of resistance and empowerment. However, the trials do not bring about these effects overnight; it is rather a gradual process. The hearings represent new social and institutional spaces in which the victims can talk and be heard even as they confront their fears. Previously unattainable spaces can now become areas disputed by the victims. As a plaintiff from Buenos Aires stated:

> There were people who [in the past] did not testify because they were afraid and now they can, because the conditions are different if still not ideal.
>
> (Int. 65, October 2012, Buenos Aires)

While, as the interviewees emphasise, the context is not "ideal" – and it will probably never be – it represents a break away from the previous context. Therefore, conducting human rights trials where previously terror and impunity were the norm is a sign of change. In this context, fear wanes as a consequence of the collective practices of solidarity that take place in the trials. As Pilar Calveiro (2015,

104) states: fear decreases with company. The restoration of support bonds plays a key role in controlling fear. Many interviewees have stressed the importance of being accompanied by their families and friends when they went to testify. A witness, whose parents are disappeared, highlighted how important it was for him to be accompanied by his relatives and friends on the day he gave testimony and stressed the close attention everyone paid to his statement:

> It wouldn't have been the same if [the courtroom] had been empty. One of the things a friend told me was that everyone was very attentive to what I was saying, there was total silence in the room.
>
> (Int. 74, September 2012, La Plata)

In turn, other interviewees also stated that the support of their families and friends at the hearings gave them the strength to face the accused, which in many cases meant seeing them again for the first time after enduring their tortures in the CDCs:

> [The day of my testimony] I was with my family and friends, and the others [the accused] were there, too. I was with my people. I could see my people behind the glass, my friends, my husband, my youngest daughter, my son-in-law, my lawyers. I looked at my husband and daughter so as to have their support when I could not look at the repressors. But then I managed to look at them.
>
> (Int. 63, September 2012, Buenos Aires)

The presence of relatives, friends and colleagues during testimony operates as an all-important network of support for the witnesses, and many interviewees have described such presence as a key factor in overcoming fear and dealing with the exposure of giving testimony at trial. While fear is reinforced by loneliness and isolation, it is diminished by the support of others. The feeling of collective action in the trials operates as an important mechanism of empowerment. In this vein, a plaintiff from La Plata stated that, in his opinion, fear increases when the links with human rights organisations are weaker:

> [P]robably the ones who were most afraid were those who had no daily contact with human rights groups and the trials.
>
> (Int. 74, September 2012, La Plata)

Breaking isolation helps counter fear. Courage undoubtedly seems to be as contagious as fear itself; it is transmitted from one person to another (Calveiro 2015, 104). The collective spirit of the trials, in which the victims feel accompanied by others, is also part of the reparative effect of these processes. An interviewee, a member of HIJOS organisation in Buenos Aires, recounted how fellow members of the organisation were glad when in 2010 a sentence was handed down in the case of his mother's disappearance:

> My mates were really moved. I feel that my mum's case, that my story was also theirs (. . .). They took this story as if it were their own. And they were more excited than me the day when the sentence was handed down. To arrive [at the sentence] like this, to understand that this is a collective fight, this was what really had a restorative effect, what really moved me.
>
> (Int. 15, April 2011, Buenos Aires)

7.2 Breaking the silence inside and outside of court

Societal silence is a product of terror and fear as well as of the complicity of those who support those regimes. When fear is countered, silence begins to be gradually broken. State terror led to social silence and impunity contributed to its reproduction over time. On the contrary, trials may create new institutional conditions, which make it possible for the victims to break that silence. Many interviewees have perceived this, especially in the more conservative northern provinces of the country. When asked whether the trials in Santiago del Estero were a turning point in the city, an ex-political prisoner, also a plaintiff in the trials, answered:

> Absolutely (. . .). Where do I see it? They've taken off all the gags, people can now name something that was shrouded in silence or not said at all. We can name people. We can name events, name things (. . .), previously everything was silenced.
>
> (Int. 53, April 2011, Santiago del Estero)

If the impunity laws "silenced," as discussed in Chapter 4, the current trials create an institutional and social framework that invites the victims to speak, to "*take off all the gags*," both in and out of court. Needless to say, this is a slow process, especially in the cities in the north of the country, where the breaking of silence has taken longer than in other urban centres. As explained by a human rights activist from Tucumán:

A: The society in Tucumán was gripped by authoritarianism and fear. It is only now that people approach you shyly and whisper: "I was also kept in a clandestine centre."

Q: Do you think the trials have something to do with that?

A: Sure, I think they do have something to do with the fact that people have started to speak.

(Int. 42, April 2011, Tucumán)

The fact that many victims "have started to speak" has also resulted in the uncovering of past crimes in a quantitative and qualitative sense. From a quantitative standpoint, victims that had never brought charges or testified before filed their own criminal complaints for the first time. This was particularly the case in the northern provinces of Córdoba, Tucumán and Santiago del Estero and reveals the changes in the social, political and legal context effected by the trials. Officially acknowledging the crimes rather than ignoring them enables the victims to report them, after years of silence. Many interviewees from those provinces gave an account of this process. A plaintiff's attorney explained:

> Many people approached us during the trial, there are new cases of people from Santiago del Estero who had disappeared that had never been reported before. (. . .) Sixteen new cases have now appeared that had never been reported before. (. . .) Many people from outside the province and from the province itself [have appeared] and said: "I was detained."
>
> (Int. 60, April 2011, Santiago del Estero)

Prosecutors and judges have also mentioned that new complaints have been filed in the course of the current trials. As explained by one of the judges presiding over the trials in Tucumán:

> What I can see is that there are more and more requests for investigation (. . .) made by people who report that they were abducted [and] (. . .) tortured. I'm very surprised. We are now in 2011. (. . .) I'd say that every month [I get] two or three new complaints. (. . .) I think there's still a lot to investigate.
>
> (Int. 49, April 2011, Tucumán)

A human rights activist from Tucumán capital city also pointed out:

> Unexpected witnesses began to appear [in the trials] (. . .) [with] invaluable testimonies.
>
> (Int. 42, April 2011, Tucumán)

Similarly, a witness from the same province stated:

> The amount of testimonies appearing in the trials is impressive. People have a huge need to speak about what they have experienced and suffered. So many stories that were not known.
>
> (Int. 68, September 2012, Tucumán)

Especially in the small towns in the north of Argentina where everyone knows each other, the co-existence of victims and former members of the dictatorship was an everyday event that created a threatening and intimidating atmosphere. People would not dare to speak out and report criminal acts. But once the perpetrators are sent to prison, fear diminishes and the victims begin to feel a certain level of freedom to speak. The trials have laid the foundations for a new social openness towards the victims and their unheard stories. The emergence of new legal and institutional conditions has enabled these new narratives. The court, as a public state-sponsored space, gives the victims' accounts a legitimacy that impunity had taken away, and disseminates them more broadly. Legitimacy contributes to decreasing stigmatisation. The fact that new victim-witnesses have begun to speak has had significant reparative consequences for themselves and for those who can find out what happened to their loved ones. Being able to tell the truth turns survivors from objects into subjects (Mertus 2000, 149; Sieder 2003, 228).

In addition, the breaking of silence not only leads to an increase in the amount of new information provided by new testimonies but also, as I show in the next section, the contents of those testimonies have become more and more comprehensive. Throughout Argentina's struggle for truth and justice (expressed in the CONADEP, the Juntas Trial, the "Truth Trials," trials held abroad, and especially the recent re-opening of criminal prosecutions) it is possible to see how the testimonies of survivors and even relatives of disappeared people have evolved. In the current trials, the victims dare to expand their statements, thus making possible the public discussion of aspects of state repression which were either taboo or ignored in previous testimonies. Against this background, silenced topics such as the political militancy of the disappeared and survivors as well as the sexualised violence suffered by many victims in the CDCs have gradually started to acquire great relevance in court. This possibility of addressing previously denied or tabooed events has been considered by many surviving victims a crucial element of the reparative process, though not free of difficulties.

7.2.1 Taboo 1: denouncing sexualised violence

Sexual abuses were systematically committed against male and female detainees in the CDCs during the Argentine dictatorship. While these crimes were prosecutable in the 1990s since they were not included in the amnesty laws, no denunciations were presented to the courts. However, as the trials advance over the years, this state of affairs has seen a gradual change. As part of their testimony, many women who had been victims of sexualised violence during the dictatorship began to tell their stories for the first time. As a matter of fact, sexualised violence had already been harshly exposed in the first oral trial held after the repeal of the amnesty laws in 2005, known as the "Hlaczik/Poblete case." As Balardini, Oberlin and Sobredo (2011, 136) explain, during that trial the cruelty of the abuse to which detainees were submitted came as a surprise, especially because the acts of sexualised violence also involved male detainees. According to the survivors, degrading practices included enforced homosexual relations between cell mates and rape by repressors at the CDCs.

Before the current prosecutions, cases of sexualised violence in particular were shrouded in silence not only in society but also within the victims' family ambit. As stated by a survivor and witness in a trial in the province of Buenos Aires: "I was only recently able to say it out loud. I had never put it into words before. We didn't tell our families because we didn't want to upset them" (quoted in Balardini, Oberlin and Sobredo 2011, 111). Indeed, the survivors have consistently played down the violence they personally suffered during their captivity in front of their partners, relatives and friends. However, the trials have started to provide the victims with a space for the public denunciation of these crimes and for the communication of such tabooed experiences of violence in their own families. In a trial in Santiago del Estero, a plaintiff's lawyer referred to testimony that shocked her:

> In a recent trial, one of the witnesses recounted the story of his wife, who had committed suicide. He said [at the trial] that his partner had been raped [during captivity under the dictatorship]. He had never spoken about it before. Their daughter was there and she didn't know about it. (. . .) And it was hard to hear him say: "I apologise to my daughter, who doesn't know about this, but I have to say it so that everyone knows what these people did to us." (. . .) His wife was the mother of his four children.
>
> (Int. 57, April 2011, Santiago del Estero)

In many cases the family was told nothing; in others, it was tacit knowledge that was never put into words. Another interviewee who gave testimony at the trial about the rape she endured in prison narrated her experience with her family:

> My son knew. And so did my mother, but we didn't speak about it. My sister didn't speak to me about it either, she found it very hard.
>
> (Int. 52, April 2011, Santiago del Estero)

The court presents itself as a legitimate public space in which the witnesses not only tell their stories to the judges but also to and for their own families. This in itself is an important and reparative event.

The courage to give testimony about sexualised violence is reflective of a change in the victims' perceptions of the social and institutional conditions. These conditions provide the victims with a certain level of trust or safety that makes it possible for them to speak about such experiences. The trials – which operate as a means of communication – convey a message-mandate to society, including the victims, about what can and cannot be said. Thus, the victims' testimony in court, along with the judges' decisions to consider rape as a crime against humanity, is slowly giving rise to a process of delegitimisation and denunciation of this type of violence. The gradual breakdown of silence in this respect has also triggered a domino effect, as more and more women report these cases in court and give testimony about them (Vassallo 2016, 95). In this sense, the justice system can also operate as a state tool that either perpetuates or challenges unequal gendered structures of power in society.

However, while there has been significant progress in regard to the prosecution of sexualised violence, many different obstacles must also be overcome, such as the sexist and discriminatory attitude of the judiciary, the lack of sensitivity of judicial officers and the fact that sexualised crimes are still offences for which charges can only be brought by the victims (Balardini, Oberlin and Sobredo 2011, 196–200). This conceptualisation of sexualised violence as a private act which only concerns the victim, in contrast to other offences such as torture or murder, denies the political and disciplining character of this kind of violence, especially – though not only – when it was committed in contexts of state repression. In addition, by putting all the responsibility for reporting the crime on the victims, the legal system may reinforce their feelings of isolation and fear.

The judicial system and its members – who in Argentina usually belong to upper-class and conservative sectors, virtually feudal in some provinces – is still permeated by strong traditional moral values, patriarchal structures and regulations which undermine the prosecution of sexualised violence, thus hindering the reparative potential that the legal treatment of these cases may have for the victims and society. Indeed, and although it has been proven that rape was a systematic practice in the majority of the CDCs in Argentina, there were only sixteen convictions for sexualised violence between 2006 and 2016, which compared to the total of 174 judgments passed in that period represents a small percentage (see Figure 7.1). In the early years of the trials, the number of court decisions addressing sexualised violence was deemed minimal. Cases of sexualised abuse and rape accounted for only 0.5 per cent of the offences warranting a conviction

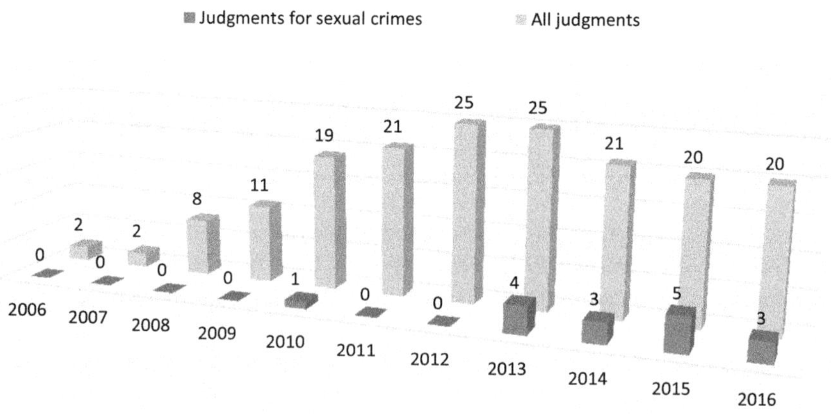

Figure 7.1 Judgments for sexual crimes in contrast to total judgments 2006–2016

Source: Table prepared with information provided by reports of the Office of Crimes against Humanity (2016; 2015a, 2015b).

between 2006 and 2011. Until then only one decision out of sixty-three had included a conviction for sexual abuse and rape (CELS 2012, 46).

Although there has been a gradual increase in the number of convictions for sexualised crimes between 2013 and 2016, this is a relatively small figure compared with the total number of convictions per year. While the victims' silence is a reason for this, it is not the only one. Especially in the initial years of the prosecutions, the courts regarded cases of rape as isolated cases, rather than as the systematic practice it actually was (Balardini, Oberlin and Sobredo 2011). In contrast to torture, sexualised crimes were not initially categorised by the courts as crimes against humanity, which are not subject to the statutes of limitations. Instead, sexualised violence was considered as a separate crime subject to a thirty-year limitations period (Carbajal 2011). These criteria are not applied when it comes to prosecuting torture. Several courts have held that captivity in a CDC implied torture. Another reason for the few convictions for rape is that many judges, though decreasingly, include this crime within the definition of torture, thus not treating it as an independent offence (Balardini, Oberlin and Sobredo 2011, 137). This leads to the invisibility of sexualised violence, which was used to discipline and demean, and to its going unpunished.

The manner in which the courts address sexualised violence can prompt or inhibit testimony about this crime in the future. As shown in other contexts in which trials were held, such as the ICTY and Sierra Leone, excluding the question of sexualised violence can reinforce silence and victimise women once again (Mertus 2004, Staggs Kelsall and Stepakoff 2007, Buckley-Zistel 2013). This can be very damaging to the victims given that, when they dare to speak out, the judicial system does not afford them proper treatment and often even ignores their testimony. A survivor from Santiago del Estero narrated her experience in court and the judge's response when she gave testimony in the trials:

> To me, rape was the most difficult issue to speak about, because it's a topic that's only now coming out (. . .) I was the first one here who dared to speak about it in public (. . .) and they didn't even take it into account when asking questions, that's an issue they wouldn't speak about. When I said "I was raped," (. . .) the judges never asked me any questions.
>
> (Int. 52, April 2011, Santiago del Estero)

Giving no value to the victim's testimony as a key piece of evidence of the rape is perhaps a paradigmatic example of how gender inequality relations are entrenched in the judiciary. When the courts neglect crimes of sexualised violence, this not only leads to their impunity, but also entails that rape victims become victims for a second time: the first time as a victim of the crime, the second time as a victim of a judicial system that shows itself incapable of action. Criminal trials may lead to a *secondary traumatisation* of the victims. Sabine Rupp (2003) defines *secondary traumatisation* as damage that occurs not at the hands of the immediate perpetrator of sexualised violence, but indirectly through the behaviour or actions of the occupational groups involved, persons in contact with the victims, or state institutions and agencies, in our case, the judicial system. As explained by a plaintiff's lawyer from Córdoba, this re-victimisation is not unique to these specific human rights trials, but is also present in cases of sexualised violence in the private sphere:

> It is a common occurrence with this type of crime. This happens not only within the framework of [the trials of] state terror but also with the law in general. Many women refuse to speak about it because telling the prosecutor about the experience results in re-victimisation. Prosecutors or the officials under their charge are not often tactful enough to realise who they are dealing with and how traumatic the event has been for the victim.
>
> (Int. 37, March 2011, Córdoba)

Judges, prosecutors and even lawyers often lack the psychological training to deal with these sensitive cases, which leads to potentially highly unpleasant and embarrassing situations for the victims at the hearings. The mistreatment of surviving victims of sexualised violence only reproduces silence and precludes them from giving testimony. Proof of this lies in the fact that the issue is still covered in silence, albeit to a lesser extent. This is confirmed by an interviewee from Santiago del Estero who knows about other cases of rape besides her own:

> I think there were many more cases of rape here in Santiago. Women don't dare to speak about it.
>
> (Int. 52, April 2011, Santiago del Estero)

While these are persistent problems in the prosecution and delegitimisation of these crimes, the mere fact that they are on trial makes them visible, which was not the case during the previous impunity period. In this sense, the few convictions for rape emerging from these trials have already had a positive impact on creating a public debate about sexual abuses that had not been addressed before. This can be seen in the way sexualised violence during the dictatorship has become an increasingly discussed topic in newspaper articles, NGO reports and books published over the past year based on the evidence given by witnesses in the trials. Sexual abuse has been a taboo subject for the past forty years, and remains so when its targets were men. This is still a pending issue which involves a more generalised taboo and not one specific to the Argentine courts.

7.2.2 Taboo 2: testifying on political militancy

Testimony in court gives public access to information about facts and crimes committed by the state and to the victims' voices. Valuing the survivors' voice as victim–witnesses and as social and political actors during the period of repression seems to be one of the most significant consequences of the trials in Argentina.

Survivors had in the post-Junta years been marginalised and stigmatised. As shown in Chapters 3 and 4, survivors were stigmatised because of their political activism – that is, because they belonged to armed political or social groups, trade unions, student movements and all those groups considered as "dangerous" by the military. During the criminal trial against the military Juntas in the 1980s and even later, most survivors kept their stories of militancy to themselves. In contrast, victim-witnesses in the current trials have tended to speak more willingly and in greater detail about their political activities. As social scientist Ana Longoni explains, even though the survivors have testified on different occasions, such as at CONADEP, in the Juntas Trial, and in international forums as well, the social audibility of survivors has been significantly low in the past three decades (Longoni 2007, 23). Both the experience of prior political activism and the survival of state terrorism have in many cases resulted in distrust, if not in the stigmatisation and isolation of the survivors. When the interviewees spoke about their experience of giving testimony in the current trials, they could not avoid comparing it with their more restricted contributions in the Juntas Trial in 1984 and 1985. The difference between testimony then and now has been highlighted by many interviewees. A survivor and witness in the current trials in Buenos Aires, who also gave testimony in the Juntas Trial, explained how the focus of testimony has shifted: at the beginning of the 1980s testimony was limited to a narrative of torture, to what some labelled "the horror show" (Kordon 1997), as stated by this witness:

> The testimonies of witnesses [in the Juntas Trial] were pouring in and they mainly concerned accounts of terror, physical torture, how children had been stolen, the torments inflicted upon the survivors and the disappeared. It is different now.
>
> (Int. 7, March 2011, Buenos Aires)

The "difference" in the trials now is that testimony can be amplified, framing the tortures and crimes that victims experienced in a historical and political context. Similarly, a former political prisoner from Santiago del Estero, also a witness in the trials, made the following comparison:

> There are some people [in the current trials] that, by way of introduction, name the organisation to which they belonged when they were detained. This would never have happened in the Juntas Trial, because until then, the *compañeros* that gave testimony denied their involvement in any type of [political and social] organisation.
>
> (Int. 53, April 2011, Santiago del Estero)

It is of critical importance for the surviving victims to be able to narrate and reclaim in court their previously stigmatised social and political activism and/or militancy, given that such militancy was precisely the reason why they and their comrades were abducted and made to disappear. Another interviewee, a survivor from Buenos Aires, explained the significance of this narrative in the following terms:

> This issue has become significant with the trials. We want to reclaim [our] militancy. Those of us who were militants and are survivors want to reclaim above all the militancy of those *compañeros* that are disappeared. (. . .) That is also a big difference [with the Juntas Trial]. Because (. . .) we want to reclaim those *compañeros* that are disappeared and [that] were not playing games (. . .). A political group was persecuted here with the goal (. . .) of dismantling political and social organisations to implement the neoliberal model. So, if we don't reclaim militancy, we fail to understand the aim of the dictatorship, why it happened.
>
> (Int. 7, March 2011, Buenos Aires)

Many interviewees expressed their hopes that their testimony would create a public record that might help to pursue justice for their specific cases and at the same time reach the entire society. The inclusion of the political militancy of the survivors and disappeared persons and their role as political opposition during the repression period in that official court record of the past is crucial as it helps to reconstruct and understand the reasons underlying state violence. On the contrary, the depoliticisation of victims leads to the creation of a decontextualised narrative of the dictatorship's crimes as merely inhuman or perverse acts hiding their political and economic goals for which human rights violations were merely a means. In this regard, a survivor from Rosario asserted:

> I think that these trials are much more positive and significant [than the Juntas Trial]. When they persecuted and made our *compañeros* disappear, it wasn't only people they were disappearing or erasing, but the political projects or the ideologies behind them. (. . .) that is what they were trying to make disappear. If our disappeared *compañeros* are deprived of their political and ideological identity, I feel we're making them disappear once again. For this reason, I think it's very important to highlight the fact that [the disappeared] were militants in political organisations and had political and ideological projects for the construction of a society different from the one existing back then.
>
> (Int. 28, March 2011, Rosario)

The fact that people who were part of resistance movements no longer have to hide their identities as militants is crucial to many of them. Victims of human rights violations are not abstract and generalisable figures but are the result of historical and political processes. As psychologist Elina Aguiar states, the lives of the disappeared had a social and political meaning. Their identity cannot be restored if they cannot recover their agency as social and political actors, with their political projects, utopias, successes and failures (Aguiar 1993, 13).

As the trials progress, more and more witnesses and victims make reference to political militancy and affiliation. As lawyer Carolina Varsky explains, "some victims' relatives wished to mention that the disappeared person had been a political militant, others merely mentioned their 'base work' or visits to '*villas*' (slums)" (2011, 41). While some are open about their past as *Montoneros*, others instead refer to local or university-based activism. The survivors' feeling that they can now speak publicly about their own political commitments and that of their disappeared fellows has a reparative effect. This new freedom is the result of a long and gradual social struggle of the human rights movement that finally found some echo in the judicial system. In this sense, several survivors have pointed out the role of the state in this process of – partial and gradual – destigmatisation of the survivors:

> It was a years-long process until I could say: "I was a militant in *Montoneros*." (. . .). It was the result of the policies implemented by the state.
>
> (Int. 7, March 2011, Buenos Aires)

The fact that the state is no longer an accomplice in the stigmatisation of political militancy fosters this process of reparation. By making it possible to give an account of the militancy of the disappeared, the trials call into question the model of the "ideal victim," that is, a passive and "innocent" victim who is depoliticised and pure, as often portrayed in the literature (Bouris 2007; Bonacker, Oettler and Safferling 2013). An individual's political activities cannot mitigate his or her victimisation by the state. Political activism and opposition (individual, groups and political parties etc.) are one of the essential components of a well-functioning democracy. By acknowledging and not criminalising the previous political militancy of the witnesses, the trials recognise that, on the one hand, opposition is not a legitimate reason for criminalisation and, on the other hand, that victimisation refers to the acts carried out by the perpetrator rather than to those of the victim. Thus, the inclusion in testimony of the political militancy of the disappeared helps to clarify the political reasons underlying their murders. In fact, it becomes obvious that those persons were not victimised despite their political activism but *because of* it, as has been held by several courts (e.g. Labolita Judgment 2009, 214; Jefatura Judgment 2010, 376–382). According to these judgments, in no way can the political contextualisation of human rights violations minimise or justify the crimes committed.

The possibility of discussing the victims' previous militancy permits an understanding not only of the historical context, but also of today's relations of power in society and the state. Depending on the regional and political context, the current trials allow different narratives of the past. Unlike the Juntas Trial, the current trials are characterised by the depth with which the victims' experiences are explored; more structured testimonies give way to an expanded concept of testimony. Testimony need no longer be confined to an account of torture but can cover other aspects such as the political biography of the disappeared and survivors, including their political militancy, without fear of being stigmatised or criminalised. This change in testimonial narrative has been underscored by many of the interviewees, and it is part of the reparative nature of these trials for the victims. In this regard, several survivors have mentioned that an important factor that also influenced the contents of their testimonies was the treatment afforded to them by the court, which – compared with that of the Juntas Trial in the 1980s – was much more respectful. A survivor and witness in both trials described the treatment in the current trials in the following terms:

> [The current trials give you] (. . .) that feeling of respect and [you feel] that you were not the guilty party, which is how I felt in the Juntas Trial.
>
> (Int. 65, September 2012, Buenos Aires)

However, despite the empathy and respect shown by judges and prosecutors, much remains to be done. Some interviewees have stressed the need to improve the training of the judiciary personnel in order to make it more sensitive to the victims' feelings. Many witnesses have pointed to the insensitiveness of the judiciary staff – well known for its impersonal and distant bureaucratic attitude – and stated that they felt very anxious before giving testimony. But in spite of these shortcomings, when compared with the Juntas Trial, the current prosecutions are seen as a much more victim-centred judicial process.

7.2.3 The other face of testimony

While it is worth acknowledging the reparatory aspects of truth-telling in testimony, breaking the silence in court cannot be compared to a therapeutic effect. Indeed, many scholars have asserted that an adversarial judicial setting makes therapeutic storytelling impossible and that there is always a risk of retraumatisation (Minow 1998; Hayner 2002). This is a sensitive issue in the current prosecutions, especially in those cases in which the survivors have to repeat their testimony in different trials. While empowering, giving testimony can also be very painful for survivors since it means having to remember their experiences of captivity and torture again and again:

> [When you give testimony] you have to sit there again [in the courtroom], go over the pain and memories. It is not easy for us to sit there and tell the whole story. (. . .) I'm back in the concentration camp again when I give testimony. In order to remember I [must] see myself in the camp: I see the hall, I see the "*quirofano*" (*operation room*[2]), the execution wall, the bathroom, the cell, I remember everything, you walk through the CDC to remember.
>
> (Int. 63, September 2012, Buenos Aires)

The pain reappears when survivors relive their experiences through their testimony (Beckerman 2010). Thus, the repetition of testimony becomes exhausting for them.[3] In addition, and as briefly explained in Chapter 6, the survivors experience great pressure and are burdened with the responsibility of not forgetting any details about what they saw when they were in captivity. Many of them fear that forgetting an important piece of evidence can have an impact on the court's decision.

In recognition of these risks, all the survivors interviewed referred to the feelings of reparation they had and also to the pain of testifying. In this sense, asserting that the trials provide feelings of reparation and relief is not the same as suggesting that the trauma is automatically overcome through them. Reparation and empowerment are not understood here as therapeutic rehabilitation. That is not the purpose of the judicial system. To allocate that function of healing trauma would be to expect too much of the trials. There are significant differences between truth-telling between a therapist and a patient in a controlled clinical setting and public truth-telling in the aftermath of mass violence (Mendeloff 2004, 365).

Against this background, it is important to acknowledge that giving testimony in court may lead to re-victimisation and to deepen the survivors' wounds. Many scholars working on international and hybrid tribunals critically point out that the dynamic and legal requirements of trials do not permit witnesses to tell their stories, and tend to silence and retraumatise survivors rather than relieve them (Hayner 2002; Dembour and Haslam 2004; Mertus 2004; Staggs Kelsall and Shanee Stepakoff 2007). While these observations are reflective of the risks and difficulties posed by the trials, they should not be generalised to all cases. As shown above, without denying the legal constraints that circumscribe the trials, the Argentine experience shows that progress has been made towards other forms of testimony in judicial inquiries which open reparative possibilities for the victims. For this to happen, a sensitive and respectful victim-centred perspective of the judiciary staff is essential.

To conclude, this chapter has shown how the new judicial conditions, including the incarceration of perpetrators and an increased openness towards more comprehensive testimony, have begun to enable the emergence of new attitudes and practices on the part of the victims. I address in what follows the social effects of the trials, which reach not only the victims but also other segments of society. For such purpose, I examine in Chapter 8 the social and institutional repercussions of the prosecutions on the victims' local contexts, in which they seem to encounter new attitudes of respect and inclusion due to their participation in the trials.

Notes

1 Jorge Alberto D'Amico was accused and convicted of crimes committed during the period of state terrorism both in Santiago del Estero and Tucumán (Poder Judicial de la Nación 2014).

2 *Quirofano* was a euphemism used by the military to refer to the torture room.

3 For more details on the psychological implications and pressure for victims when providing testimony in the trials, see the work of psychologist Silvina Beckerman (2010).

Chapter 8

The restorative effects of trials on the victims' social context

Whereas Chapters 6 and 7 looked at how the trials have gradually contributed to civic and personal reparation by dissipating fear, breaking the silence among the victims, and allowing access to new information on the past, this chapter explores the effects of human rights trials on the victims' social context arising from their being recognised as victims in the trials. The trials have made the victims visible and paved the way for new and more respectful and inclusive forms of treatment towards them.

As briefly outlined in Chapter 1, the "restorative versus retributive justice debate" calls into question the reparative function of criminal trials by claiming that they ignore the victims' needs and that there are greater benefits in other justice alternatives which exclude the punishment of perpetrators. However, domestic prosecutions dealing with human rights violations can expand the traditional notion of retributive justice and incorporate restorative elements. In fact, as this chapter shows, when judging human rights violations in Argentina, criminal justice shares many common grounds with restorative initiatives, blurring the boundaries between restorative and retributive justice.

Thus, in what follows I examine how human rights trials, when properly held, can have not only a reparative but also a restorative function. The trials have the potential to transform, at least partially, the social and institutional local context of the victims: the public and official establishment of responsibilities sends an all-important message not only to the victims but also to society. This in turn generates different responses from society at the local level and can modify social perceptions and attitudes towards the survivors and the relatives of the disappeared. With higher intensity in some contexts than in others, the trials fulfil a restorative function by causing a major social impact on the communities in which the victims are immersed. This translates, for example, into the restoration of social bonds, social acknowledgment and inclusion in new social and public spaces.

This chapter is divided into five sections. In Section 1, I analyse the notion of restorative justice as a possible function of domestic human rights prosecutions. In doing so, I also discuss the "restorative–retributive justice debate." In Section 2, I draw on some of the theoretical approaches introduced in Chapter 1 in order to explain the social scope of the trials, which goes beyond the victims themselves to affect their social contexts and relationships. For this purpose, I also provide an overview of the particular features of prosecutions in Argentina, which contribute to amplifying their impact at the local level. In Section 3, I discuss specific changes in local community attitudes towards the survivors and the relatives of the disappeared, both during and after the trials held in their cities. In Section 4, I discuss how this change in attitudes is accompanied by a decrease in public support for perpetrators. Finally, I analyse the advances and limits of what I call "a social framework of reparation," that is, the specific legal, social and political conditions which contribute to the redress of victims of mass human rights violations.

8.1 Trials as restorative justice

The findings in this study reveal that, along with civic and personal reparation, domestic human rights trials have the potential to produce crucial restorative effects for survivors and relatives of disappeared persons. Restorative justice is defined in the literature as a form of justice aiming to repair the harm done not only to the direct victims but also to their communities. In this sense, it is usually described as "relational," since it seeks to address and restore the harm that violence caused to social relationships (Zehr 1990; Walgrave 2003; McCold, Llewellyn and Van Ness 2007; Laplante 2014). As shown in the previous chapters, through state terror and impunity many survivors, ex-political prisoners and relatives of disappeared people experienced a rupture with social and even family relations. Many in their social contexts ignored, stigmatised and isolated them. As described by many of the interviewees, both they and the crimes committed against them had become socially invisible. Against this background, human rights prosecutions can have broader effects that go beyond the individual victims involved in the legal processes as plaintiffs or witnesses. Because trials in Argentina involve oral and public hearings, with space for storytelling, they allow the presence of the public and the media, having an impact on other sectors of society, with significant effects on the victims' everyday lives.

Like restorative justice initiatives, criminal justice can also acquire specific modalities with restorative effects. Human rights trials in Argentina have distinctive features that move beyond the accusatorial system to include other aspects that contribute to the redress of victims, although this may vary from context to context. However, much of the literature on restorative justice in the "restorative versus retributive justice debate" often questions whether criminal justice can harbour a reparative potential for victims. An overview of this discussion is outlined below.

8.1.1 The restorative versus retributive justice debate

The idea of restorative justice as opposed to that of retributive justice has been the subject of debate in the human rights literature since the 1990s (Zehr 1990; Daly 2000; McElrea 2013; Clamps 2014). A pioneering and influential text on this dichotomy in that period was Howard Zehr's "*Changing Lens: A New Focus for Crime and Justice.*" Zehr's work contrasted restorative and retributive views of accountability by emphasising the defects of the latter. Indeed, most advocates of restorative justice are highly critical of retributive justice. They argue that criminal justice fails to achieve any of its professed objectives (rehabilitation, deterrence and inclusion) in a satisfactory manner (Parent 2010, 282; Clamp 2014, 16). They mainly understand retributive justice as the mere punishment of perpetrators, through a process of judging guilt and imposing penalties commensurate with the nature of the crime, leaving victims' interests and needs aside (Sherman and Strang 2007). Although these arguments might be adequate when applied to the regular criminal system for minor offences, they present a very limited view of criminal trials when applied to human rights violations.

Restorative justice, by contrast, is regarded as an alternative form of justice – which can take place within or outside the formal court system – that excludes punishment for perpetrators and envisages a wider range of initiatives such as public apologies, meetings between victims and perpetrators,[1] and truth and reconciliation commissions. Its main focus, according to its advocates, is on the notion of reconciliation and reparation for the harm done to the victim and to society (McElrea 2013, 93–94; Sherman and Strang 2007, 13). Due to the broad aims and wide range of forms that restorative justice can take, there is no agreed definition of what kind of justice this is (Clamp 2014). Thus, almost all forms of traditional and alternative justice initiatives that exclude judicial sanctions could be considered as restorative justice.

Advocates of restorative justice often overlook the fact that retributive accountability can also incorporate new elements which reinforce its reparative function. The denial of this diversity within criminal justice results in a highly stereotyped conceptualisation of the retributive approach. Table 8.1 shows the habitual contrasts between restorative and retributive justice made by advocates of restorative justice. They point out the following aspects:

Table 8.1 Assumed contrasts between retributive and restorative justice

	Retributive justice	*Restorative justice*
1	The goal of the process is to punish perpetrators	The goal of the process is to offer reparation to victims and the affected community
2	It addresses individual and personal damage	It addresses the harm done to social relationships ("relational perspective")
3	Victims are peripheral to or excluded from the process	Victims are central to the process
4	Little incentive for offenders to speak. Truth is often suppressed	Offenders are more prone to speaking and confessing their crimes. Truth is highly valued
5	Two-party system: the process is characterised by adversarial relationships among the parties. No reconciliation is possible	Multi-party system: the process is characterised by negotiation between the parties. It fosters dialogue between offenders, victims and the wider community. It supports reconciliation

Source: Prepared by the author

First, many supporters of restorative justice argue that, unlike retributive justice, the restorative approach is based on a different principle, and looks to repair (as far as possible) the harm that the crime caused to the victim and the wider community since it provides a space for communication and the participation of both (Mallinder 2013, 145). However, while criminal justice has a strong focus on the punishment of perpetrators, when dealing with human rights violations it can acquire a wider perspective by including the victims and the community in the process. When trials are oral and public, as is the case in Argentina, the community can attend the hearings and listen to all the testimonies. In addition, when the media are permitted to attend the hearings, the trials have an even greater dissemination and impact on society.

Second, advocates of restorative justice describe it as "relational" (McCold, Llewellyn and Van Ness 2007) since, according to them, restorative justice aims to address and restore the harm that violence caused to social relationships rather than only to individuals, as is the case with retributive justice. However, again this is a very narrow conceptualisation of the potential of retributive justice. As mentioned above, human rights trials act as a public forum that can also allow the restoration of the social ties broken by state violence and impunity. Needless to say, the restoration of these relationships can vary from one context to another and be very profound or only superficial. However, such restoration is a relevant change perceived by many victims in Argentina. Many interviewees stated they have experienced solidarity and recognition at the community level since the trials started.

Third, it is usually claimed that victims' interests are peripheral to the judicial process, while restorative initiatives would have a victim-centred perspective (Hayner 2002; Blom-Cooper 2013). Those who support this perspective state that formal court proceedings often marginalise victims and deny them a forum to speak and tell their stories (McCold, Llewellyn and Van Ness 2007; Parent 2010). Similarly, it is often argued that restorative justice is a process through which victims are given back ownership of their dispute, in contrast to retributive justice, where the state appropriates the role of victims by defining injustice as an act of breaking the law (Van der Merwe, Baxter and Chapman 2009, 119). In this vein, Mertus argues that victims are not the focus of attention for their own sake but only in order to reveal something about the perpetrator (2004, 115). However, as noted in previous chapters, human rights prosecutions in Argentina have shown that the victims can acquire a crucial status in the judicial process in diverse forms. The state, in its role as prosecutor, is not the only accuser: the victims can also become fully involved as private plaintiffs ("*querellantes*") through the representation of counsel and have the right to ask questions and file accusations. In several cases, the accusations lodged by the victims are different from those presented by the public prosecutor. Both perspectives are considered by the court, which eventually convicts or acquits the defendant. In addition, the victims are crucial to the trials, and if they so choose, they can become active contributors. As a matter of fact, the feasibility of the trials in Argentina depends on the participation of the victims, especially survivors, who are the main witnesses in the processes. Furthermore, the opportunity that human rights trials in Argentina give to the victims to narrate their stories marks a significant difference from regular court trials, which as a rule are limited to narrative matters relevant to the criminal offence. In this sense, these trials challenge the conception that judicial inquiries only focus on the acts of perpetrators. The public hearings in which the survivors describe their experiences have provided many victims with a public voice, and this has contributed to removing the veil of silence and denial that obscured a critical and painful period of history. The fact that an institutional space such as a courtroom with state officials such as judges and prosecutors was used allows the testimony of the victims to be viewed not only as a symbolic valorisation of their words, but also as a legitimation of their experiences as evidence for the trials.

Fourth, advocates of restorative justice claim that in the absence of potential punishment, perpetrators are more willing to collaborate in the process (Mallinder 2013, 145), tell the truth, confess their crimes and even assist the victims (Clamp 2014, 6). Similarly, Kathleen Daly asserts that restorative justice processes involve direct exchanges between victims and perpetrators that "permit the potential for honesty and humanity to emerge in ways foreclosed in a courtroom process" (Daly 2000, 19). Jennifer Llewellyn also argues that the encounter of victims with perpetrators would provide the opportunity for dialogue and understanding about the nature of the harm experienced (2006). McElrea also stresses that, while for the restorative justice model access to the truth is highly valued, its suppression is common in criminal procedures since they tend to "silence the accused" (2013, 102, 103). However, the assumption that perpetrators would collaborate with victims merely because they do not run the risk of being punished for their crimes is not a *sine qua non* condition. The fact that there is no sanction does not automatically lead to perpetrators asking for forgiveness from or collaborating with the people they victimised years ago. Many of them remain convinced of their crimes and offer justifications for their actions, as is the case with the military in Argentina. People do not change their mind about their crimes simply because there is no threat of a jail sentence. In fact, in many cases they believe they are entitled to the freedom they enjoy. In several well-known initiatives that aimed to establish the truth, such as the so-called Truth Trials in the late 1990s in Argentina, army officers summoned to give evidence have frequently refused to do so. As Roht-Arriaza (2004) and the Human Rights Watch report (2006) show, military perpetrators in Argentina showed almost no cooperation in providing information about their crimes even though they did not face punishment because of the amnesty laws (see Chapter 4).[2] In addition, within the framework of the current human rights trials, even in those cases where several perpetrators have already been convicted for life and are in prison – and thus, their confessions cannot change their current situation – they have shown no regret and have chosen not to speak. As a consequence, a great deal of vital information remains unavailable.[3] However, this silence is not necessarily the result of prosecutions or the threat of punishment, as those who deny the value of the trials claim, but of other factors, such as rational decision-making, ideological conviction and loyalty to other perpetrators. On the other hand, one can ask how sincere the repentance of perpetrators is when it is based solely on the granting of impunity. Furthermore, many victims of atrocities have no interest in having a dialogue with their torturers or rapists, who in many cases kept on harassing them for years even when the authoritarian regime was over, as was the case in Argentina.

Fifth, it is usually argued that, while retributive justice is a two-party process characterised by contentious and adversarial relationships between the victim and the perpetrator, restorative initiatives promote dialogue and a negotiated solution between different parties. According to this perspective, restorative justice tends to re-integrate offenders rather than punish and isolate them as retributive justice does (Mallinder 2013, 145). The underlying idea of this perspective is that restorative justice strategies are based on the achievement of consensus and reconciliation among all the parties (Sherman and Strang 2007, 32) and the active participation of stakeholders, victims and perpetrators (Van Ness and Strong 2010). Similarly, Marshall defines restorative justice as a process "whereby parties with a stake in a specific offence collectively resolve how to deal with the aftermath of the offence and its implications for the future" (1999, 5).

Much of the literature equates restorative justice with reconciliation. As discussed in Chapter 1, reconciliation is a highly controversial and vague concept with varying implications in different contexts (Hermann 2004; Little 2012). In the academic research on restorative justice there tends to be a strong emphasis on reconciliation as a normative project: one inspired by the pursuit of truth and forgiveness to reach the objective of peaceful co-existence and the renewal of a society (Hamber and Kelly 2004). The idea of a process that brings victims and perpetrators together can work in individual criminal cases, minor offences or in countries in which this is a traditional and widespread practice. However, in the Latin American context, where the criminal system is usually perceived as a means from which political and economic elites benefit (O'Donnell 1998), the non-prosecution of major state criminals is understood, as many interviewees have asserted, as another manifestation of the privileges those powerful groups are accustomed to having. When it comes to state repression – which is a vertical, top-to-bottom kind of violence – the history of the selective impunity of law and punishment in Latin America converts restorative initiatives without sanctions into another expression of the unequal application of the law to the benefit of those who hold power. In the Argentine case specifically, the notion of reconciliation has always been used as a synonym for impunity (Figari Layús 2015). Against this background, the only relationships to be restored at least at a basic level are the ones of the victims, as members of the community, with other members of their social environment – but not with the perpetrators.

Now, without denying the procedural limitations of trials (which are also discussed in this work), retributive justice should not be viewed in opposition to restorative justice. Instead, when properly implemented, the one can borrow and blend elements from the other. In fact, when judging human rights violations in Argentina, criminal justice can share many common grounds with restorative initiatives. The boundaries between restorative and retributive justice are blurred in practice, as when we consider how different elements of restorative justice are present in human rights trials. However, it is important at this point to stress again that no trial is per se restorative. As discussed above, in many other cases, trials which lack a victim-centred perspective (i.e. one which includes victims' rights and needs) are not reparative and can even retraumatise victims, as has been mentioned in the literature on Sierra Leone, Rwanda and ICTY (Corey and Joireman 2004; Campbell 2007; Dougherty 2004; Kelsall and Stepakoff 2007). Even in Argentina, the first Juntas Trial in the 1980s, though very important, did not have the strong reparative impact that the current prosecutions are having. Thus, a strictly dichotomous and schematic view of retributive and restorative justice runs the risk of ignoring or underestimating the scope and forms that criminal trials of systematic human rights violations can acquire and achieve when conducted under specific considerations with safeguards for the victims. The Argentine case is a good example of this.

8.2 Beyond the victims: the social scope of prosecutions

The question now is why do human rights trials have this restorative potential for victims? Drawing on some of the theoretical contributions outlined in Chapter 1, it is possible to state that the role of the law to communicate, legitimise and influence social behaviour is crucial to understanding the social scope of the trials. As argued by Duff (2001), the law as a communication instrument has the power to transmit a clear official message to society and, as the case may be, exert a total or partial influence. The legal system penetrates and textures society and social relations (O'Donnell 1998, 15). The law is largely a dynamic condensation of power relations, not just a rationalised technique for the ordering of social relations. The state, through the formulation and implementation of the law, has the aim and the power to influence and even shape public social behaviour in favour of a certain social order according to the prevailing power relations in each historical context (Tyler 2006). Therefore, the justice system plays a crucial role in shaping social perceptions and attitudes to mass atrocities. Changes in the ways criminal justice deals with human rights violations can affect those power relations within the state and have an impact on social interactions and ultimately on the victims' lives.

The trials not only communicate explicitly that a certain act-crime is prohibited, but also convey underlying implicit messages which influence social perceptions and the attitudes of some sectors of society towards the victims. As described in Chapter 7, several interviewees stated that many victims began to talk after having seen others providing testimony in the trial hearings. The legitimation and acknowledgement provided by human rights trials to the survivors and relatives of the disappeared and their narratives have a domino effect on other victims and on their social environment. The trials express a new attitude of the state towards the victims, which is very different from the denial and exclusion of the impunity period, and the effects go beyond the courtroom to reach other sectors of society. Public hearings make accessible information not only about the specific crimes but also about the causes for repression, and allow allocating clear responsibilities. Acknowledging the victims as such, rather than making them responsible for the crimes they endured, as the military wanted the population to believe, is a crucial reparative dimension of the trials. This act of official visibilisation fosters new social attitudes towards survivors and relatives of disappeared persons, and leads to a partial reconstruction of social ties and relationships of trust, breaking down isolation and restoring networks of solidarity among the victims and those who had previously mistrusted them or treated them with indifference. The trials have opened up – to a greater or lesser degree according to the political contexts in which they have been conducted – a possibility for dialogue and the reunion of groups that had long been separated. As many interviewees have asserted, the day of the sentence is one to share with others. Public events organised around the trials, such as demonstrations or even festivals held the day on which the sentences are passed, have allowed survivors and activists to come together (Varela 2011), perhaps with other members of society who had remained largely uninvolved before.

As will be discussed below, many survivors, political prisoners and relatives of the disappeared interviewed stated that they perceived a relevant change in the attitudes of others towards them during and after the trials. They have experienced attitudes of greater *solidarity*, *respect* and *recognition* by others since the trials started. Again, the magnitude of this change varies significantly among the victims depending, for example, on the regional and political context. Whereas in provincial and small towns the change in social attitudes was markedly highlighted by the interviewees, this was not the case of those living in large urban centres such as Buenos Aires, Rosario and La Plata.

There are several factors that contribute to amplifying the restorative scope and impact of domestic human rights trials on the victims' local contexts in Argentina. First, the trials are oral and public, and thus allow the presence of larger audiences than those cases governed by written procedures, as is the case with Chile (Collins 2010). Second, the fact that the prosecutions are being conducted locally has played a crucial role.

8.2.1 The public modality of the trials

The trials held in many provinces comprise oral and public hearings. This public modality offers the possibility for anyone to attend the hearings and hear the survivors' testimonies. Furthermore, the national government, together with the judicial system, has implemented several strategies in order to make available the information provided in the trials and reach other sectors of society. Against this background, in 2014 the national government launched an educational programme called *La Escuela va a los Juicios* ("School Goes to the Trials"), in which groups of secondary school students of up to 16 years of age are invited to attend the hearings.[4] Fifty schools attended the trials in the first year of the programme, and as of October 2015, other ninety-five educational institutions also participated (Vujassin 2015).[5] It is worth noting that the trials are bringing about a change in how the issue is addressed. A secondary school student who attended the hearings in the case of the ex-CDC ESMA in the city of Buenos Aires narrated:

> At the beginning, it was like a movie to me, I felt as if I was not there. It was too shocking. I even looked at the screen above the judges so that I didn't have to look at the actual person who was testifying at that moment. But then I gradually began to look at the person speaking. I began to look at him, at the judges, at the defence attorneys.
>
> (quoted in Vujassin 2015)

The courage to be able to look at others giving testimony of such heinous crimes plays a key role when dealing with the past. For survivors, the act of daring to look the perpetrators in the eye is perceived as an act of empowerment. In this case instead, those who attend the hearings and belong to a generation different from that of the victims go through a symbolic process or *movement* of approaching that past. The transformation from a feeling of alienation and distance ("it was like a movie to me, I felt as if I was not there") and even evasion of what happened, to another of increased proximity and confrontation with this violent past is reflected in the ability to look at those protagonists of the past who are in the courtroom giving their testimonies.

Many (though not all) of the hearings are broadcast on radio and television. In order to protect victim–witnesses and ensure the rights of the defendants,[6] the only hearings that can be broadcast on television are the initial hearing of a trial and the final hearing when the court's decision is handed down (Dandan 2012). However, the judges are vested with discretion to decide whether to permit media coverage and hence not all judges allow the media into their courtrooms.[7] Furthermore, all the judicial decisions are available on the Internet. The judiciary publishes on its website called *Centro de Información Judicial* (Judicial Information Centre) not only the decisions of all the courts in the country but also quarterly reports and daily news of the developments in the human rights trials. Along with these state-sponsored strategies, NGOs have supported the trials (see Chapter 5), organising events such as festivals, updating blogs and holding open radio broadcasts informing about the trials in different parts of the country. With more or less efficiency and scope, these kinds of measures aim to make the trials a public issue by offering society an array of means to access the information generated and disclosed in the judicial processes.

8.2.2 The federal scope of the trials: "this also happened to us"

The fact that the trials are being conducted across the country extends their impact and the above-mentioned legitimisation effects for the victims at the local level. The responsibility of the state itself is acknowledged in regions away from the capital – the city of Buenos Aires. As described in Chapter 3, this had not been the case with the Juntas Trial hearings in the 1980s. Those trials had been exclusively conducted in Buenos Aires, which diminished their impact in other regions of the country, such as the northern province of Santiago del Estero. In the rural areas of those provinces, the transition to constitutional rule and the policies of truth and justice – the Juntas Trial and the creation of CONADEP – were perceived as distant experiences. The lack of trials in other parts of the country perpetuated denial about the state crimes committed in such locations. It was something that had happened to other people in the country's capital. As an attorney of Santiago del Estero explained:

> Before these trials people said, "This [the human rights violations] happened in Buenos Aires, (. . .) this didn't happen in Santiago." They didn't understand the true scale of horror that had also occurred in Santiago del Estero. (. . .) Every town wanted to have its own trials. (. . .) Because of the social impact of the trial in the city. (. . .) [Since the trial took place here] people have changed their feelings, their understanding and realise that (. . .) after the trial in their city (. . .) this [the crimes] also happened to us in Santiago del Estero.
>
> (Int. 60, April 2011, Santiago del Estero)

Thus, the interviewee stresses the change that took place after prosecutions were held at the local level. The fact that trials are being carried out in nearly every province, with convictions not only of senior, well-known military officers but also of the lower ranks who people met on a day-to-day basis, had a greater impact on the local community than the Juntas Trials in the 1980s. On trial now are not only those high commanders who were responsible at the national military government level, whose faces and names, though known by everyone, were often perceived as remote figures. To also prosecute provincial officers and functionaries who actually perpetrated the crimes in their own communities has a greater impact for survivors and relatives of the disappeared as well as for the social environment. Hence, several interviewees stressed how important it was for each city to have "its" own trials prosecuting "its" perpetrators and "its" victims. The proximity of victims and perpetrators, who in small locations are always neighbours, makes the consequences of the trials – such as the convictions of those neighbours – more palpable and visible. The repercussions of the trials in their cities evidence that those crimes "also happened" there. Domestic human rights trials that take place simultaneously in many different regional contexts in a country have a greater effect on local communities than when they are conducted only in one specific city.

8.3 Social inclusion. Making victims visible

Many of those interviewed, especially in Argentina's central and northern provinces (such as Córdoba, Tucumán and Santiago del Estero), perceived positive changes in the attitudes of neighbours and even strangers towards them. Some of the interviewees said, for instance, that during and after the trial, people who had previously ignored them began to greet them. Neighbours started to show more interest in them, asking questions about their lives and about their disappeared relatives. Other interviewees stated that they were even congratulated by people in the street or by neighbours for their testimonies in court. A plaintiff from Córdoba narrated the following anecdote:

> Back at home my mother's neighbours always knew that my father had been taken away by the military (. . .) but that was all. After the first trial against Menéndez [in the city of Córdoba] the neighbours phoned my mother, they were happy about what was going on, believing that that trial had been conducted to look into the disappearance of my father.
>
> (Int. 34, March 2011, Córdoba)

Several interviewees stated that, following the trials in their cities, they were recognised in public ceremonies in schools. Thus, since the beginning of the trials, victims have begun to be valued socially, as have their relatives and their fight against impunity. In this regard, several interviewees said that, after the trials in their cities, the human rights organisations they belong to were honoured by institutions that used to ignore them before. A former political prisoner from Santiago del Estero gives an account of a tribute made to ex-political prisoners in the nearby province of Salta. This would have been unthinkable several years ago:

> There was a tribute to ex-political prisoners in the city of Salta, it was organised (. . .) in commemoration of the Memory Day. In my opinion, this is the best thing that has happened so far, because (. . .) paying a tribute to ex-political prisoners, people who until not so long were demons, terrorist subversives (. . .). Do you know how they referred to us [during the dictatorship]?: "A Detained Terrorist." Now, saying that a tribute has been paid is quite a change.
>
> (Int. 53, April 2011, Santiago del Estero)

Another interviewee from Tucumán whose entire family was disappeared also referred to how public institutions have changed their attitude towards them. While for years such institutions were inaccessible to victims' organisations, after the first trials they started to honour and acknowledge them in public commemorations of their struggle for truth and justice:

> Despite the fact that many students had joined us, we couldn't gain access to the universities, [the authorities] never [received us] at an institutional level. By the end of the year, after the trial, the School of Humanities gave our Association an award in recognition of our activity (. . .), which says "our recognition to the Association for Memory, Truth and Justice for its dedication and work."
>
> (Int. 70, October 2012, Tucumán)

Similarly, many other interviewees have stated that since the trials started, they have felt that their voices are finally being heard by society and by the relevant institutions. This leads not only to public tributes being paid to them but also to their being included and invited to participate in institutional spaces which had been closed to them before. A plaintiff 's attorney from Santiago del Estero said that since the day when the court in his city handed down the sentence in his case, he has begun to notice:

> the respect and solidarity of people that had barely greeted us before. We are now treated differently. We notice that society is with us now. (. . .) [There is] more respect now that people know that what we said was true, that we were not lying or overdoing it. For example, in the universities of Santiago del Estero [they] have opened their doors to us. Before that, they used to regard us with suspicion.
>
> (Int. 60, April 2011, Santiago del Estero)

This shows how these gestures of "respect and solidarity" mark a change in society's approach to the victims and its support for human rights organisations. The contrast with the period of impunity has been highlighted by several interviewees. As described in Chapter 4, in the 1980s and 1990s, the absence of justice and of allocation of responsibilities helped stigmatise the victims, especially the survivors. Such stigmatisation was possible because impunity relies on the vagueness and lack of definition of legal silence. This created uncertainty about who was responsible for acts committed during the period of violence, and was in turn reflected in official discourse. These circumstances make it difficult to build social ties of trust and solidarity with the victims (Cohen 2001, 14–15). By contrast, the trials undermine practices of social indifference, which are typical of impunity. In effect, oral and public trials – where the survivors' testimony, not only about the tortures inflicted upon them but also about the historical context and even previous political militancy – make it difficult to deny state violence. In addition, the trials recognise the victims as such and make it clear that the perpetrators are the accused. Thus, rather than being treated "with suspicion," the survivors begin to feel that more sectors of society are "with them." Solidarity and understanding depend on knowledge. Such knowledge is difficult to acquire in contexts of impunity, where silence and denial prevail. Public hearings and official juridical records provide information, allowing victims to become visible and others to feel closer to them. Along these lines, a survivor from Tucumán recounted how, after the first trial in the city, he began to be invited to public lectures at different secondary schools to give his testimony:

> The Physical Education school has called me on two different occasions. They have an auditorium – which was even used [during the dictatorship] as a CDC for some months – that can accommodate up to 300 students. And even though quite some time has passed, people find it hard [to listen to these things]. We are speaking to very young people about events that took place more than thirty years ago. (. . .) From the questions I was asked [after my testimony], especially in my latest talk, I could see that the students have become more sensitive, more interested (. . .). They were moved, their eyes were filled with tears. The same happened in the secondary school in my town (. . .), where I've spoken on two different occasions.
>
> (Int. 68, September 2012, Tucumán)

Many interviewees pointed out this institutional openness. As explained by one of the plaintiffs:

> [The trials] have opened institutional spaces for us, in the government, in universities, in many places that, while they had not previously closed their doors on us, had been wary of meeting with us.
>
> (Int. 42, April 2011, Tucumán)

The public and official acknowledgement of the crimes committed has enabled a gradual reconstruction of the victims' social ties, which had been damaged in times of terror and impunity. Such changes operate as a significant process of reparation for the victims. Michael Humphrey (2013) points out that the trials may result in a new consensus about past violence and thereby change the social status of victims and perpetrators in society. Because human rights trials are not just about individual criminal acts but deal with large-scale collective political crimes, they can also produce a historical narrative which contextualises those individual acts (Humphrey 2013, 69). The public nature of the hearings has paved the way for the legitimisation and dissemination of new narratives of the past in wider sectors of society. This process of making the victims' experiences visible, while at the same time disseminating and legitimising them, challenges and deconstructs previous stigmatising narratives of them. Several interviewees underscored the fact that, although not completely eliminated, stigmatisation has decreased. Echoing the attorney's previous comment, many others have also stated that after their participation in the trials, they began to be invited to other public events and to deliver speeches at schools about the period of the dictatorship: they were integrated into social and institutional spaces from which they had been previously excluded. The work of Bourdieu (1987) and Foucault (2007) accounts for the ways in which legal discourse becomes a powerful and legitimate producer of knowledge and truth. The way in which legal processes reconstruct and represent a past of systematic human rights violations perpetrated by agents of the state has important symbolic and performative effects on society and on its attitudes towards the victims. Indeed, the legitimacy of the role of judicial narrative as a producer of historical truth is often presented as unquestionable (Orentlicher 1991, 32). Through the widespread acceptance of judicial methodology, criminal trials confer heightened legitimacy on the victims' narratives and produce very concrete effects. Therefore, to provide testimony at a trial becomes important, not only because it means an institutional recognition of the victims, but also because of its resonances outside the courtroom.

It should be noted at this point that the interviewees have different perceptions about the social repercussions of the trials. Although one of the most significant contributions made by the prosecutions is to make their findings public and thus have an impact on wider sections of society, many victims – especially those living in large urban centres such as the city of Buenos Aires – were disappointed by the scale of interest shown for the trials by society as a whole. Some plaintiffs and witnesses stressed that in the course of the trials there was a decrease in media attention and public attendance. After the major impact of the first trials in each of the locations, there seems to have been a decline in social, media and even political attention and interest in subsequent trials.[8] At the same time, attendance at the trials has gradually diminished. The reasons for this decline are manifold. One such reason is eminently practical. As pointed out by several interviewees, everyday obligations and activities – work, study and family commitments, among others – do not allow a regular attendance at the trials, which take place during working hours. While several interviewees stated they had even asked for permission at work to attend the hearings, this was not possible for many of them. Another factor mentioned in the interviews that accounted for the decline in public attention and interest in the trials was the void left by the state, both at the national and provincial levels, in failing to publicise the outcomes of the processes, especially in the initial years. As was explained in Chapter 5, this task of spreading information about the trials and the convictions that the state has left unfulfilled is often undertaken by human rights organisations.

Interviewees from large urban centres highlighted the role played by those close to them such as friends and relatives. Especially after testifying, many underscored the attitude of those who listened to their statements at the hearings. A son of disappeared parents from La Plata told me:

> When I left the courtroom [after testifying], they [family and friends] hugged me, they were all crying. Me too. Then I relaxed a bit (. . .). I cried but I felt

> very satisfied, (. . .) and everyone was surprised by all that I had said, everyone congratulated me.
>
> (Int. 74, September 2012, La Plata)

Those victims that were more isolated and with fewer possibilities of engaging in collective action during the period of impunity due to the continuity of local strongholds of the dictatorship (as is the case in Tucumán and Santiago del Estero) placed more emphasis on the social impact of the trials than the interviewees living in large cities. In large urban centres such as La Plata or Buenos Aires, the presence of human rights organisations was stronger during the 1980s and 1990s. The more favourable context – though still troublesome as explained in Chapter 4 – allowed more opportunities for human rights activism and social protest. This contributed to the establishment of stronger networks of support for more victims than in some provincial contexts. Thus, many interviewees of those populated areas did not notice a big contrast in the reactions of other sectors of society because they could rely on stronger solidarity networks.

Regardless of their place of origin, one aspect that almost all the interviewees have underscored is the change in the approach adopted by the national state towards the victims during the government of Néstor Kirchner first and Cristina Fernández later. Unfortunately, this victim-centred approach of the state seems to have changed again with the new government of Mauricio Macri (December 2015–ongoing). Indeed, as described in Chapter 5, several human rights organisations have voiced their concern that in 2016 there were important cuts in the budget for the trials and increased delays in the conduct of public hearings. In turn, there have been varied responses from the provincial governments, depending on the different provincial political contexts. For example, while the provincial government in Córdoba has been more present, the government of the city of Buenos Aires took no action with respect to the trials or the victims.

8.4 Decrease in public support for perpetrators

This emerging social and official recognition of the victims has had social consequences for the perpetrators. Human rights trials officially allocating criminal responsibilities have partially undermined public support for well-known perpetrators. Many interviewees, especially in the north of the country, stressed that the trials in their city had an impact on how former supporters of the perpetrators behave and refer to them in public. For example, in Tucumán, former governor Antonio Bussi was sentenced to life imprisonment in 2008 for the murder and disappearance of Peronist Senator Guillermo Vargas Aignasse – a conviction that was crucial not only to the struggle for justice but also to a change in consciousness of society in Tucumán. Public support for Bussi decreased after the first trial against him in 2008. As some interviewees recalled, before the trial was held, many people in Tucumán had no problem in admitting that they supported Bussi. As a matter of fact, during that trial, there were several public demonstrations to show support for Bussi and to protest against the trial. However, once Bussi was convicted, public support waned significantly. At the subsequent trials in the province, there were no such demonstrations in support of the perpetrators. As members of the organisation HIJOS in Tucumán explained, such withdrawal of support for the perpetrators was also reflected in the trials themselves. While the first trial in the city saw large numbers of people supporting the accused, the number fell significantly in the second trial.

> In the second trial, fewer seats were allocated to the defence in the courtroom because they realised that those guilty of genocide didn't have so many friends and relatives [as in the first trial] (. . .). In sum, in the trial held in connection with [the crimes committed in the ex-CDC] *Jefatura* there must have been four or five people supporting the defence. Sometimes there was only one person, and sometimes no one at all during the trial. In fact, when the sentence was read out, there were only three people (. . .). The situation was different in the case of the sentence handed down [in the first trial] for the disappearance of Vargas Aignasse. There were a lot of people [there] (. . .). But as time went by, those people that supported [the accused] throughout the first trial just vanished in the second one.
>
> (Int. 43, April 2011, Tucumán)

Former state officials who are being prosecuted for human rights violations are less valuable icons than they were in the past. While impunity made the criminal liability of the accused invisible, and even justified their actions, the trials and the sentences handed down recently have made this no longer possible. As a survivor from Tucumán explained:

> Most people didn't want to see it, to know about it (. . .) because this is what it was all about all this time, denying a reality, (. . .) I think that in the case of this genocidaire [Bussi], thanks to the conviction [obtained in the trial] (. . .), today Bussi is officially acknowledged as a murderer. And that [his conviction] had a strong political impact because after that, no one dared to stand up for him any longer.
>
> (Int. 73, October 2012, Tucumán)

Thus, many supporters and other political and social actors often find it more convenient to distance themselves from those – now legally convicted and sentenced – perpetrators whose involvement in the repression was revealed or exposed in the trials. A lawyer from Santiago del Estero explains that public justifications for the crimes committed by the military are not so easily accepted, as was the case before the trials:

> These societies have been shaken [with the trial] and today no one would dare to justify what happened to Cecilio Kamenetzky.[9]
>
> (Int. 60, April 2011, Santiago del Estero)

Even though public justification and support for former perpetrators have decreased, this does not automatically mean that people have changed their way of thinking about the perpetrators and their crimes. However, it does show a change in the way people behave in public: Those perpetrators – such as Bussi in Tucumán – who were still running for elections before the trials have at least lost "public legitimacy." Thus, for the perpetrators the trials bring about not only the legal and economic costs of the formal sanction (a conviction, lost wages, legal fees, inability to participate in elections while on trial, etc.), but also an informal social and political cost that arises from the publicity surrounding the prosecutions. All of this translates into a loss of reputation or legitimacy and a resulting loss of public support. Once again, this is not an absolute phenomenon and can vary from one context to the other. However, one thing is for certain: as stated by some interviewees, trials do not go unnoticed in Argentina. They have had, as described above, significant social and political effects inside and outside the courtroom and have generated what can be described as a "social framework of reparation."

8.5 Towards a social framework of reparation

It follows from the above that the trials can have a reparative and restorative impact on the victims since they not only contribute to the reconstruction of the past and the re-establishment of the victims' rights, but also – in a partial and gradual manner – facilitate an active restoration of the social bonds destroyed by state violence and impunity. Once domestic human rights trials are launched, they also begin to influence and transform the social and political context in which they take place. Thus, the trials promote a social framework that is conducive to reparation and the empowerment of victims. This social framework is very different from the one that existed before the trials. In this connection, a survivor from Tucumán stated that thanks to the trials:

> Today we can speak and breathe a different air.
>
> (Int. 73, October 2012, Tucumán)

Another survivor from the same province also referred in similar terms to the changes brought about by the trials:

> All this came as a refreshing and restoring rain in an environment that had always been very painful for us.
>
> (Int. 68, September 2012, Tucumán)

In contrast with the previous framework of denial sustained by impunity, prosecutions are partially and gradually helping to rebuild the victims' social context and enhance the social and legal conditions needed for their empowerment and fulfilment of their rights.

To summarise the findings and analyses presented in this work, a social framework of reparation brings with it the following changes:

1 A legal and civic change: this entails the end of a justice system of privileges and legal asymmetries which weighs in favour of the perpetrators and against the victims. Trials support the principle of equality before the law – that is, that no one is above the law (the perpetrators) or excluded from the law (the victims). This is reflected in the prosecution of perpetrators previously facing no charges and in the recognition of the legal status of the victims. The legal change also involves the enactment and the recognition of the rights to justice and truth (including new investigations and access to new information). Thus, the victims are recognised as citizens and the rights of which they were deprived in the impunity period are restored. In turn, the legal acknowledgment of the victims' status also means an end to the official and social denial of human rights violations, along with the public acknowledgement of state responsibility.

2 Changes in the personal sphere: the trials provide the victims with new possibilities of action, such as the gradual confrontation of fear and the breaking of silence. This is reflected, for example, in the opportunity that the survivors had to access new information about their relatives or other people they knew and to talk about their own history of victimisation and also about their political militancy without being stigmatised or punished for it. The courts have started to provide a space for the communication of such tabooed experiences of violence not only to the judges but also to and for the victims' own families. This was very important for many survivors and ex-political prisoners that stated that before the trial, their families preferred not to talk about their pasts. It was tacit knowledge that nobody wanted to put into words. Thus, the possibility of speaking about that within the family setting as well as in other social spaces also contributes to the empowerment of the victims.

3 A social and institutional change: there are new social attitudes and perceptions of the victims, which translate into practices of greater solidarity with, and interest in, them. Furthermore, the trials have given the victims recognition and visibility, and have fostered their inclusion in social and institutional spaces and activities. The prosecution of those perpetrators who still belonged to state institutions during the period of impunity has important consequences for generating new social attitudes towards the victims at the local level, especially in small towns and semi-rural and conservative areas. It is precisely in these areas where the survivors, the relatives of the disappeared and others who had been silenced during many years started to mobilise and to act and voice their political demands, as they fought more openly for their rights. As shown above, the victims and those who had been previously silenced and paralysed became politically active by taking part in protests in public spaces and in public lectures in relevant institutions such as

> universities. As argued by John Rawls: "The law defines the basic framework within which the pursuit of all other activities takes place" (1971, 236). The law sends a message to society. The same as legal impunity translated into social impunity, legal destigmatisation also has repercussions in the social field of the victims. The trials foster certain attitudes in favour of a higher support and inclusion of those who survived state repression. In Bourdieu's words, the law *creates* the social world and the possibilities of actions in it (1987, 829). In contrast to the period of impunity, the "social world" or framework supported by the trials promotes speech and provides the victims with the opportunity to express themselves in public.

The two contrasting social frameworks – the one of impunity and that of prosecutions – reflect different prevailing political, legal and social conditions, in which the victims have to live with very different levels of freedom and possibilities of action. During the period of impunity, the social framework in which the survivors and relatives of the disappeared were embedded tended to reproduce the damage generated by state terror and made them invisible. The social framework of prosecutions provides an environment conducive to the empowerment of the victims. The degree of achievement of this change can vary according to the local context. As shown above, in more conservative and small locations, such as in the north of the country, the change in the social and the political context brought about by the trials is more visible. This was also mentioned by some interviewees in the large urban centres, though with less emphasis. In this regard, a survivor from Buenos Aires affirmed:

> There are still people who believe that a victim can be "innocent" or "guilty" (. . .) and they say: "after all, they were guerrilla members, weren't they?"
>
> (Int. 7, March 2011, Buenos Aires)

The interviewee's statement shows once again that social changes and the accompanying reparation process are slow, conflictual and actually endless. The damage is irreparable and irreversible: there is no return from the traumatic experience of captivity in a CDC to a previous state. It is impossible to make people reappear or to erase the pain caused by their loss. Many survivors of enforced disappearance, despite the feelings of reparation that accompany the trials, say that the damage suffered thirty years ago can never be healed. There will always be something irreparable which the victims have to learn to live with. A survivor from Tucumán, whose brother was made to disappear, explained this in the following way:

> More than thirty years have passed and the tragedy still shakes us, it is as if time had never passed. What's more, sometimes it is as if the events were happening right now (. . .) It cannot be easily forgotten, (. . .) what happened is too terrible for time to erase it.
>
> (Int. 68, September 2012, Tucumán)

Other survivors have also referred to this feeling of time not passing or of their reliving the events as if they were happening "right now." Another survivor from Buenos Aires stated that:

A: As the date on which I was abducted approaches, August 5, I begin to feel down; from August 5 to November 4 I feel worse and worse because it is as if I'm living the concentration camp experience again.

Q: Every year?

A: All my life, since I was released. Every year August 5 is in black in the calendars, and I begin to feel down. (. . .) [And] September 20 is a particularly terrible date. To me, spring doesn't exist. Spring Day[10] is the day after (. . .) [my partner] was taken away.

(Int. 63, September 2012, Buenos Aires)

The interviewee also recounts how the experience of captivity changed her personality forever:

> I used to be very funny, [but] the concentration camp took it away from me. I can have fun, I can be happy, but the person I was before [being detained in] the camp is not the same as the one who came out and continued her life. Despite having raised a family – I have my husband, my daughters – there is a part of me, of my life, that the CDC took away from me.
>
> (Ibid.)

Many relatives and friends of disappeared persons have yet to fully comprehend their loss. In the cases of enforced disappearance, it is difficult to mourn without a body. As a survivor explained:

> There is still an illusion, without having seen the corpse [of the disappeared person], you cannot mourn (. . .). It has happened to me that, you think you see someone [in the street] who is actually disappeared, then you look closer and you realise it's not them. It happened to me with a friend. For a child, a mother or a wife [of a disappeared person], it must be much worse.
>
> (Int. 10, March 2011, Buenos Aires)

However, despite these insurmountable limitations, there are important reparative effects that flow from the recognition provided by the state through the trials, as many interviewees have affirmed. A daughter of disappeared parents from Buenos Aires described the day when those who had been guilty of the disappearance of her parents were sentenced as follows:

> The courtroom was full and you have the feeling that justice does exist. (. . .) It gave me hope, belief in justice and in the democratic system. It's not that one is happy (. . .). I have no feelings of fulfilment and happiness. [But] there's been a recognition that heinous crimes were committed, that

> [people] were hunted, kidnapped, disappeared and tortured, on such a large scale, (. . .) and it is the justice system that is saying it now.
>
> (Int. 63, September 2012, Buenos Aires)

Similar answers were provided by another interviewee from the province of Tucumán, a survivor of a CDC, who expressed his feelings regarding the trials as follows:

> [E]ven with all the limits surrounding the actions of the judiciary (. . .), progress has been made. It's opening up a path and this has given us hope.
>
> (Int. 68, September 2012, Tucumán)

Both interviewees testified to the reparative function of the trials while at the same time acknowledged their limitations. Feelings of "hope" and of "believing a little more" mark the beginning of a process of reparation. Of course, personal and social reparation is a gradual and endless process, rather than a spontaneous and automatic change in people's reality and ways of feeling. Furthermore, such processes can also be interrupted or undermined if state policies do not persist over time. In this sense, it is clear that the reparation process which could have been produced by the Juntas Trial in the 1980s did not have sufficient time to "mature," since the adoption of the amnesty laws in 1986 and 1987 interrupted any possibility of reparation. Thus, in order to be as integral as possible, a reparation process requires both time to have durable effects and a continued and appropriate performance from public institutions. Policies aiming at the reparation of victims of human rights violations requires serious and sustained commitment and state support, both at the national and local levels.

The above-mentioned contrasting frameworks are not absolute phenomena but nuances and prevailing tendencies promoted and supported by the state in its different levels (national and local). As shown in Chapter 4, during the period of impunity there were some sectors of society such as human rights activists, survivors and relatives of the disappeared who were very active in the search for truth and justice. In this sense, in this new period of judicial accountability, there are also sectors of society that remain untouched. A personal and social process of reparation does not entail a radical 180-degree shift but it does mean a change that acknowledges the victims' rights and narratives, and promotes their integration into social and institutional spaces. This process of opening up and recognition is still ongoing, partial and limited. Yet, it is an important one for an inclusive and real process of democratisation.

Notes

1 According to Sherman and Strang, these initiatives can embrace many varieties. These include: face-to-face conferences of victims, offenders and stakeholders; face-to-face mediation (without supporters present); indirect, "shuttle

diplomacy" mediation; discussions about the crime in the absence of the victim with the offender and supporters; discussions about the crime in the absence of the offender with the victim and supporters; etc. (2007, 32).

2 Another example in which judicial concessions did not necessarily yield all the required information was the Colombian demobilisation of paramilitaries in 2005, where a threshold of justice for truth was the key to the whole process. Although there were some important positive developments in the location of bodies of disappeared people, thanks in part to information provided by the paramilitaries in exchange for having their sentences reduced under the so-called Justice and Peace Law, no progress was made in finding persons taken hostage (despite an explicit requirement that paramilitaries release or account for them). In many cases the fate of the hostages was still unknown by 2008 and paramilitaries have yet to account for their whereabouts (Human Rights Watch 2008, 73).

3 See Chapter 6.

4 The programme was first implemented for the prosecutions in the city of Buenos Aires (for example in the trials for the crimes committed at the ex-CDCs ESMA and Automotores Orletti). Though at a slow pace, it is being implemented in other provinces.

5 This was initially met with stiff resistance from the judiciary since Argentine law stipulates that the minimum age for admission to the courtrooms is 18 years old. However, the Buenos Aires Court of Appeals hearing the cases finally admitted the students, under the argument that the history of the dictatorship in Argentina is already part of the secondary school curriculum.

6 In 2008 the Supreme Court issued a decision prohibiting the use of cameras or video cameras in the judicial phase called *etapa de prueba* ("evidence phase") (Dandan 2012). This measure should prevent future witnesses from becoming acquainted with the testimonies of other victims and changing their testimony at trial, which may infringe the rights of the accused. In fact, witnesses are not allowed to attend any hearings until they have testified themselves.

7 While federal courts in cities such as La Plata, Córdoba and even Tucumán showed more flexibility in allowing access to journalists and the media, other judges – for example in the city of Buenos Aires – were more restrictive (Filippini 2009).

8 Exceptions to this are the so-called mega-cases, which include a multiplicity of perpetrators and victims, and those cases where well-known perpetrators, such as high-ranking officers in the armed forces, were convicted. These cases usually received more attention from the media than others.

9 The first trial in Santiago del Estero was held in connection with the abduction, torture and execution of Cecilio Kamenetzky in November 1976. As explained before, the victim was a law student and a militant in the Guevarist Youth. In 2010, several ex-members of the provincial police were sentenced to life in prison.

10 In Argentina, spring begins on 21 September and is usually celebrated in parks and other public places.

Concluding reflections

In this work, I have analysed how prosecutions can operate as a mechanism of reparation for victims of human rights violations. While acknowledging the impossibility of truly repairing the harm caused by torture, sexualised violence, extrajudicial killings and enforced disappearance, I have shown how human rights trials in Argentina have produced important changes in the victims' lives. Specifically, analysis shows how the different uses of the law – either as amnesty laws or in the form of prosecutions – can have opposing consequences for the survivors and relatives of disappeared people. While impunity tends to deepen the damage generated by violence and excludes victims from the justice system, prosecutions tend to create favourable institutional and social premises for their inclusion, empowerment and redress. Both modalities generate specific conditions that give rise to what can be defined as either a framework of exclusion, where impunity prevails, or a framework of reparation where prosecutions are undertaken. The two contrasting frameworks – one of impunity and the other of prosecutions – reflect different prevailing political, legal and social conditions. Each framework enables very different levels of freedom, inclusion, credibility, expression and possibilities of action for the victims.

However, it is important to note that the relationship between the trials, as an implementation of the law, and society is a dialectic one. In the same way that the conduct of prosecutions may influence social attitudes and perceptions, so also the trials reflect the social contexts and their contradictions. In this sense, it is important not to forget that domestic trials as a state-sponsored mechanism are riddled with the internal contradictions, conflicts and ambiguities that are present in the state itself. Thus, the dynamics of the prosecutions reflect the legal and political constraints and power struggles within the state and its institutions, such as the judiciary. The trials are not an isolated phenomenon but exist in a specific social and political context that, to a greater or lesser extent, shapes them. In this sense, the implementation of human rights trials in Argentina is a process in which, as described by one prosecutor, the "state reconfigures and judges itself." That the state judges itself, while also judging the past actions of its agents, has led to a "confrontation of the state against the state." In this confrontation it is possible to distinguish two different dimensions. On the one hand, there is a *diachronic historical dimension* that refers to the confrontation of the state of today with the state of a recent past, through the judging of public servants, civilians and the military, who carried out a systematic criminal policy.

On the other hand, there is a *synchronic contemporary dimension* which refers to a confrontation of the state against itself during the current implementation of the trials. The state is a heterogeneous political unit in which its different institutions and individuals have different interests leading to power struggles. Thus, the implementation of domestic prosecutions has to deal with different kinds of difficulties and resistances that come from within the state itself and, in several cases, limit the scope and reparative potential that trials could achieve.

Towards a distinction in criminal prosecutions and human rights trials

This book has shown how criminal trials acquire some specific characteristics that help to distinguish them from ordinary criminal proceedings, resulting in a more integrated perspective that includes retributive and restorative aspects for the victims. The fact that these trials are conducted within the framework of the ordinary criminal justice system does not mean that they work like ordinary criminal trials. Even though ordinary criminal trials and human rights trials have much in common, they present some significant differences, as the Argentine case shows. Domestic human rights trials are a subtype of criminal trials. Thus, in order to understand the peculiarities of human rights trials as well as their reparative potential for the victims, it is necessary to make some important distinctions between both types of trials. Table C1.1 below provides an overview of ten differences and similarities.

Table C1.1 An overview of criminal and human rights trials: similarities and differences

Features	*Ordinary criminal trials*	*Human rights trials*
1 Type of court	Permanent	Permanent
2 Jurisdiction	Domestic	Domestic
3 Type of crimes prosecuted	Crimes committed by private actors	Crimes committed by agents of the state or by persons or groups of persons acting with the authorisation, support, or acquiescence of the state
4 Contextual framework	Reference to the individual case being tried	Historical and political reconstruction and framing of the crimes in the context in which they took place.
5 Legal framework	Domestic criminal code	Domestic criminal code and international human rights law

(*Continued*)

Table Cl.1 (Continued)

Features	*Ordinary criminal trials*	*Human rights trials*
6 **Institutional structure**	Ordinary domestic institutions of the criminal justice system	Ordinary domestic institutions are supported by the creation of new complementary institutions and programmes (e.g.: Special Prosecutions Units, Programme of Witness Protection, Programmes of Psychological Support for Plaintiffs and Witnesses, etc.)
7 **Focus and goal of the judicial process**	Focus on perpetrators and punishment	Focus on victims (support for active participation, access to previously denied rights) and perpetrators (punished if found guilty).
8 **Features of witnesses**	Witnesses are not necessarily victims	"Victim-witnesses": witnesses are usually also direct victims (survivors) or indirect victims (related to the disappeared)
9 **Kinds of testimony**	Limited: testimonies are usually restricted to the specific facts of the offence being tried	Extensive: testimonies go beyond the specific crime and can include personal and political history and experiences of the victims
10 **Scope and consequences**	Regulation of social behaviour	Regulation of state agents' behaviour through the incorporation of human rights prosecutions as standards in the legal criminal system

Source: Table prepared by the author

The first two aspects refer to common features. Both kinds of trials work with permanent domestic courts and procedures instead of temporary and external courts, and both use the same legal procedures and national domestic jurisdiction.

The third point refers to the kinds of offences prosecuted in these trials. Whereas ordinary criminal trials deal with offences committed by private individuals or collective actors, human rights processes prosecute a special category of crimes: human rights violations. From a legal perspective, not all abuses or crimes or forms of violence are technically violations of human rights. The main characteristic of human rights violations is that they are committed by agents of the state or by persons or groups acting with the authorisation, support or acquiescence of the state (Nikken 1994, 28–29; Sikkink 2011, 135). As set forth by international treaties, human rights violations are either perpetrated by the state or supported by it. Human rights violations are the result of a state's active policy against human dignity, or result from the lack of political will and concrete measures to stop crimes and guarantee fundamental rights, many of which are established in international conventions. Thus, the state can violate human rights by action or omission.

The fourth point accounts for the difference in scope and nature of the crimes committed. While ordinary trials often deal with specific cases, human rights trials deal with mass and systematic state-supported violence. This means that the understanding of the historical context in which that violence took place plays a crucial role in the testimonies and judgments. In regular criminal trials, in which the main goal is to prove a certain specific crime, the judicial process and investigations may refer to the personal history of the victim or/and of the perpetrator to explain the case, but not to a more general historical framework that may seem irrelevant to the particular case. On the contrary, in cases of human rights violations, whose perpetrators were agents of a state´s policy of violence, the reference to history plays an important role. A significant difference between these two kinds of criminal trials, regular and human rights cases, is that the latter usually deal with a crime that was committed in the framework of a more widespread practice, as for instance the enforced disappearance of persons in Argentina. In that context, adjudicating a particular case of a state's systematic violence means understanding that case as "another one" in a more general historical framework of repression. There are many more victims of the same type of crime – in this case, enforced disappearance – than in any particular case. In this sense, human rights prosecutions usually incorporate, reconstruct and interpret the historical and political context. This contextual framing of the particular case, which is to be found in most of the courts' decisions dealing with human rights cases – not only in Argentina – provides the specific crime with a broader historical and political understanding of what happened, which for the victims brings a very important reparative dimension.

The fifth point stresses that even though both types of criminal trials use the same domestic criminal code, the prosecution of human rights crimes also requires resorting to international law and jurisprudence. The jurisprudence of the international courts, such as the Inter-American Human Rights Court, provides an important tool for framing and supporting the local sentencing process (see e.g.: Judgment Simón 2006; Judgment Jefatura 2010, etc.).

Furthermore, as the sixth category shows, human rights trials usually require the support of additional institutions and programmes, which are unusual in ordinary criminal processes, such as the Programme of Witness Protection and Programme of Psychological Support for Victims and Witnesses. Due to the large scope, massiveness, cruelty and systematic nature of the crimes as well as the security risks and emotional stress that the judicial process involves, victims participating in the trials require adequate and sensitive treatment, psychological support, attention and security measures.

The seventh point refers to the focus of both trial modalities. Ordinary criminal trials place great emphasis on perpetrators. The victims are not regarded as parties to criminal proceedings (McElrea 2013, 93–94; Blom-Cooper 2013, 157–158). However, the case of Argentina reveals that human rights prosecutions, while not ignoring perpetrators, also focus on victims, with the ensuing reparative effect. These judicial processes offer the chance for victims to be officially recognised; to tell their stories before the judges; to be heard by members of their families, communities and friends; to obtain information that is important to them; to confront offenders; and simultaneously to have a supportive environment. Furthermore, in human rights trials, victims have the possibility, if they so wish, to be active contributors to the trials. They are involved in, and central to, the judicial process. This is not necessarily the case in ordinary criminal cases.

The eighth point highlights the difference between witnesses in both types of judicial proceedings. In ordinary criminal trials witnesses are not necessarily victims; in contrast, most of the principal witnesses in human rights trials acquire the status of "victim-witnesses." Witnesses who testify in such trials are compelled to speak from the standpoint of a victim. This implies both the experience of incarceration in the detention centres and ultimately of survival, or of being a relative of one of the victims.

The ninth point refers to the difference between the testimonies delivered in the two types of trials. The kind of narrative allowed in human rights trials is different to that of ordinary criminal processes. As discussed in Chapter 7, the opportunity that human rights trials in Argentina give the victims to narrate their stories marks a significant difference with regular court trials, which as a rule are limited to a narrative of those courses of action pertaining to the specific criminal offence under investigation. Indeed, in human rights trials in Argentina, not only survivors but also relatives of the disappeared are able to speak in greater detail about their personal and political stories as well as what consequences these crimes had in their lives. In this sense, human rights trials challenge the narrow perspective of regular trials that only focus on the acts of perpetrators. In the latter, testimony in court can only take the form of giving legal evidence. This opportunity that survivors have to narrate their stories is unique to human rights trials.

Finally, both kinds of trials differ in their scope or consequences. Whereas regular criminal trials regulate and punish offences committed by private individuals, human rights trials are focused on state-sponsored crimes. Thus, domestic accountability in cases of systematic human rights violations represents the internal mechanism that the state uses to send a message within the state institutions and outside them. Prosecution of human rights violations aims to prevent these kinds of atrocities in the future and sends a message to state agents, thus operating as a mechanism of self-control and accountability. This message of trials influences perceptions and attitudes of and towards victims, while simultaneously fulfilling their rights.

Although this typology has its basis in the domestic trials in Argentina, several of the characteristics discussed above can also be found, to a greater or lesser extent, in judicial processes dealing with human rights violations in other countries. Many of the features specific to local human rights prosecutions differentiate them from ordinary criminal trials, and make these processes a means of redress for victims of mass atrocities. A more integrated perspective that includes retributive and restorative aspects for victims can be incorporated into trials when there is the political and judicial will, as well as the capacity and knowledge, to do so. This implies an engagement with prosecutions which goes beyond the classical focus on perpetrators and encompasses a more victim-centred, integrative and sensitive perspective.

However considering the importance of the reparative potential of trials in Argentina is not the same as treating it as a universalised experience. To what extent retributive justice can acquire reparative dimensions will depend on several factors, some of which are described above and others are related to the social contexts in which they are conducted. A trial does not necessarily lead to reparation nor is it always desired by victims, as cases in Rwanda and Sierra Leone show (Corey and Joireman 2004; Kelsall and Stepakoff 2007; Campbell 2007). The importance and the effect of prosecutions are linked to the social contexts as well as the modality of violence in which they take place. In contrast with other cases of mass atrocities, such as in the Balkans, in Argentina there was no civil war but rather state-sponsored violence was executed through terror and repression. Systematically enforced disappearance was directed against all those in society considered as opposition. Impunity in this case just reproduces the unequal application of the law. Against this background, judicial acknowledgement and sanction acquire a relevant role as mechanisms of control of the state and its agents, as well as operate as a means of democratisation, recognition and inclusion of victims in the justice system.

Outstanding matters for further research include to what extent the reparative function of domestic human rights trials can be replicated by international and hybrid courts also dealing with victims of mass atrocities and crimes against humanity. To improve the reparative potential of those tribunals is a challenge for the future. After so much criticism of the way in which victims of mass atrocities are treated, especially by international courts (see e.g. Fletcher and Weinstein 2002, Mertus 2004, Dembour and Haslam 2004, Kelsall and Stepakoff 2007), this book shows that prosecutions can assume reparative modalities. Although retributive justice in its origins has a narrow approach centred on perpetrators, it does not mean that it always needs to be like this. Changes can be undertaken by treating victims differently and including them in the legal processes. For example, changes in legal procedures that help support victims before, during and after their testimonies can have reparative implications. Public hearings and publicity of the content and outcomes of the prosecutions are also important conditions that extend and improve the scope and impact of trials on other sectors of society. Trials can have reparative and restorative implications that are often typical of those initiatives classified as "restorative justice" but the judicial authorities involved must be amenable for these goals to be achieved.

The analysis and discussion of the reparative impact of domestic prosecutions dealing with crimes against humanity, committed years ago (almost forty years in the case of Argentina), is not only a matter of the past. As shown throughout this book, human rights trials deal with very concrete consequences of that past in the present and for the future of a country that claims to be democratic. A reparation process – even though incomplete – creates important changes in victims' realities or, as one survivor put it, "small victories."

Bibliography

Abudara, O. Amati, S. Aragones, R. Arias, L., Berkowiez, L. Bodni, O. and Carpman, J. (1986). *Argentina, Psicoanálisis, Represión Política*. Buenos Aires: Ediciones Karigeman.

Acuña, C. and Smulovitz, C. (1991). *¿Ni olvido ni perdón? Derechos humanos y tensiones cívico-militares en la transición argentina*. Buenos Aires: Centro de Estudios de Estado y Sociedad.

Acuña, C. and Smulovitz, C. (1995). *Militares en la Transición*. Buenos Aires: Centro de Estudios de Estado y Sociedad.

Adelman, H. (1998). "Why Refugee Warriors are Threats." *The Journal of Conflict Studies* 18 (1): 49–69.

Aguiar, E. (1993). *Efectos psicosociales de la impunidad*. Paper presented in the Internaitonal Conference of the Liga Internacional de los Pueblos. Session Impunity. Impunidad, Ginebra, 1–10.

Aguiar, E. (2006). *30 años después*. La Rioja: instituto de Configuraciones vinculares de La Rioja.

Águila, G. (2006). "Dictatorship, Society, and Genocide in Argentina: Repression in Rosario, 1976–1983." *Journal of Genocide Research* 8 (2): 169–180.

Ainley, K. (2008). "Individual Agency and Responsibility for Atrocity." In: R. Jeffery (ed.), *Confronting Evil in International Relations: Ethical Responses to Problems of Moral Agency*. Basingstoke: Palgrave Macmillan: 37–60.

Akhavan, P. (1998). "Justice in the Hague, Peace in the Former Yugoslavia? A Commentary on the United Nations War CrimesTribunal." *Human Rights Quarterly* 20: 737–816.

Ambos, K. (1999). *Impunidad y Derecho Penal Internacional*. Buenos Aires: AD – HOC SRL.

Arendt, H. (1964). *Eichmann in Jerusalem: A Report on the Banality of Evil*. New York: Viking Press.

Arendt, H. (1985). *Totalitarianism: Part Three of the Origins of Totalitarianism*. New York, London: Harvest Book.

Armony, A. (1997). *Argentina, the United States, and the Anti-Communist Crusade in Central America*. Athens, OH: Ohio University Press.

Arthur, P. (2009). "How 'Transitions' Reshaped Human Rights: A Conceptual History of Transitional Justice." *Human Rights Quarterly* 31 (2): 321–367.

Balardini, L., Oberlin, A. and Sobredo, L. (2011). "Gender Violence and Sexual Abuse in Clandestine Detention Centers." In: Center for Legal and Social Studies and International Center for Transitional Justice (eds.), *Making Justice Further Discussions on the Prosecution of Crimes against Humanity in Argentina*. Buenos Aires: Siglo Veintiuno Editores: 106–142.

Barahoma de Brito, A., Gonzalez-Enriquez, C. and Aguilar, P. (2001). *The Politics of Memory: Transitional Justice in Democratizing Societies*.Oxford: Oxford University Press.

Bayer, O., Boro, A., Gambina, J., Barillaro, E. and La Greca, F. (2010). *El terrorismo de estado en la Argentina*. Buenos Aires: Instituto Espacio para la Memoria.

Beckerman, S. (2010). "Retraumatización: una nueva vieja historia." In: D. Kordon, L. Edelman, D. Lagos and D. Kersner (eds.), *Sur, Dictadura y Después . . . Elaboración psicosocial y clínica de los traumas colectivos*. Buenos Aires: EATPI. Psicolibro Ediciones: 126–135.

Bell, C. and O'Rourke, C. (2007). "Does Feminism Need a Theory of Transitional Justice? An Introductory Essay." *International Journal of Transitional Justice* 1 (1): 23–44.

Beristain, C. (2009). *Dialogos sobre la Reparación: Que reparar en los casos de Violaciones de los Derechos Humanos*. Ecuador: V&M Graficas.

Binningsbø, H., Elster, J. and Scott, G. (2005). *Civil War and Transitional Justice, 1946–2003: A Dataset*. Paper presented at the 'Transitional Justice and Civil War Settlements' workshop in Bogotá, Colombia 18–19 October.

Blake, J. (2014). "Should Domestic Courts Prosecute Genocide? Examining the Trial of Efrain Rios Montt." *Brooklyn Journal of International Law* 39 (2): 564–611.

Blom-Cooper, L. (2013). "Crime and Justice: A Shrift in Perspective." In: D. Cornwell, J. Blad and M. Wright (eds.), *Civilising Criminal Justice: An International Restorative Agenda for Penal Reform*. United Kingdom: Waterside Press: 151–170.

Bonacker, T. (2012). "Globale Opferschaft: Zum Charisma des Opfers in Transitional-Justice-Prozessen." *Zeitschrift für Internationale Beziehungen* 19: 5–36.

Bonacker, T., Form, W. and Pfeiffer, D. (2011). "Transitional Justice and Victim Participation in Cambodia: A World Polity Perspective." *Global Society* 25 (1): 113–134.

Bonacker, T., Oettler, A. and Safferling, C. (2013). "Valorising Victims' Ambivalences in Contemporary Trends in Transitional Justice." In: T. Bonacker and C. Safferling (eds.), *Victims of International Crimes: An Interdisciplinary Discourse*. The Hague: Springer: 279–296.

Bonacker, T. and Safferling, C. (2013). *Victims of International Crimes: An Interdisciplinary Discourse*. The Hague: Springer.

Borello, F. (2010). *La protección de testigos de violaciones graves de derechos humanos: casos en Argentina. Report for the UN High Commissioner of Human Rights*.

Bosco, F. (2004). "Human Rights Politics and Scaled Performance of Memory: Conflicts Among the Madres de Plaza de Mayo in Argentina." *Social and Cultural Geography* 5 (3): 381–402.

Bosniak, L. (2000). "Citizenship Denationalized." *Indiana Journal of Global Legal Studies* 7 (2): 447–509.

Bourdieu, P. (1987). "The Force of Law: Toward a Sociology of the Juridical." *Hastings Law Journal* 38 (5): 817–818.

Bouris, E. (2007). *Complex Political Victims*. Bloomfield: Kumarian Pr Inc.

Brubaker, R. (1992). "Civic and ethnic nations in France and Germany". In Hutchinson John and Smith Anthony (ed.): *Ethnicity*, Oxford – New York: Oxford University press: 168–173.

Brysk, A. (1995). *Politics of Human Rights in Argentina: Protest, Change, and Democratization*. Stanford: Stanford University Press.

Buckley-Zistel, S. (2006). "Remembering to Forget: Chosen Amnesia as a Strategy for Local Coexistence in Post-Genocide Rwanda." *Africa: Journal of the International African Institute* 76 (2): 131–150.

Buckley-Zistel, S. (2013). "Redressing Sexual Violence in Transitional Justice and the Labelling of Women as 'Victims'." In: T. Bonacker and C. Safferling (eds.), *Victims of International Crimes: An Interdisciplinary Discourse*. The Hague: Springer: 91–100.

Burt, Jo-Marie. (2009). "Guilty as Charged: The Trial of Former Peruvian President Alberto Fujimori for Human Rights Violations." *The International Journal of Transitional Justice* 3: 384–405.

Call, C. (2004). "Is Transitional Justice Really Just?" *Brown Journal of World Affairs* 6 (1): 101–113.

Calloni, S. (2016). "Macri ubica en 6 mil 348 la cifra de desaparecidos en la dictadura." *La Jornada*, November 9.

Calveiro, P. (1998). *Poder y Desaparición: Los campos de concentración en Argentina*. Buenos Aires: Colihue.

Calveiro, P. (2015). "Sobrepasar el miedo." In: M. Alonso and S. Mansolessi (eds.), *Estudios sobre memoria: Perspectivas actuales y nuevos escenarios*. Córdoba and Argentina: Editorial Universitaria de Villa María: 103–118.

Campbell, K. (2007). "The Gender of Transitional Justice: Law, Sexual Violence and the International Criminal Tribunal for the Former Yugoslavia." *The International Journal of Transitional Justice* 1: 411–432.

Canelo, P. (2004). "La política contra la eocnomia: Los elencos militares frente al plan económico de Martinez de Hoz durante el Proceso de Reorganización social (1976–1981)." In: A. Pucciarelli (ed.), *Empresarios, tecnocratas y militares. La trama corporativa de la última dictadura*. Buenos Aires: Siglo Veintiuno Editores S.A: 173–218.

Capdepon, U. (2015). *Vom Fall Pinochet zu den Verschwundenen des Spanischen Bürgerkrieges*. Transcript.

Capiello, H. (2014). "Estela de Carlotto encontró a su nieto después de 36 años de búsqueda." *La Nacion*, August 6.

Carbajal, G. (2003). "La historia secreta del doble crimen que conmueve a Santiago." *La Nación*, June 8.

Carbajal, M. (2011). "Casi todas sufrieorn abusos." *Página 12*, January 17.

Cavarozzi, M. (1997). *Autoritarismo y Democracia (1955–1996)*. Buenos Aires: Ariel.

CELS. (2005). *Las leyes de Punto Final y Obediencia Debida son inconstitucionales*. Buenos Aires: CELS. Accessed May 10, 2017. http://www.cels.org.ar/common/documentos/sintesis_fallo_csjn_caso_poblete.pdf

CELS. (2010). *Informe 2010 sobre la situación de los derechos humanos en Argentina*. Buenos Aires: Siglo Ventiuno Editores S.A.

CELS. (2011). *Making Justice Further Discussions on the Prosecution of Crimes Against Humanity in Argentina* edited by Center for Legal and Social Studies and International Center for Transitional Justice. Buenos Aires: Siglo Veintiuno Editores.

CELS. (2012). *Informe 2012 sobre la situación de los derechos humanos en Argentina*. Buenos Aires: Siglo Ventiuno Editores S.A.

CELS. (2016). *Derechos humanos en la Argentina Informe 2016*. Buenos Aires: Siglo Ventiuno Editores S.A.

Centro de Información Judicial (Judicial Information Centre) (2013). *Lesa humanidad: condenan a Musa Azar a prisión perpetua en el juicio oral por crímenes en Santiago del Estero*. Accessed December 14, 2016. www.cij.gov.ar/nota-12783-Lesa-humanidad–condenan-a-Musa-Azar-a-prisi-n-perpetua-en-el-juicio-oral-por-cr-menes-en-Santiago-del-Estero.html

Clamp, K. (2014). *Restorative Justice in Transition*. New York: Routledge.

Clarín. (2011). "Duro informe de la ONU sobre protección de testigos." *Clarín*, April 8.

Clarin. (2016). "Condenas por los crímenes del Plan Cóndor: 20 años para el dictador Bignone." *Clarín*, May 27.

Cohen, S. (2001). *States of Denial: Knowing About Atrocities and Suffering*. Cambridge, UK: Polity Press.

Collins, C. (2006). "Grounding Blobalised Justice – International Networks and Domestic Human Rights Accountability in Chile and El Salvador." *Journal of Latin American Studies* 38: 711–738.

Collins, C. (2010). *Post-Transitional Justice: Human Rights Trials in Chile and El Salvador*. USA: Pennsylvania State University.

Collins, C. (2013). "The Politics of Prosecutions." In: C. Collins, K. Hite and A. Joignant (eds.), *The Politics of Memory in Chile: From Pinochet to Bachelet*. London: First Forum Press: 61–89.

Collins, C., Balardini, L. and Burt, J. M. (2012). "Mapping Perpetrator Prosecutions in Latin America." *International Journal of Transitional Justice* 1: 1–21.

CONADEP, Comisión Nacional sobre la Desaparición de Personas (National Commission on the Disappearance of Persons). (2013). *Nunca más: Informe de la Comisión Nacional sobre Desapirición Forzada*. Buenos Aires: Eudeba-Editorial Universitaria de Buenos Aires.

Corey, A. and Joireman, S. (2004). "Retributive Justice: The Gacaca Courts in Rwanda." *African Affairs* 103: 73–89.

Corradi, J. (1987). "The Culture of Fear in Civil Society." In: M. P. Ramos and C. Waisman (eds.), *From Military Rule to Liberal Democracy in Argentina*. London: Westview Press: 113–129.

Corradi, J., Weiss Fagen, P. and Garreton, M. (1992). *Fear at the Edge: State Terror and Resistance in Latin America*. Berkeley: University of California Press.

Crawford, A. and Hucklesby, A. (2013). "Introduction: Compliance and Legitimacy in Criminal Justice." In: A. Crawford and A. Hucklesby (eds.), *Legitimacy and Compliance in Criminal Justice*. New York: Rotledge: 1–7.

Crenzel, E. (2001). *Memorias Enfrentadas: El Voto a Bussi en Tucumán*. Tucumán: Colección Diálogos. Universidad Nacional de Tucumán.

Crenzel, E. (2008). *La Historia Política del Nunca Más: La memoria de las desapariciones en la Argentina*. Buenos Aires: Siglo Veintiuno Editores.

Daly, K. (2000). "Revisiting the Relationship Between Retributive and Restorative Justice." In: H. Strang and J. Braithwaite (eds.), *Restorative Justice: From Philosophy to Practice*. Aldershot: Dartmouth: 33–54.

Dandan, A. (2010). "La definitiva muerte de un caudillo." *Página 12*, July 4.

Dandan, A. (2011). "Juicios demorados por falta de sala." *Página 12*, August 22.

Dandan, A. (2012). "El Ojo de la Cámara." *Página 12*, July 22.

Dandan, A. (2016). "Un funcionario que no transmite seguridad." *Página 12*, April 3.

Dargoltz, R, Gerez, O. and Cao, H. (2006). *El nuevo Santiagueñazo: cambio político y régimen caudillista*. Buenos Aires: Biblos.

De Gregorio, J. C. (2007). *Teoria del Derecho.* Madrid: Uned, Universidad Nacional de Educación a Distancia.

De Greiff, P. (2008). "Justice and Reparations." In: P. De Greiff (ed.), *The Handbook of Reparations.* New York: Oxford University Press: 451–477.

Dembour, M. and Haslam, E. (2004). "Silencing Hearings? Victim-Witnesses at War Crimes Trials." *European Journal of International Law* 15 (1): 151–177.

Di Paolantonio, M. (2004). "Tracking the Transitional Demand for Legal Recall: The Foreclosing and Promise of Law in Argentina." *Social and Legal Studies* 13 (3): 351–375.

Diaz, E. (1980). *Sociologia y Filosofia del Derecho.* Madrid: Taurus.

Doak, J. (2011). "Therapeutic Dimension of Transitional Justice: Emotional Repair and Victim Satisfaction in International Trials and Truth Commissions." *International Criminal Law Review* 11: 263–298.

Dougherty, B. (2004). "Right-Sizing International Criminal Justice: The Hybrid Experiment at the Special Court for Sierra Leone." *International Affairs* 80 (2): 311–328.

Doxtader, E. (2001). "Making Rhetorical History in a Time of Transition: The Occasion, Constitution, and Representation of South African Reconciliation." *Rhetoric and Public Affairs* 4: 223–260.

Druliolle, V. (2013). "H.I.J.O.S. and the Spectacular Denunciation of Impunity: The Struggle for Memory, Truth, and Justice and the (Re)Construction of Democracy in Argentina." *Journal of Human Rights* 12(2): 259–276.

Drumbl, M. (2005). "Collective Violence and Individual Punishment: The Criminality of Mass Atrocity." *Northwestern University Law Review* 99: 539–510.

Duff, R. A. (2001). *Punishment, Communication and Community.* Oxford/New York: Oxford University Press.

Duhalde, E. (1999). *El Estado terrorista argentino: Quince años después, una mirada crítica.* Buenos Aires: Eudeba.

Eckelmans, F. (2013). "The ICC's Practice on Victim Participation." In: T. Bonacker and C. Safferling (eds.), *Victims of International Crimes: An Interdisciplinary Discourse.* The Hague: Springer: 189–222.

Edelman, L. (2010). "Testigos." In: D. Kordon, L. Edelman, D. Lagos and D. Kersner (eds.), *Sur, Dictadura y Después. . .Elaboración psicosocial y clínica de los traumas colectivos.* Buenos Aires: EATPI. Psicolibro Ediciones: 107–113.

Eliaschev, J. (2011). *Los hombres del Juicio.* Buenos Aires: Sudamericana.

Feierstein, D. (2006). "Political Violence in Argentina and Its Genocidal Characteristics." *Journal of Genocide Research* 8 (2): 149–168.

Feierstein, D. (2011). *El genocidio como practica social: Entre el nazismo y la experiencia argentina: Hacia un analisis del aniquilamiento como reorganizador de las relaciones sociales* Buenos Aires: Fondo de Cultura Económica.

Feitlowitz, M. (1998). *A Lexicon of Terror.* Oxford: Oxford University Press.

Feinsberg, J. (1970). *On doing and deserving in the theory of responsibility.* Princeton, New Jersey. Princeton University Press.

FIDH – International Federation for Human Rights. (2009). *Argentina, Advances and Obstacles in Legal Proceedings Against Those Responsible for Crimes Against Humanity Commited During the Dictatorship.* FIDH.

Figari Layús, R. (2010). *The Role of Transitional Justice in the Midst of Ongoing Armed Conflicts: The Case of Colombia.* Potsdamer Studien zu Staat, Recht und Politik 5. Potsdam: Potsdam University.

Figari Layús, R. (2015). "What Do You Mean by Transitional Justice?" Local Perspectives on Human Rights Trials in Argentina." In: M. Esparza and N. Schneider (eds.), *Legacies of State Violence and Transitional Justice in Latin America: A Janus-Faced Paradigm?* London: Lexington Books: 1–16.

Filc, J. (1997). *Entre el parentesco y la política: Familia y dictadura 1976–1983*. Buenos Aires: Biblos.

Filippini, L. (2009). *ICTJ Briefing Criminal Prosecutions for Human Rights Violations in Argentina*. Buenos Aires: International Center for Transitional Justice.

Filippini, L. (2010). "Criminal Prosecution in the Search for Justice." In: Center for Legal and Social Studies and International Center for Transitional Justice (eds.), *Making Justice Further Discussions on the Prosecution of Crimes Against Humanity in Argentina*. Buenos Aires: Siglo Veintiuno Editores: 11–29.

Findlay, M. (2009). "Activating a Victim Constituency in International Criminal Justice." *International Journal of Transitional Justice* 3: 183–206.

Findlay, M. and Ralph, H. (2012). *Transforming International Criminal Justice*. London: Routledge.

Finnemore, M. and Sikkink, K. (1998). "International Norm Dynamics and Political Change." *International Organization* 52 (4): 887–917.

Fletcher, L. and Weinstein, H. (2002). "Violence and Social Repair: Rethinking the Contribution of Justice to Reconciliation." *Human Rights Quarterly* 24 (3): 573–639.

Floria, C. and Garcia Belsunce, C. (2005). *La Argentina Política*. Buenos Aires: El Ateneo.

Forsberg, T. (2003). "The Philosophy and Practice of Dealing With the Past: Some Conceptual and Normative Issues." In: N. Biggar (ed.), *Burying the Past: Making Peace and Doing Justice After Civil Conflict*. Washington, DC: Georgetown University Press: 65–84.

Foucault, M. (2004). *Society Must Be Defended*. London: Penguin Books.

Foucault, M. (2007). *La verdad y las formas jurídicas*. Barcelona: Gedisa.

Garbett, C. (2013). "The Truth and the Trial: Victim Participation, Restorative Justice, and the International Criminal Court." *Contemporary Justice Review* 16 (2): 193–213.

García-Godos, J. (2008). "Victim Reparations in Transitional Justice – What is at Stake and Why?" *Nordisk Tidsskrift for Menneskerettigheter* 26 (2): 111–130.

Gill, L. (2004). *The School of the Americas: Military Training and Political Violence in the Americas*. Durham: Duke University Press.

Gillespie, R. (1982). *Soldiers of Peron: Argentina's Montoneros*. Oxford: Clarendon Press.

Gingold, L. (1991). *Crónica de muertes anunciadas: El caso de Ingeniero Bunge*. Buenos Aires: Centro del Estudios de Estado y Sociedad.

Ginzberg, V. (2002). "El embajador y el plan sistemático." *Página 12*, August 20.

Ginzberg, V. (2015). "La memoria es también mirar al futuro." *Página 12*, December 3.

Ginzberg, V. (2016a). "Macri mostró desprecio y desinterés." *Página 12*, August 11.

Ginzberg, V. (2016b). "Del hecho al dicho." *Página 12*, August 15.

Gloppen, S. (2005). "Social Rights Litigation as Transformation: South African Perspectives." In: P. Jones and K. Stokke (eds.), *Democratising Development: The Politics of Socio- Economic Rights in South Africa*. Irland: Brill Academic Publishers: 153–180.

Goldstone, R. (1996). "Justice as a Tool for Peacemaking: Truth Commissions and International Criminal Tribunals." *New York University Journal of International Law and Politics* 28: 485–503.

Guembe, M. J. (2008). "Economic Reparations for Grave Human Rights Violations: The Argentinean Experience." In: P. De Greiff (ed.), *The Handbook of Reparations.* Oxford/New York: Oxford University Press: 21–54.

Guglielmucci, A. (2015). "Transición política y reparación a las víctimas del terrorismo de Estado en la Argentina: Al gunos debates pendientes." *Taller Segunda Epoca. Revista de Sociedad, Cultura y Política en América Latina* 4 (5): 24–42.

Guissé, E. H. (1996). *Final Report on the Question of the Impunity of Perpetrators of Human Rights Violations (Economic, Social and Cultural Rights)*, Special Rapporteur, pursuant to Sub-Commission resolution 1996/24.

Hafner-Burton, E., Tsutsui, K. and Meyer, J. (2008). "International Human Rights Law and the Politics of Legitimation: Repressive States and Human Rights Treaties." *International Sociology* 23: 115–141.

Hamber, B. and Kelly, G. (2004). *A Working Definition of Reconciliation.* Working Paper. Belfast: Democratic Dialogue.

Hamber, B. and Van der Merwe, H. (1998). "What Is This Thing Called Reconciliation? *Reconciliation in Review* 1 (1): 3–6.

Hayner, P. (2002). *Unspeakable Truths: Facing the Challenge of Truth Commissions.* New York: Routledge.

Hermann, T. (2004). "Reconciliation: Reflections on the Theoretical and Practical Utility of the Term." In: Y. Bar-Siman-Tov (ed.), *From Conflict Resolution to Reconciliation.* Oxford: Oxford University Press: 39–60.

Hollander, E. (1978). *Leaderships Dynamics.* New York. Free Press.

Human Rights Watch. (2006). *Reluctant Partner: The Argentine Government's Failure to Back Trials of Human Rights Violators.* Human Rights Watch.

Human Rights Watch. (2008). *Breaking the Grip? Obstacles to Justice for Paramilitary Mafias in Colombia.* New York: Human Rights Watch.

Humphrey, M. (2000). "From Tterror to Trauma: Commissioning Truth for National Reconciliation." *Social Identities* 6: 7–27.

Humphrey, M. (2013). "The Individualising and Universalising Discourse of Law: Victims in Truth Commissions and Trials." In: T. Bonacker and C. Safferling (eds.), *Victims of International Crimes: An Interdisciplinary Discourse.* The Hague: Springer: 67–89.

Humphrey, M. and Valverde, E. (2007). "Human Rights, Victimhood and Impunity." *Social Analysis: International Journal of Social and Cultural Practice* 51 (1): 179–197.

Huntington, S. (1991). *The Third Wave: Democratization in the Late twentieth Century.* USA: University of Oklahoma Press.

Huyse, L. (1995). "Justice After Transitions: On the Choices Successor Elites Make in Dealing With the Past." In. N. J. Kritz (ed.), *Transitional Justice: How Emerging Democracies Reckon With Former Regimes*, Vol. 1. Washington, DC: United States Institute of Peace Press: 104–115.

Huyse, L. (2005). "Victims." In: D. Bloomfield, T. Barnes and L. Huyse (eds.), *Reconciliation After Violent Conflict: A Handbook.* Stockholm: International Institute for Democracy and Electoral Assistance: 54–66.

International Criminal Court. (2002). *Rules of Procedure and Evidence.* Accessed December 14, 2016. www.icc-cpi.int/iccdocs/PIDS/legal-texts/RulesProcedure EvidenceEng.pdf

Izaguirre, I. (2004). "Los primeros años de la represión." *Puentes*, año 4 n°. 12.

Izaguirre, I. (2009). *Lucha de clases, guerra civil, y genocidio en la Argentina 1973–1983: Antecedentes, desarrollo, complicidades*. Buenos Aires: Eudeba.

Jacobs, J. and Maldonado, M. (2005). "Civil Society in Argentina: Opportunities and Changes for National and Transnational Organisations." *Journal of Latin American Studies* 37 (1): 141–172.

Jelin, E. (1995). *Juicio, castigos y memoria: Derechos humanos y justicia en la política argentina*. Buenos Aires: Nueva Visión.

Junta Militar (Military Junta) (1980) [1976]. *Documentos Básicos y Bases Políticas de las Fuerzas Armadas para el Proceso de Reorganización Nacional*. Buenos Aires: Congreso de la Nación.

Kaiser, S. (2002). "Escraches: Demonstrations, Communication and Political Memory in Postdictatorial Argentina." *Media, Culture & Society* 24 (4): 499–516.

Keck, M. and Sikkink, K. (1998). *Activists Beyong Borders: Advocacy Networks in International Politics*. Ithaca: Cornell.

Kelly, M. (2013). "The Status of Victims Under the Rome Statute of the International Criminal Court." In: T. Bonacker and C. Safferling (eds.), *Victims of International Crimes: An Interdisciplinary Discourse*. The Hague: Springer: 47–66.

Koomen, J. (2013). "'Without These Women, the Tribunal Cannot Do Anything': The Politics of Witness Testimony on Sexual Violence at the International Criminal Tribunal for Rwanda." *Signs* 38 (2): 253–277.

Kordon, D. (1997). "Impunity's Psychological Effects: Its Ethical Consequences." *Journal of Medical Ethics* 17: 29–32.

Kordon, D., Edelman, L., Lagos, D. and Kersner, D. (2010). *Sur, Dictadura y Después. . .Elaboración psicosocial y clínica de los traumas colectivos*. Buenos Aires: EATPI. Psicolibro Ediciones.

Kordon, D. and Edelmann, E. (1986). *Efectos pscológicos de la represión política*. Buenos Aires: Sudamericana Planeta.

Kordon, D. and Edelmann, E. (1988). *Psychological Effects of Political Repression*. Buenos Aires: Sudamericana.

Kotler, R. (2007). "Analisis del informe de la comisión Bicamaeral investigadora de las violaciones de los DD.HH. en la provincia de Tucumán (1974–1983)." *Prohistoria 11:*. 29–47.

La Gaceta. (2015). "Condenan a un ex juez por su labor en la dictadura." *La Gaceta*, June 13.

La Izquierda Diario. (2016). "Megacausa La Perla: 716 víctimas y solo 43 acusados. 26, August." *La Izquierda Diario*, August 26.

La Nación. (2011). "Condenaron a Luis Patti a prisión perpetua." *La Nación*, April 15.

La Rue, F. (1995). "The Right to truth in Central America." In: R. Sieder (ed.), *Impunity in Latin America*. London: Institute of Latin American Studies: 73–81.

Lagos, M. (2010). "Juicio a Represores: Testimonios y Testigos: Algumas implicancias psicológicas y psicosociales." In: D. Kordon, L. Edelman, D. Lagos and D. Kersner (eds.), *Sur, Dictadura y Despues. . .Elaboración psicosocial y clínica de los traumas colectivos*. Buenos Aires: EATPI. Psicolibro Ediciones: 114–125.

Lampasona, J. (2012). "La figura del *sobreviviente*: en torno a las especificidades del genocidio en la Argentina. Una aproximación posible." *Revista Afuera*, 12.

Laplante, L. (2014). "The Plural Justice Aims of Reparation!" In: S. Buckley-Zistel, T. Koloma Beck, C. Braun and F. Mieth (eds.), *Transitional Justice Theories.* New York: Routledge: 66–84.

Laplante, L. and Theidon, K. (2007). "Transitional Justice in Times of Conflict: Colombia's Ley de Justicia y Paz." *Michigan Journal of International Law* 28 (1): 49–107.

Lawry-White, M. (2015). "The Reparative Effect of Truth Seeking in Transitional Justice." *International and Comparative Law Quarterly* 64 (1): 141–177.

Lechner, N. (1992). "Some People Died of Fear: Fear as a Political Problem." In: J. Corradi, P. Weiss Fagen and M. Antonio Garreton (eds.), *Fear at the Edge: State Terror and Resistance in Latin America.* Berkeley: University of California Press: 26–38.

Lernoux, P. (1980). *Cry of the People: The Struggle for Human Rights in Latin America and the Catholic Church in Conflict with US Policy.* New York: Penguin Books.

Lie, T. G., Binningsbø, H. and Scott, G. (2007). "Postconflict Justice and Sustainable Peace." *Post-Conflict Transitions Working Paper* No. 5, World Bank Policy Research Working Paper.

Little, A. (2012). "Disjunctured Narratives: Rethinking Reconciliation and Conflict Transformation." *International Political Science Review/Revue Internationale de Science Politique* 33 (1): 82–98.

Llewellyn, J. (2006). "Restorative justice in transitions and beyond: The justice potential of truth telling mechanisms for post-peace accord societies." In Borer T. (Ed.), *Telling the truths: Truth telling and peace building in post-conflict societies.* South Bend, IN: Notre Dame Press: 83–114.

Longoni, A. (2007). *Traiciones: La figura del traidor en los relatos acerca de los sobrevivientes de la represión.* Buenos Aires: Norme Ediciones.

Lutz, E. and Sikkink, K. (2000). "International Human Rights Law and Practice in Latin America." *International Organization* 54 (3): 633–659.

Maculan, E. (2012). "Prosecuting International Crimes at National Level: Lessons From the Argentine Truth-Finding Trials." *Utrecht Law Review* 8 (1): 107–121.

Madlingozi, T. (2007). "Good Victim, Bad Victim: Apartheid's beneficiaries, Victims and the Struggle for Social Justice." In: W. Le Roux and K. van Marle (eds.), *Law, Memory, and the Legacy of Apartheid: Ten Years After AZAPO v. President of South Africa.* Pretoria: Pretoria University Law Press: 107–126.

Madlingozi, T. (2010). "On Transitional Justice Entrepreneurs and the Production of Victims." *Journal of Human Rights Practice* 2 (2): 208–228.

Malamud-Goti, J. (1996). *Game Without an End: State Terror and the Politics of Justice* Norman and London: University of Oklahoma Press.

Mallinder, L. (2013). "Amnesties in the Persuit of Reconciliation, Peacebuilding and Restorative justice." In: D. Cornwell, J. Blad and M. Wright (eds.), *Civilising Criminal Justice: An International Restorative Agenda for Penal Reform.* United Kingdom: Waterside Press: 138–171.

Mannergren Selimovic, J. (2010). "Perpetrators and Victims: Local Responses to the International Criminal Tribunal for the former Yugoslavia." *Journal of Global and Historical Anthropology* 57: 50–61.

Marchak, P. (1999). *God's Assassins: State Terrorism in Argentina in the 1970s.* Montreal: McGill-Queens's University Press.

Marshall, T. (1999). *Restorative Justice: An Overview*. London: Home Office, Research, Development & Statistics Directorate.

McCarthy, C. (2012). *Reparations and Victim Support in the International Criminal Court*. Cambridge: Cambridge University Press.

McCold, P., Llewellyn, J. and Van Ness, D. (2007). *An Introduction to Restorative Peacebuilding*. Working Party in Restorative Justice. Alliance of NGOs on Crime Prevention and Criminal Justice. Accessed December 14, 2016. www.restorativejustice.org/10fulltext/mccoldp

McElrea, F. (2013). "Restorative Justice as a Procedural Revolution: Some Lessons From the Adversary System." In: D. Cornwell, J. Blad and M. Wright (eds.), *Civilising Criminal Justice: An International Restorative Agenda for Penal Reform*. United Kingdom: Waterside Press: 81–114.

McEvoy, K. and McConnachie, K. (2012). "Victimology in Transitional Justice: Victimhood, Innocence and Hierarchy." *European Journal of Criminology* 9 (5): 527–538.

McEvoy, K. and McConnachie, K. (2013). "Victims and Transitional Justice: Voice, Agency and Blame." *Social and Legal Studies* 22 (4): 489–513.

McGonigle Leyh, B. (2011). *Procedural Justice? Victim Participation in International Criminal Proceedings*. Cambridge: Intersentia.

McSherry, P. (1997). *Incomplete Transition: Military Power and Democracy in Argentina*. Blomington: Universe. Inc.

Mendeloff, D. (2004). "Truth-Seeking, Truth-Telling, and Postconflict Peacebuilding: Curb the Enthusiasm?" *International Studies Review* 6 (3): 355–380.

Méndez, J. (1997). "In Defense of Transitional Justice." In: A. J. McAdams (ed.), *Transitional Justice and the Rule of Law in New Democracies*. Notre Dame and London: University of Notre Dame Press: 1–26.

Mertus, J. (2000). "The Truth in a Box: The Limits of Justice Through Judicial Mechanisms." In: L. Amadiume and A. An-Na'im (eds.), *The Politics of Memory, Truth, Healing and Social Justice*. London: Zed Books: 142–161.

Mertus, J. (2004). "Shouting From the Bottom of the Well: The Impact of International Trials for Wartime Rape on Women's Agency." *International Feminist Journal of Politics* 6 (1): 110–128.

Meyer, L. and Mena, J. (1989). "Introducción." In: L. Meyer and J. Mena (eds.), *Los Sistemas Políticos en América Latina*. México City: Siglo Veintiuno Editores / Universidad de las Naciones Unidas. Mills, M: 17–21.

Meyers, D. (2011). "Two Victim Paradigms and the Problem of 'Impure' Victims." *Humanity: An International Journal of Human Rights, Humanitarianism and Development* 2(2): 255–275.

Ministerio de Justicia y Derechos Humanos (Ministry of Justice and Human Rights). (2015). *Responsabilidad empresarial en delitos de lesa humanidad Represión a trabajadores durante el terrorismo de Estado*. Argentina: Joint report edited by the Human Rights Secretariat, Cels and Flacso. Accessed January 4, 2017. www.saij.gob.ar/docs-f/ediciones/libros/Responsabilidad_empresarial_delitos_lesa_humanidad_t.2.pdf

Minow, M. (1998). *Between Vengeance and Forgiveness: Facing History after Genocide and Mass Violence*. Boston: Beacon Press.

Molesworth, C. L. (2007). "Knowledge Versus Acknowledgment: Rethinking the Alford Plea in Sexual Assault Cases." *Seatle Journal for Social Justice* 6: 907–951.

Neier, A. (1990). "What Should Be Done About the Guilty?" *New York Review of Books* 37 (1): 32–35.

Nikken, P. (1994). "El concepto de Derechos Humanos." *Estudios de Derechios Humanos* 1: 15–35.
Nilson, C. (1998). *Operación Cóndor: Terrorismo de Estado en el Cono Sur.* Buenos Aires: Lholé Lumen.
Nino, C. (2006). *Juicio al Mal Absoluto.* Buenos Aires: Ariel.
Nizkor (2013). "Denuncian intimidaciones contra abogados querellantes", December 19. Accessed May 10, 2017: http://www.derechos.org/nizkor/arg/doc/tucuman25.html
Novaro, M. and Palermo, V. (2003). *La dictadura militar (1976/1983): Del golpe de Estado a la restauración democrática.* Buenos Aires: Paidos.
O'Donnell, G. (1993). "On the State, Democratization and Some Conceptual Problems: A Latin American View With Glances at Some Postcommunist Countries." *World Development* 21 (8): 1355–1369.
O'Donnell, G. (1998). *Polyarchies and the (Un) Rule of Law in Latin America.* Paper presented at the Meeting of the Latin American Studies Association, Chicago. Kellogg Institute and Department of Government University of Notre Dame.
O'Donnell, G. and Schmitter, P. (1995). "Transitions From Authoritarian Rule: Tentative Conclusions About Uncertain Democracies." In: N. J. Kritz (ed.), *Transitional Justice: How Emerging Democracies Reckon With Former Regimes,* Vol. 1. Washington, DC: United States Institute of Peace Press: 57–64.
Olsen, T., Payne, L. and Reiter, A. (2010). *Transitional Justice in Balance: Comparing Processes: Weighing Efficacy.* Washington, DC: United States Institute of Peace Press.
Orentlicher, D. (1991). "Settling Accounts: The Duty to Prosecute Human Rights Violations of a Prior Regime." *100 Yale Law Journal* 2537: 25–37.
Orentlicher, D. (2005). *Report of the Independent Expert to Update the Set of Principles to Combat Impunity.* E/CN/4/2005/102/Add. United Nation, Economic and Social Council.
Osiel, M. (1986). "The Making of Human Rights Policy in Argentina: The Impact of Ideas and Interests on a Legal Conflict." *Journal of Latin American Studies* 18: 135–180.
Página 12. (2009). "Juicio en la cancha." *Página 12,* November 2.
Página 12. (2016a). "Atentan contra la lucha por la verdad." *Página 12,* January 22.
Página 12. (2016b). "Fueron dictadas 20 sentencias por crímenes de lesa humanidad en 2016." *Página 12,* December 30.
Palmer, N. (2012). "Understanding of International Law in Rwanda: A contextual approach." In: E. Kristtjansdottir, A. Nollkaemper and C. Ryngaert (eds.), *International Law in Domestic Courts: Rule of Law Reform in Post-Conflict States.* Cambridge: Intersentia: 153–174.
Parent, G. (2010). "Reconciliation and Justice After Genocide: A Theoretical Exploration." *Genocide Studies and Prevention: An International Journal* 5 (3): 277–292.
Parlevliet, M. (1998). "Considering Truth: Dealing With a Legacy of Gross Human Rights Violations." *Netherlands Quarterly of Human Rights* 16 (2): 141–174.
Pertot, W. (2014). "Otra de Macri y los derechos humanos." *Página 12,* December 24.
Pham, P., Stover, E. and Vinck, P. (2009). *So We Will Never Forget: A Population-Based Survey on Attitudes About Social Reconstruction and the Extraordinary Chambers in the Courts of Cambodia.* USA:University of California Berkeley.
Picco, E. (2012). *Medios, Política y Poder en Santiago del Estero (1859–2012).* Santiago del Eszero/Argentina: Indes-Universidad Nacional de Santiago del Estero.

Picker, R. (2005). *Victims' Perspectives About the Human Rights Violations Hearings*. Center for the Study of violence and Reconciliation. Accessed December 14, 2016. www.csvr.org.za/docs/humanrights/victimsperspectivshearings.pdf

Pion-Berlin, D. (1997). *Through Corridors of Power: Institutions and Civil-Military Relations in Argentina*. University Park: Pennsylvania State University Press.

Poder Judicial de la Nación. (2014). *Causa: "Cantos Germán, Cantos Anabel y Cantos Luis s/ privación ilegítima de libertad y otros delitos", Expte. N° 401304/07*. Septiembre 11. Accessed January 14, 2017. www.bc-consultores.com.ar/articulos/fallos/Lesa-humanidad – difunden-fallo-que-condeno-a-prision-perpetua-a-un-acusado-en-un-juicio-oral-en-Tucuman.pdf

Posner E. and Vermeule, A. (2003). "Transitional Justice as Ordinary justice". *Public Law and Legal Theory: Working Paper* 40, University of Chicago: 3–50.

Procuración General de la Nación (Attorney General's Office). (2013). *Resolución PGN 1442/13*. Accessed January 14, 2016. www.mpf.gov.ar/resoluciones/pgn/2013/PGN-1442-2013-001.pdf

Procuraduría de Crímenes contra la Humanidad (Office of Crimes against Humanity). (2015a). *A diez años del fallo "Simón." Un balance sobre el estado actual del proceso de justicia por crímenes de lesa humanidad*. Accessed December 14, 2016. www.fiscales.gob.ar/wp-content/uploads/2015/06/20150612-Informe-Procuradur%C3%ADa-de-Cr%C3%ADmenes-contra-la-Humanidad.pdf

Procuraduría de Crímenes contra la Humanidad (Office of Crimes against Humanity). (2015b). *El estado de las causas por delitos de lesa humanidad en Argentina. Balances y Desafíos: Datos actualizados al 23 de diciembre del 2015*. Accessed January 14, 2017. www.fiscales.gob.ar/lesa-humanidad/wp-content/uploads/sites/4/2015/12/Ver-Informe.pdf

Procuraduría de Crímenes contra la Humanidad (Office of Crimes against Humanity). (2016). *Informe estadístico sobre el estado de las causas por delitos de lesa humanidad en Argentina: Balance 2016*. Public Ministry of Prosecution. Accessed January 4, 2017. www.fiscales.gob.ar/wp-content/uploads/2016/12/Informe-Lesa-Humanidad-2016.pdf

Pucciarelli, A. (2004). "La Patria contratista. El nuevo discurso liberal de la dictadura militar encubre una vieja práctica corporativa." In: A. Pucciarelli (ed.), *Empresarios, tecnocratas y militares: La trama corporativa de la última dictadura*. Buenos Aires: Siglo Veintiuno Editores S.A: 99–172.

Rawls, J. (1971). *A Theory of Justice*. Cambridge: The Belknap Press of Harvard University Press.

Redress. (2001). *Torture Survivors' Perceptions of Reparations*. Surrey, UK: The REDRESS Trust.

Risse, T. (1995). *Bringing Transnational Relations Back in: Non-State Actors, Domestic Structures, and International Institutions*. Cambridge: Cambridge University Press.

Risse, T. and Sikkink, K. (1999). "The Socialization of International Human Rights Norms into Domestic Practices: Introduction." In: T. Risse, K. Sikkink, and S. Ropp (eds.), *The Power of Human Rights: International Norms and Domestic Change*. Cambridge: Cambridge University Press: 1–38.

Robben, A. (2007). *Political Violence and Trauma in Argentina: The Ethnography of Political Violence*. Philadelphia: University of Pensylvania Press.

Rodriguez, C. (2003). "La historia negra de un represor que se recicló como funcionario." *Página 12*, June 22.

Roehrig, T. (2009). "Executive Leadership and the Continuing Quest for Justice in Argentina." *Human Rights Quarterly* 31 (3): 721–747.

Roht-Arriaza, N. (1990). "State Responsibility to Investigate and Prosecute Grave Human Rights Violations." *International Law* 78: 449–505.

Roht-Arriaza, N. (2004). *The Pinochet Effect. Thansnational Justice in the Age of Human Rights.* Philadelphia: University of Pennsylvania Press.

Roniger, L. and Sznajder, M. (1998). *Constructing Collective Identities and Shaping Public Spheres: Latin American Paths.* Brighton: Sussex Academic.

Rousseaux, F. (2014). "Testigo-víctima." *Página 12*, May 29.

Rupp, S. (2003). "Sekundäre Traumatisierung Durch Behördenprozesse." *Fachtagung: Nachhaltiger Opferschutz Durch interdisziplinäre Zusammenarbeit*: 30–52.

Salimovich, S., Lira, E. and Weinstein, E. (1992). "Victims of Fear: The Social Psychology of Repression." In: J. Corradi, P. Weiss Fagen and M. Garreton (eds.), *Fear at the Edge: State Terror and Resistance in Latin America.* Berkeley: University of California Press: 72–89.

Schaap, A. (2005). *Political Reconciliation.* London: Routledge.

Schindel, E. (2002). "Verschwunden, aber nicht vergessen: Die Konstruktion der Erinnerung an die 'Desaparecidos.' "In: K. Bodemer, A. Pagni, P. Waldmann (Eds.): *Argentinien heute. Politik, Wirtschaft, Kultur.* Frankfurt am Main: 105–134.

Schindel, E. (2012). "'Now the Neighbors Lose Their Fear': Restoring the Social Network around Former Sites of Terror in Argentina." *International Journal for Transitional Justice* 6 (3): 467–485.

Schindel, E. (2014). "Ghosts and *Compañeros*: Haunting Stories and the Quest for Justice around Argentina's Former Terror ites."*Rethinking History: The Journal of Theory and Practice* 18 (2): 244–264.

Seidel, K. (2014). *The Power of Absence: An Ethnography of Justice, Memories of Genocide, and Political Activism of a New Generation in Post-Transitional Argentina.* PhD Thesis. NUI Maynooth, Faculty of Social Sciences.

Servetto, A. (2004). "Córdoba en los Prolegómenos de la Dictadura: La política del Miedo en el gobierno de Lacabanne." *Estudios 15*, CEA-UNC.

Shelton, D. (1999). *Remedies in International Human Rights Law.* Oxford: Oxford University Press.

Shelton, D. (2006). "The Jurisprudence of Human Rights Tribunals on Remedies for Human Rights Violations." *Introductory Lessons and Thematic Courses. Internaitonal Protection of Human Rights and Victims' Rights.* Documentary File. Vol. 1: 113–156. Strasburg: International Institute of Huma Rights.

Sherman, L. and Strang, H. (2007). *Restorative Justice: The Evidence.* London: The Smith Institute.

Shklar, J. (1991). *American Citizenship: The Quest for Inclusion.* Cambridge, MA: Harvard University Press.

Sieder, R. (1995). *Impunity in Latin America.* London: Institute of Latin American Studies.

Sieder, R. (2003). "War, Peace and the Politics of Memory in Guatemala." In: N. Biggar (ed.), *Burying the Past: Making Peace and Doing Justice Acivil Conflict.* Washington, DC: Georgetown University Press: 209–234.

Sikkink, K. (1993). "Human Rights, Principled Issue-Networks, and Sovereignty in Latin America." *International Organization* 47 (3): 411–441.

Sikkink, K. (1998). "Transnational Politics, International Relations Theory and Human Rights." *PS: Political Science and Politics* 31 (3): 516–523.

Sikkink, K. (2011). *The Justice Cascade: How Human Rights Prosecutions Are Changing World Politics.* New York: W. W. Norton.

Sikkink, K. and Booth Walling, C. (2007). "The Impact of Human Rights Trials in Latin America." *Journal of Peace Research* 44 (4): 427–445.

Smith, R. (1998). *Civic Ideals: Conflicting Visions of Citizenships in US History.* New Heaven: Yale University Press.

Smulovitz, C. (2002). "The Discovery of Law: Political Consequences in the Argentine Case." In: Y. Dezalay and B. Garth (eds.), *Global Prescriptions: The Production, Exportation and Importation of a New Legal Orthodoxy.* Ann Arbor: University of Michigan Press: 249–275.

Sriram, C. L. (2005). *Globalizing Justice for Mass Atrocities: A Revolution in Accountability.* New York: Routledge.

Staggs Kelsall, M. and Stepakoff, S. (2007). " 'When We Wanted to Talk About Rape': Silencing Sexual Violence at the Special Court for Sierra Leone." *The International Journal of Transitional Justice* 1 (3): 355–374.

Stewart, M. and Hodgkinson, P. (1988). "Missing: Presumed Dead." *Disaster Management* 1: 11–14.

Suarez-Orozco, M. (1992). "Grammar of Terror: Psychocultural Responses to State: Terrorism in Dirty War and Post Dirty War in Argentina." In: C. Nordstrom and M. Joann (eds.), *The Paths to Domination, Resistance and Terror.* Berkeley: University of California Press: 219–259.

Sveaas, N. and Lavik, N. (2000). "Psychological Aspects of Human Rights: The Importance of Justice and Reconciliation." *Nordic Journal of International Law* 69 (1): 35–52.

Tedesco, L. (1999). *Democracy in Argentina: Hope and Disillusion.* London: Frank Cass.

Teitel, R. (2000). *Transitional Justice.* New York: Oxford University Press.

Teitel, R. (2003). "Transitional Justice Genealogy." *Harvard Human Rights Journal* 16: 69–94.

Telam. (2013). "El 24 de marzo de 2004, el día que Kirchner hizo bajar el cuadro del Colegio Militar." *Telam*, May 17.

Telam. (2014). "Atentado en San Juan: "¿Te gusta declarar contra los militares? Ya tenemos dos en libertad." *Telam*, July 10.

Todorov, T. (1996). "The Touvier Affair." In: R. Golsan (ed.), *Memory, the Holocaust and French Justice: The Bousquet and Touvier Affairs.* Hanover and New Heaven: University Press of New England: 114–121.

Tumini, C., Plaza, S, Molas and Molas, M., Pomares, N., Vazquez, V., Calabrese, S. (2008). *Informe: Experiencia del Acompañamiento Psicologico realizado a Testigos y Querellants del primer juicio por crimenes de Lesa Humanidad en Córdoba.* Córdoba: Equipo de Acompañamiento Psicológico.

Tyler, T. (2006). *Why People Obey the Law.* Princeton: Princeton University Press.

United Nations. (1985). *Annex of the Declaration of Basic Principles of Justice for Victims of Crime and Abuse of Power.* Accessed December 22, 2016. www.unodc.org/pdf/compendium/compendium_2006_part_03_02.pdf

United Nations. (2006). *International Convention for the Protection of All Persons From Enforced Disappearance.* Accessed December 22, 2016 www.ohchr.org/en/hrbodies/ced/pages/conventionced.aspx

United Nations General Assembly. (1998). *Rome Statute of the International Criminal Court.* Accessed January 22, 2017. www.icc-cpi.int/nr/rdonlyres/ea9aeff7-5752-4f84-be94-0a655eb30e16/0/rome_statute_english.pdf

Van Boven, T. (2005). *Basic Principles and Guidelines on the Right to a Remedy and Reparation for Victims of Gross Violations of International Human Rights Law and Serious Violations of International Humanitarian Law*, United Nations Doc. E/CN.4/2005 L.

Van der Merwe, H., Baxter, V. and Chapman, A. (2009). *Assessing the Impact of Transitional Justice: Clallenges for Empirical Research.* Washington, DC: United State bInstitute of Peace.

Van Drunen, S. (2010). *Struggling With the Past: The Human Rights Movement and the Politics of Memory in Post-Dictatorship in Argentina (1983–2006).* Amsterdam: Rozenberg Publishers.

Van Ness, D. and Strong K. (2010). Restoring Justice: An Introduction to Restorative Justice. Cincinnati: Anderson Publishing Co.

Varela, J. C. (2011). "Habrá un festival de música popular para recibir el fallo." *El Diario*, October 21.

Varsky, C. (2011). "Testimonies as Evidence in Criminal Prosecutions for Crimes Against Humanity." In: Center for Legal and Social Studies and International Center for Transitional Justice (eds.), *Making Justice Further Discussions on the Prosecution of Crimes against Humanity in Argentina.* Buenos Aires: Siglo Veintiuno Editores: 30–49.

Vassallo, M. (2016). *Salir del Silencio.* Dossier. Universidad de Buenos Aires. Accessed December 10, 2016. www.sociales.uba.ar/wp-content/blogs.dir/219/files/2016/03/18.-DOSSIER_VASSALLO_90.pdf

Ventura, A. (2008). "Según la Corte, Patti debería haber asumido en diputados." *La Nación*, April 9.

Verbitsky, H. (1985). *Ezeiza.* Buenos Aires: Contrapunto.

Verbitsky, H. (2017). "Macrì envía a la CIDH a un defensor de represores, banqueros y servicios ¿Son o se hacen?" *Página 12*, February 5.

Verwoerd, W. (2000). "Towards a Recognition of Our Past Injustices." In: C. Villa-Vicencio and W. Verwoerd (eds.), *Looking Back, Reaching Forward: Reflections on the Truth and Reconciliation Process of South Africa.* Cape Town: University of Cape Town Press: 155–165.

Viau, S. and Ginzberg, V. (2001). "La Justicia tardó pero llegó a los marinos." *Página 12*, October 3.

Vinjamuti, L. and Snyder, J. (2004). "Advocacy and Scholarship in the Study of International War Crimes Tribunals and Transitional Justice." *Annual Review Political Science* 7: 345–362.

Vujassin, P. (2015). "La Escuela va a los Juicios a Sembrar Memoria." *El diario.es*, September 13. Accessed January 4, 2017. www.eldiario.es/internacional/Escuela-va-Juicios_0_429758045.html

Walgrave, L. (2003). *Repositioning Restorative Justice.* Villan: Cullompton.

Weber, G. (1999). "Die Verschwundenen von Mercedes Benz: der Automobilkonzern und die argentinische Militardiktatur." *ILA/Informationsstelle Lateinamerika* 229: 4–6.

Weschler, L. (1990). *A Miracle, a Universe: Settling Accounts With Torturers.* New York: Penguin Books.

Wilson, R. (2005). "Judging History: The Historical Record of the International Criminal Tribunal for the Former Yugoslavia." *Human Rights Quarterly* 27 (3): 908–942.

Yapur, F. (1999). "Los hombres del gobernador." *Página 12*, November 5.

Zaffaroni, E. (1983). *Tratado de Derecho Penal: Parte General.* Buenos Aires: Ediar.

Zalaquett, J. (1995). "Confronting Human Rights Violations Committed by Former Governments: Principles Applicable and Political Constraints." In: N. J. Kritz (ed.), *Transitional Justice: How Emerging Democracies Reckon With Former Regimes*, Vol. 1. Washington, DC: United States Institute of Peace Press: 3–31.

Zarankin, A. and Salerno, M. (2008). "Después de la Tormenta: Arqueología de la Represión en América Latina." *Complutum* 19 (2): 21–32.

Zehr, H. (1990). *Changing Lenses.* Scottdale, PA: Herald Press.

Zorbas, E. (2004). "Reconciliation in Post Genocide Rwanda." *African Journal of Legal Studies* 1 (1): 30–52.

Zur, J. (1994). "The Psychological Impact of Impunity." *Anthropology Today* 10 (3): 12–17.

Judgments

Judgment Velásquez Rodríguez. (1989). *Caso Velásquez Rodríguez Vs. Honduras.* Accessed January 4, 2017. www.corteidh.or.cr/docs/casos/articulos/seriec_09_esp.pdf

Judgment Simón. (2006). *Buenos Aires, agosto 11 de 2006 y Vistos.* Accessed January 4, 2017. www.cels.org.ar/blogs/blogs-2012/2006/Sentencia%20Julio%20H%C3%A9ctor%20Sim%C3%B3n.pdf

Judgment Von Wernich. (2007). *Vistos, del Plata, noviembre 2007.* Accessed January 4, 2017. www.cij.gov.ar/adj/ADJ-0.803708001226937477.pdf

Judgment Vargas Aignasse. (2008). *Causa: "Vargas Aignasse Guillermo S/Secuestro y Parición". – Expte. V – 03/08.* Accessed January 4, 2017. www.cels.org.ar/blogs/2008/Vargas%20Aignasse.pdf

Judgment massacre of Fatima. (2008). *CAUSA Nro. 9673 "GALLONE, Carlos Enrique y otros s/ recurso de casación.* Accessed January 4, 2017. www.mpf.gob.ar/wp-content/uploads/2016/03/9-20100930-Sala-IV-Gallone-MASACRE-DE-F%C3%81TIMA.pdf

Judgment "Labolita". (2009). *Vistos, del Plata, 7 de agosto de 2009.* Accessed January 4, 2017. www.cels.org.ar/blogs/2009/Labolita.pdf

Judgment "Jefatura". (2010). CAUSA*: "Jefatura de Policía de Tucumán s/secuestros y desapariciones," Expte. J – 29/09.-.* Accessed January 4, 2017. www.cels.org.ar/blogs/2010/Jefatura%20de%20polic%C3%ADa.pdf

Judgment Mansión Seré. (2008). *CAUSA Nro. 10178 -SALA IV- COMES, César Miguel y otros s/recurso de casación.* Accessed January 4, 2017.

Annex: list of interviews

No of interview	*Date of the interview*	*Brief description of interviewee and type of participation in the trials:*
2011		
City of Buenos Aires		
1	23/02/2011	Sociology professor at the University of Buenos Aires and conceptual witness in the trials of the city of Buenos Aires
2	23/02/2011	Former presidential adviser and law professor
3	24/02/2011	Witness in a trial in the city of Buenos Aires. His brother is disappeared.
4	25/02/2011	Staff of National Ministry of Justice
5	28/02/2011	Plaintiff in the trials in the province of Buenos Aires. Her cousin is a disappeared.
6	01/03/2011	Prosecutor in one of the trials in the city of Buenos Aires
7	03/03/2011	Survivor and plaintiff in two trials in the city of Buenos Aires
8	09/03/2011	Instruction judge in the trials taking place in the city of Buenos Aires
9	09/03/2011	Plaintiff lawyer of the human rights organisation "Justicia Ya" (in English "Justice Now") litigating in the trials in the city of Buenos Aires
10	14/03/2011	Survivor and witness in one trial in the city of Buenos Aires
11	23/03/2011	Instruction judge in the trials taking place in the city of Buenos Aires
12	27/03/2011	Plaintiff lawyer in the trials in the province of Buenos Aires.
13	28/03/2011	Staff of human rights organisation EATIP that provides psychological support for victims in the trials
14	25/04/2011	Director of the Human Rights Unit of the Supreme Court (Consejo de la Magistratura)
15	26/04/2011	Member of the human rights organisation HIJOS in the city of Buenos Aires. Plaintiff and witness in two trials in the city of Buenos Aires.

(*Continued*)

(Continued)

No of interview	*Date of the interview*	*Brief description of interviewee and type of participation in the trials:*
City of La Plata		
16	11/03/2011	Judge of the Federal Oral Tribunal of the trials in the city of La Plata
17	11/03/2011	Plaintiff lawyer of the organisation *Liga por los DDHH* (in English "League for Human Rights") in the cases of the city of La Plata
18	22/03/2011	Historian of the Memory Provincial Commission of the city of La Plata
19	22/03/2011	Lawyers of the Human Rights Secretary of the government of the province of Buenos Aires
20	22/03/2011	Plaintiff lawyer of the human rights organisation "Justicia Ya" in the trial in the city of La Plata
21	19/04/2011	Plaintiff lawyer of the human rights organisation Permanent Assembly for Human Rights in the trials in the city of La Plata
22	26/04/2011	Independent plaintiff lawyer in the trials of the city of La Plata
City of Rosario		
23	16/03/2011	Plaintiff and witness in the trials in the city of Rosario. His parents are disappeared. Member of the organisation HIJOS in the city of Rosario.
24	16/03/2011	Member of the human rights organisation Permanent Assembly for Human Rights (APDH) in Rosario
25	17/03/2011	Professor of history at the National University of Rosario
26	17/03/2011	Member of the human rights organisation HIJOS
27	17/03/2011	Member of the human rights organisation "*Familiares de Ex Detenidos Desaparecidos por Razones Políticas*" (in English "Association of Families of the Detained-Disappeared for Political Reasons")
28	18/03/2011	Survivor and witness in trials in the city of Rosario
29	18/03/2011	Plaintiff lawyer of the human rights organisation HIJOS
30	18/03/2011	Survivor and witness in the trials of the province of Santa Fe
31	18/03/2011	Friend of Silvia Suppo, witness killed in 2010 in the province of Santa Fe
32	18/03/2011	Director of the Plan of Protection of Witnesses in the province of Santa Fe
City of Córdoba		
33	30/03/2011	Staff of the *Archivo Provincial de la Memoria* (Memory Archive) in Córdoba
34	31/03/2011	Member of the human rights organisation HIJOS in Córdoba. Her father is disappeared.
35	31/03/2011	Lawyer of the human rights organisation HIJOS in Córdoba

No of interview	Date of the interview	Brief description of interviewee and type of participation in the trials:
36	31/03/2011	Director of the Provincial Plan for Victims of State Terrorism
37	31/03/2011	Lawyer of the human rights organisation *Servicio de Paz y Justicia* (SERPAJ, in English "Peace and Justice Service") in Córdoba. His father was killed during the dictatorship.
38	31/03/2011	Member of the staff of the Plan of Psychological Support for Plaintiffs, Witnesses and Victims in the province of Córdoba
39	01/04/2011	Director of the Human Rights Secretary of the province of Córdoba
40	01/04/2011	Member of the human rights organisation HIJOS in the province of Córdoba. Her father is disappeared and she is plaintiff in a trial in the city of Buenos Aires.
41	01/04/2011	Plaintiff lawyer of the human rights organisation HIJOS in the province of Córdoba. Both of his parents are disappeared.
City of Tucumán		
42	05/04/2011	Member of the human rights organisation Permanent Assembly for Human Rights (APDH), accompanying the trials in Tucumán
43	05/04/2011	Two members of the human rights organisation HIJOS in Tucumán
44	05/04/2011	Plaintiff lawyer of the human rights organisation ANDES in the province of Tucumán
45	06/04/2011	Member of the human rights organisation *Familiares de Ex Detenidos Desaparecidos por Razones Políticas* (in English "Association of Families of the Detained-Disappeared for Political Reasons"). Her husband is disappeared.
46	06/04/2011	Staff of the Human Rights Unit of the Federal Court in the province of Tucumán
47	06/04/2011	Member of the human rights organisation *Madres de Plaza de Mayo* in the province of Tucumán ("Mothers of Plaza de Mayo")
48	06/04/2011	Psychologist of the Plan of Psychological Support for Witnesses in the province of Tucumán
49	07/04/2011	Instruction judge of the Federal Court in the province of Tucumán
50	07/04/2011	Prosecutor in the province of Tucumán
51	07/04/2011	Plaintiff lawyer of the human rights organisation HIJOS in the province of Tucumán. Both of his parents are disappeared.
City of Santiago del Estero		
52	07/04/2011	Former political prisoner. Witness and plaintiff in the trials in Santiago del Estero.

(*Continued*)

(Continued)

No of interview	*Date of the interview*	*Brief description of interviewee and type of participation in the trials:*
53	08/04/2011	Former political prisoner
54	08/04/2011	Prosecutor of the province of Santiago del Estero
55	08/04/2011	Former political prisoner. Witness and plaintiff in the trials in Santiago del Estero.
56	08/04/2011	Former political prisoner. Witness in one trial in Santiago del Estero.
57	09/04/2011	Plaintiff lawyer of the National Secretary of Human Rights
58	09/04/2011	Plaintiff lawyer of the human rights organisation *Colectivo Juicio y Castigo* ("Association Trial and Punishment") in the province of Santiago del Estero
59	09/04/2011	Artist accompanying the trial in the province of Santiago del Estero
60	09/04/2011	Plaintiff lawyer in the trials in Santiago del Estero
2012		
City of Buenos Aires		
61	20/09/2012	Survivor, plaintiff and witness in the trials in the city of Buenos Aires
62	21/09/2012	Plaintiff and witness in the trials in the city of Buenos Aires. Her parents are disappeared. Member of the organisation HIJOS in the city of Buenos Aires.
63	25/09/2012	Survivor, plaintiff and witness in the trials in the city of Buenos Aires
64	26/09/2012	Sociology professor and witness in a trial in the province of Tucumán. Her brother is disappeared.
65	05/10/2012	Survivor, plaintiff and witness in the trials in the city of Buenos Aires
66	05/09/2012	Plaintiff lawyer of the human rights organisation CELS
City of Tucumán		
67	28/09/2012	Plaintiff lawyer of the human rights organisation HIJOS in the province of Tucumán
68	29/09/2012	Survivor, plaintiff and witness in the trials in the province of Tucumán. His brother and sister are disappeared.
69	30/09/2012	Member of the staff of the Plan of Psychological Accompaniment to Plaintiffs, Witnesses and Victims in the province of Tucumán
70	01/10/2012	Plaintiff and witness in the trials in the province of Tucumán. Her parents and brother are disappeared.
71	02/10/2012	Plaintiff lawyer of the National Secretary of Human Rights

No of interview	Date of the interview	Brief description of interviewee and type of participation in the trials:
72	02/10/2012	Plaintiff and witness in the trials in the province of Tucumán. Her father is disappeared.
73	03/10/2012	Former political prisoner. Witness and plaintiff in the trials in Tucumán.
City of La Plata		
74	20/09/2012	Plaintiff and witness in the trials in the city of Buenos Aires. His parents are disappeared. Member of the organisation HIJOS in the city of La Plata.
75	04/10/2012	Plaintiff and witness in the trials in the city of Buenos Aires. His parents are disappeared. Member of the organisation HIJOS in the city of La Plata.

Index

For Product Safety Concerns and Information please contact our EU representative GPSR@taylorandfrancis.com
Taylor & Francis Verlag GmbH, Kaufingerstraße 24, 80331 München, Germany

www.ingramcontent.com/pod-product-compliance
Ingram Content Group UK Ltd.
Pitfield, Milton Keynes, MK11 3LW, UK
UKHW021302190926
475701UK00009B/576
* 9 7 8 0 3 6 7 1 9 1 8 3 2 *